Empires of Knowledge in International Relations

This volume offers the first systematic account of how education and science have become sources of power for the states in international relations and what factors have effected this development.

Drawing together extensive empirical data on the USA, the EU, Japan, Korea, Singapore, and China, Wojciuk explores the factors and mechanisms through which education and science translate into the international position of different states, highlighting how they continue to contribute to the reproduction of the centre-periphery system in global politics. Written in an accessible style, the author argues that these factors increase the likelihood of success for states in international relations, even if in themselves, they cannot guarantee it. Specifying the ways in which education and science contribute to the power of a state in international relations, Wojciuk focuses on mechanisms involved in state-building processes and economic development, and invokes cases of successful competitive strategies involving education and science.

This work will be of interest to scholars in a wide range of subjects including education research, international relations and international political economy.

Anna Wojciuk is Associate Professor in the Institute of International Relations, University of Warsaw, Poland.

Routledge Advances in International Relations and Global Politics

131 **Neutrality in International Law**
From the Sixteenth Century to 1945
Kentaro Wani

132 **Reconciling with the Past**
Resources and Obstacles in a Global Perspective
Edited by Annika Frieberg and C.K. Martin Chung

133 **Order Wars and Floating Balance**
How the Rising Powers Are Reshaping Our Worldview in the Twenty-First Century
Andreas Herberg-Rothe and Key-young Son

134 **The Political Psychology of Attitudes towards the West**
An Empirical Analysis from Tamil Nadu
Björn Goldstein

135 **Resistance, Power, and Conceptions of Political Order in Islamist Organizations**
Comparing Hezbollah and Hamas
Maren Koss

136 **Christianity and American State Violence in Iraq**
Priestly or Prophetic?
Christopher A. Morrissey

137 **Small States and Hegemonic Competition in Southeast Asia**
Pursuing Autonomy, Security and Development amid Great Power Politics
Chih-Mao Tang

138 **Empires of Knowledge in International Relations**
Education and Science as Sources of Power for the State
Anna Wojciuk

Empires of Knowledge in International Relations
Education and Science as Sources of Power for the State

Anna Wojciuk
Translation by Antoni Górny

LONDON AND NEW YORK

First published 2018
by Routledge
2 Park Square, Milton Park, Abingdon, Oxon OX14 4RN

and by Routledge
711 Third Avenue, New York, NY 10017

Routledge is an imprint of the Taylor & Francis Group, an informa business

© 2018 Anna Wojciuk

The right of Anna Wojciuk to be identified as author of this work has been asserted by her in accordance with sections 77 and 78 of the Copyright, Designs and Patents Act 1988.

All rights reserved. No part of this book may be reprinted or reproduced or utilised in any form or by any electronic, mechanical, or other means, now known or hereafter invented, including photocopying and recording, or in any information storage or retrieval system, without permission in writing from the publishers.

Trademark notice: Product or corporate names may be trademarks or registered trademarks, and are used only for identification and explanation without intent to infringe.

British Library Cataloguing-in-Publication Data
A catalogue record for this book is available from the British Library

Library of Congress Cataloging-in-Publication Data
A catalog record for this book has been requested

ISBN: 978-1-138-06524-6 (hbk)
ISBN: 978-1-315-15988-1 (ebk)

Typeset in Times New Roman
by Wearset Ltd, Boldon, Tyne and Wear

For my grandmother and mother

Contents

List of illustrations   x
Acknowledgements   xii

Introduction   1

1 **Historical background and the theoretical model**   9

   From the Middle Ages until industrialisation 9
   The theoretical model 19

2 **The role of education and science in the state-building process**   29

   Education and state-building processes: political ideas and social theories 33
   The history of state education systems: from reformation to modernity 41
      Reformation: State versus Church 42
      The establishment of state bureaucracy 45
      Professionalisation 50
      Education and the citizen 54
   Examples of the use of education and science in state-building processes 59
      Great Britain – a success that became a burden 59
      France – the pros and cons of centralism 64
      Poland – integrating the state through education 69
   Conclusion 74

3 Human capital and knowledge in economic theory   84

Human capital, technological advancement, and economic growth 86
Controversies over state policy recommendations for education and science: the market and the state 93
National innovation systems and competitive advantages 99
    The concept of competitive advantages in education and science 99
    National innovation systems 104
Knowledge in the era of the Third Industrial Revolution 109
Education, knowledge, and the global value chains 113
The impact of education and science on economic development in market economies 117
    Germany – efficiency that astounded and frightened 119
    Japan – from avoiding colonisation to challenging the greatest superpower 123
Critiques of the commodification of knowledge and abilities 128
Conclusion 130

4 International distribution of power and state strategies   140

International distribution of power in education and science 141
    Primary and secondary education 141
    Higher education 146
    Scientific research 154
    Research, development, and applications 163
Examples: strategies of select states in education, science, and innovation 166
    The United States: a global magnet 167
    Europe: multiple models between internal competition and cooperation 177
    The Republic of Korea and Singapore: educational miracle in conditions of high coordination 183
    China: change in progress 187
Conclusion 190

5 Structural factors: governance, institutions, norms, transnational regimes   199

Transnational regimes as a level of governance 200
The role of international comparisons: governance by numbers 206

The PISA study as an example of a transnational regime 210
    The peculiarity of the OECD and its role in educational
        policy 210
The PISA study and state policy 213
    PISA as a set of norms and rules 215
    The impact of the PISA study on state policy 219
Conclusion 226

Conclusion   234

Index   237

Illustrations

Figures

1.1	Schematic representation of Stefano Guzzini's concept of power in international relations	23
3.1	Correlation of mean education level and GDP per capita in national economies	89
3.2	Correlation of educational attainment and GDP per capita	92
3.3	Costs and gains in iPhone's value chain	116
4.1	Percentage of literate persons in the population of people aged fifteen or more	142
4.2	Average number of years of schooling for people aged twenty-five or more	142
4.3	Correlation between average duration of schooling and literacy	143
4.4	Combined average score, PISA 2015	145
4.5	Average educational expenses, 1990–2014, represented in constant US$ (2005)	146
4.6	Gross schooling rate at ISCED 5 and 6 level	147
4.7	Average yearly expenses (public and private) on higher education, 1998–2014, per student in constant US$ (2005)	147
4.8	States exporting the most students abroad and main directions of migration	150
4.9	States hosting the most foreign students and major sources of migration	151
4.10	Analysis of network of international mobility of scientists	156
4.11	Analysis of international networks of scientific cooperation as measured by cooperative publications in 1998 and 2011	157
4.12	The number of universities in the top 100 of the Shanghai Ranking (ARWU) of higher education institutions, by state	158
4.13	The number of universities in the top 400 of the Shanghai Ranking (ARWU) of higher education institutions, by state	159
4.14	Correlation of the number of universities in the 'top 400' (AWRU) per ten million inhabitants and WEF competitiveness index	160

4.15	The share of states on all levels of development (according to HDI) in the overall amount of Nobel Prizes and Fields medals	161
4.16	The share of states on specific levels of development (according to HDI) in the overall amount of Nobel Prizes and Fields medals	162
4.17	Government expenses on research and development (GERD) per capita	164
4.18	Correlation between the number of scientists per 1,000 employees and R&D expenses in relation to GDP	165
4.19	Ties between education, science, and innovation and other sectors	192

Table

5.1	Participation in subsequent cycles of PISA	217

Acknowledgements

I would like to thank Michał Fedorowicz, who encouraged me to take up the project and offered support on various stages of its completion. Throughout the years I spent working on this book, I was repeatedly pointed in new theoretical and methodological directions and led along new paths of empirical research. The list of persons who provided me with helpful critique and guidance is extremely long. I am particularly thankful to Stefano Guzzini, whose concept of power serves as the linchpin of this work, and who devoted much of his time and patience to me. He was the source of the most accurate critical remarks at various stages of the project. I am quite sure that, in spite of all my efforts and changes introduced to the final version of this book, Stefano Guzzini would still have approached it with a critical eye. I owe a debt of gratitude to Philip Cerny, the source of many useful hints. I drew copiously from the comments and observations of lecturers and participants in the summer schools and workshops during which I presented the project, particularly the Institute for Qualitative and Multi-Method Research (2014) at Syracuse University, Essex Summer School in Social Science Data Analysis (2011), European Workshops in International Studies (2014), and workshops for young scholars at the Institute for International Relations of the University of Warsaw, conducted by Knud Erik Jørgensen and Stefano Guzzini in 2012, 2013, and 2015.

I would also like to cordially thank Jan Dzierzgowski and Maciej Bukowski, who helped me find my way in sociological and economical writings in spite of the differences in our approaches to the object of this study. I benefitted significantly from the useful comments of the reviewers, Aleksander Surdej and Andrzej Rychard, as well as the publisher of the Polish version of this volume, Jacek Raciborski, for which I am deeply grateful. My understanding of the subject owes much to years of cooperation and discussion within two formidable research teams I had the privilege of belonging to. One is my Team at the Educational Research Institute; of those unmentioned in other contexts, I wish to thank Agnieszka Dziemianowicz-Bąk, Mikołaj Herbst, Jan Herczyński, and Aneta Sobotka, who taught me a great deal about educational policy, as well as the politics of higher learning and its evaluation. The other is the team involved in the project 'School of Education of the Polish-American Freedom Foundation and the University of Warsaw'; of its members, I want to express my gratitude to

Acknowledgements xiii

Magdalena Krawczyk-Radwan, Michał Miąskiewicz, Katarzyna Znaniecka-Vogt, Tom Corcoran, and other partners from Columbia University's Teachers College for helping me better understand the mechanisms of education on a micro level. These experiences have been invaluable to me. I am also thankful for valuable inspiration and guidance from Roman Bäcker, Jacek Czaputowicz, Que Anh Dang, Maciej Drozd, Blanca Heredia-Rubio, Martyna Kobus, Łukasz Mikołajewski, Michał Sitek, Mojca Štraus, and Joanna Czeczott. Each of the persons named here is owed special thanks, particularly for the generosity and patience of those who tried to help in spite of holding theoretical or normative perspectives divergent from mine. I corrected and updated the English version of this book in the hospitable environment of Cornell University during my research stay supported by The Foundation 'Liberalna edukacja'. I especially would like to thank Peter J. Katzenstein for his apt suggestions regarding both the main argument and the structure of the book. I applied final edits to the book during my stay as Braudel Fellow at the European University Institute. I am grateful for the space for independent study and support I received throughout years of our cooperation from Roman Kuźniar, head of the Unit of Strategic Studies at the Institute of International Relations of the University of Warsaw. The English edition of this book would not have seen the light of day without support from various authorities at the University of Warsaw: the director of the Institute of International Relations, Jakub Zajączkowski, and Vice-Rector for Research, Maciej Duszczyk. I would also like to thank Bruno Kamiński, who provided me with much help in gaining access to secondary literature, Marta Stormowska, who helped me in my research query and then carefully read the manuscript of this work. I am grateful to Adam Müller and Barbara Piotrowska for their help in preparing maps and diagrams, and, last but not least, to Antoni Górny for making the translation better than the original text is. All faults are mine.

Introduction

Scholars and practitioners of international relations rarely take up an interest in education and science. While studying the literature on international relations, I noticed that questions of the knowledge and abilities of the people are almost completely absent from it, or, if present, receive only passing mentions, without any in-depth discussion, explication, or analysis of causal relations. This book offers the first systematic account of how education and science came to affect the position of states in international relations and what mechanisms effected this development. I conceptualise those factors as contributing causes, explaining the sources of their significance and the likelihood of its future increase, while conceding that they constitute neither sufficient nor necessary conditions for a build-up of state power. I treat them as factors increasing the likelihood of success for states in international relations, though in themselves, they cannot guarantee it. I adapt Stefano Guzzini's concept of power to an analysis of the selected issue-areas that constitute the object of this study. The genealogical study of processes of modern state-building and subsequent industrial revolutions allows me to identify the mechanisms by which the effect in question occurs. Specifying the ways in which education and science contribute to the power of a state in international relations, I focus on the mechanisms involved in state-building processes and economic development, and finally invoke cases of successful competitive strategies involving education and science. In reality, state-building and economic mechanisms, as well as specific choices in terms of strategy, coincide in nearly all instances. The division that is deployed in this work is meant to facilitate analysis; however, discussions of specific case studies inevitably lead to the referencing of mechanisms and strategies beyond the scope of the given chapter. Thus, the cases were chosen according to their ability to illustrate the arguments pursued in the chapters.

The proposed analysis ascribes major significance to processes, taking note of changes in both agency and structure. The existence of interaction between agents and structures and their mutual formation constitute the fundamental theoretical underpinnings of this work. These interactions are marked by various kinds of power and the potential of the actors is varied; however, it is the structural conditions that define the relative weight of factors, the available tools and the sources of authority. Only some of those effects are controllable; most occur impersonally, unintentionally, and even unconsciously. These are the contours of the theoretical model that I discuss in detail in the second part of Chapter 1.

Seeking to make this work accessible to more than just specialists in international relations (IR) and those interested in social theories, I organised it so that the main claims and relevant empirical material are readily available without diving into the theory, which constitutes the least approachable part of the text. The applied conceptualisation of power in international relations accounts for a multiplicity of dimensions and actors and deploys a broad selection of readings in political theory, international relations theory, and other major social science theories. It is neither simple, nor parsimonious, owing to the complexity of the situations it is applied to, but when used correctly, its intellectual discipline organises international realities without downplaying significant empirical data – which, in my view, are often disregarded in alternative approaches. For readers who are not IR scholars but who are interested in the significance of education and science for the international position of states, familiarity with the theoretical part is not necessary to benefit fully from this work.

Though the applied theoretical approach to power rightly involves many interacting agents, my study concentrates primarily on the state. One reason for this is empirical: in spite of the activity of numerous and varied actors in this arena and the continuing diffusion of power, the state remains the only significant actor – in the past as well as today – capable of at least limited coordination of actions aimed at the achievement of common welfare. Another reason is that the normative assumptions of this work naturally give precedence to the state. I believe that continuing globalisation and its various negative effects (notwithstanding its undoubted benefits) prove that the state has a crucial role to play. This should not be taken to mean that every public intervention is better than alternative mechanisms of coordination, including the market. The market is irreplaceable as a producer of wealth, but the uses of the market are limited and it cannot serve as a universal mechanism of coordination for social life at large. Even in the purely economic sphere, a 'guardian' is needed to protect against the pathologies that this mechanism can create due to its immanent structural weakness. A prime example of the difficulties in eradicating the deleterious effects of the market (in tandem with cynical public policy of many states) is the impossibility to coordinate global actions to limit CO_2 emissions. Furthermore, the market cannot provide many crucial public goods: while it can create elite institutions for the richest of the rich and those endowed with much cultural capital, those not privileged enough cannot depend on the market in that regard. In the case of basic research, the temporal delay and uncertainty of the profits it may yield prompts the market to offer financial support in amounts that are inadequate for the needs of the development of the state.

Maintenance of the economy is a goal in itself only insofar as work constitutes an indelible part of human life. Typically, however, the economy plays merely an instrumental role as a means to other social goals. Among such instruments, though, it stands foremost, being impossible to overlook or underplay. It is through the ingenuity of and risks taken by entrepreneurs that wealth is multiplied most effectively, allowing a broad social strata to enjoy high living standards when combined with a beneficial socio-political order. The art of governance requires the creation of a space for human creativity and entrepreneurship governed by honest rules as well as the maintenance of civic interest and social justice. In axiological terms, these elements do not always combine harmoniously, and the interests of specific groups tend to be highly polarised, especially in the short term. For this reason, the state never offers universal solutions, and specific choices are a matter of politics, not technocracy; art, not science. States whose inhabitants enjoy high living standards owe it to the cooperation between public authorities and the market. There are many tried and true institutional models for combining these two spheres.

This work delves into the heated confrontation between the concept of education as a matter resolved by the family (parentocracy) or, in extreme cases, by the children themselves, and the belief that, given its significance for the entire society, it belongs with the state rather than individuals. The proponents of the former view support a drastic limitation of the state's involvement in schooling. The other side argues that the youth should become socialised within a broader community as its future members. I am more inclined to endorse the latter perspective, which assumes that education plays a social and public role, and thus requires the involvement of public authorities. This should not be taken to mean that everything a state does in this field is correct and must be endorsed. On the contrary, this work also discusses instances of a dangerous instrumentalisation of education driven by nationalist or authoritarian state agendas or caused by the institution of limited instruction meant only to prepare the people for rivalry in the labour market.

Apparently, the state itself faces not only a daunting task, but also its own weaknesses, which can, at times, lead to pathologies. Its fundamental weakness lies in the absence of internal mechanisms guaranteeing that the rulers will pursue the common good and follow the rules of social justice to act in the interest of a broad cross-section of the citizenry. In other words, the greatest threat is that the state might be in some way intercepted by one or more interest groups to the detriment of everyone else.

Though elections are a means of control over public authorities in a democratic state, the fixed term of office that this mechanism of establishing the government imposes leads to a woeful short-sightedness. When individuals plan the lives of their own and their families, they consider the effects their decisions might have over a span of decades, as when choosing to devote years of one's own life and financial assets towards gaining an education. The impact of those decisions is only clear in the long term, when the fruits of one's labour and self-denial are clearly observable. Meanwhile, politicians and governments are assessed on the effects of actions (by themselves or others) that are readily apparent. This mechanism discourages strategic thinking and planning and promotes going with the flow, wherever that might lead.

Within the realm of public policy, education and science constitute fields in which effects can only be assessed after at least a decade, which is why they often lose funding and attention to undertakings that are more impactful in the short term. Their value for internal policy is obvious – so much so that they have become the object of a wide array of works in sociology, pedagogy, and economics, not to mention the great humanities.

My goal is to highlight the fact that education and science also play a significant role from an international perspective. This claim finds support in empirical observations (states that achieved broadly conceived success in the international arena since the Industrial Revolution had applied strategic thinking by making advances in these areas). It has also been noticed by major scholars in the field of international political economy, without, however, receiving a systematic account. As early as in the 1960s, Robert Gilpin (1968: 445) observed this fact, and education and science were later analysed as sources of state power in the hegemonic stability theory (Gilpin 1981: 175–177). According to Gilpin, the process of diffusion of knowledge from the centre to the peripheries of the international system leads the dominant powers to lose political, military, or economic advantages. Since the diffusion of knowledge cannot be prevented in the long term, this lack of control, in Gilpin's view, contributes to the redistribution of power. In addition, the dominant powers are incapable of controlling the locus of innovation (Gilpin 1981: 180–181). For Susan Strange,

> knowledge is power and whoever is able to develop or acquire and to deny the access of others to a kind of knowledge respected and sought by others; and whoever can control the channels by which it is communicated to those given access to it, will exercise a very special kind of structural power.
> (Strange 1994: 30–31)

For Strange, this kind of power is subtle and elusive, and while different kinds of knowledge were crucial in the past, today technology plays a vital role. Judging that this topic deserves a more systematic account, both in terms of theory and practice – with regard to political choices and long-term strategies of the states – I was inspired to produce this study, which is the fruit of my analyses and considerations over the past six years.

In the chapters that follow, I strive to address the major axiological controversies in particular areas. It does not follow that other aspects and functions of education are not significant for me. In fact, I consider it crucial that an answer be provided to the question, what does it mean to be an educated person today? I do not believe this question has been sufficiently answered yet. However, it is not the purpose of this work to define the contours of good education.

In Chapter 1, I provide a brief historical introduction to the problem and develop the theoretical part of the work. In Chapter 2, I investigate the role education played in the transformation from feudal to modern political structures. The mechanisms involved remain valid and operational today, even though they are taken for granted in developed countries to the point that their importance is no longer realised. The genealogical study of modernisation in France, Great Britain, and Poland allows me to demonstrate the role of education in state-building. As political modernisation still remains a challenge for many developing countries, struggling with the lack of meritocratic bureaucracy and the deficit of the skills necessary to effectively administrate public institutions and develop infrastructure in the broad sense, my study shows the role of education in overcoming those obstacles. Furthermore, a substantial part of the chapter concerns issues of citizenship, loyalty to the state, and the homogenisation of culture, whose achievement was facilitated by education. This question, which remains a challenge for numerous developing states, has recently resurfaced in developed countries in a new context: contemporary debates about the role of education in the integration of immigrants. In Chapter 3, I analyse economic mechanisms by which the level of education and science translates into state power. Engaging literature from economics and economic policies concerning human capital, growth theory, competitive advantages, and national systems of innovation, I show how skills contribute to wealth and prosperity. I also discuss what challenges the Third Industrial Revolution brings to education and science and argue that development of those issue-areas is vital for any state that seeks to achieve a favourable position in the global value chains. From this perspective, education and science serve as an additional means of gaining superiority over competitors and of establishing the boundary between economies of the centre and of the periphery. Finally, I show that, though there are different ways to succeed in education and science, successful policies are always embedded in the model of capitalism a given country represents. Chapter 3 examines the cases of Germany and Japan. In Chapter 4, I provide a thorough analysis of global inequalities as far as education and science are concerned, addressing various questions, from literacy and primary schooling, through secondary schools, up to higher education, science, and research and development (R&D). The analysis of indicators describing those fields allows me to distinguish the global centre, the peripheries and the intermediate zone, as well as to provide a general characteristic of countries belonging to each of those categories. I show that although global inequalities continue to affect all areas of education and science, the more advanced the field, the further the distance between global leaders and those closer to the global median. One should, of course, assume that the causal chain runs in both directions – the potential of knowledge and skills translates into success, and success creates possibilities for development in these areas. The case studies of the United States, the European Union, Republic of Korea, Singapore, and China allow me to identify various strategies of development of education and science, which have proved to be successful for the actors who implemented them, and which I analyse in Chapter 4. Successful policies always have to fit into the local context, either emerging incrementally from the given socio-political system (i.e. being embedded) or by way of smart imitation, which adapts the chosen model to the possibilities and limitations of the given environment. This part is particularly important from the point of view of policy and political practice.

Having presented the mechanisms through which education and science inform a state's power in international relations and indicated some of the successful strategies in those issue-areas (with the agential aspect covered in Chapters 2, 3, and 4), in Chapter 5, I look at the governance level in order to show how education and science became a part of the transnational structure (the applied concept of power explicitly links the structural dimension of power with the notion of governance). Since this structure is extremely complex and multi-layered, it is not my purpose to describe all of the structural dimensions of education and science as factors of power. I consider only one layer: transnational regimes which emerged around cross-country comparisons in those issue-areas. I do not treat the diffusion of norms in education and science via cross-country comparisons of institutions as an entirely new phenomenon, but rather as an intensification of processes described many decades ago and captured in the concept of mimetic isomorphism. The analysis of the structural dimension of education and science as sources of a state's power in international relations entails a consideration of the normative side of the changes introduced by the processes involved. On the one hand, I give an account of the values which the so-called knowledge-based economy fosters and which are broadly endorsed worldwide not only by prominent international organisations, such as the Organisation for Economic Co-operation and Development (OECD) or the World Bank, and almost all governments, but also by business and many influential NGOs. On the other hand, I show those values to be deeply controversial, contested, and charged with causing the marketisation of education and science and tacitly redefining those areas. Critics from both the conservative and progressive side argue that those changes deprive education and science of their significance in the transmission and development of the richness of human cultures. Critics also point out that the subordination of education to the needs of globalised markets frequently limits the function of education as a vehicle for emancipation and the main tool for overcoming inequalities in modern societies.

The model of education and science as factors of a state's international power thus depends on the theoretical groundwork of international relations, and on research into the conceptualisation of power in particular. The empirical material referenced in the study is mostly derived from other social sciences – mostly sociology (Chapter 2) and economics (Chapter 3). Only the part devoted to structures of governance in these fields (Chapter 5) draws to a greater extent on studies in international relations. It is an attempt to learn from different research traditions and scholarly disciplines and to tailor their findings to the identified problem (Sil and Katzenstein 2010; Lake 2013; Bennett 2013).

This study does not discuss extensively the ideological hegemony that undergirds imperialism, which has attracted widespread interest among education researchers (e.g. Connell 2006; Takayama, Sriprakash, and Connell 2015; Hartmann 2015; Connell, Collyer, and Maia 2017). This work devotes more space to institutions than to discourses, drawing heavily on the findings of institutionalism in social sciences, particularly research into varieties of capitalism. Indeed, this is an interdisciplinary project tracing a path across research areas of contemporary social sciences. Seeking to integrate findings from different disciplines, I was often forced to apply them selectively according to my own research needs. Crossing boundaries between academic disciplines inadvertently leads to trespassing – this risky approach puts the author under threat of accusations of minor or major clumsiness. Wary of the risk, the feeling of being lost in a foreign territory was my constant companion. I am also aware that, though interdisciplinary studies tend to receive rave reviews, they often fail to make full use of any of the disciplines they invoke.

The study received financial support from the National Centre for Science grant 'Education as a new source of a state's international power', SONATA UMO-2011/01/D/HS5/022064.[1] Results obtained at earlier stages were published before the completion of the project (Wojciuk 2014; Wojciuk, Michałek, and Stormowska 2015).

Note

1 Papers presenting results of this research were delivered at the following conferences: Convention of the Polish International Studies Association (2012), International Studies Association Annual Convention (2014), European International Studies Association Pan-European Conference (2013, 2015, and 2017), conference of the Institute of International Relations, University of Warsaw (May 2014), 'Research and Educational Policy' seminar of the Educational Research Institute, Warsaw (January 2014).

References

Bennett, A. (2013). The Mother of All Isms: Causal Mechanisms and Structured Pluralism in International Relations Theory. *European Journal of International Relations* 19(3): 459–481.
Connell, R. (2006). Northern Theory: The Political Geography of General Social Theory. *Theoretical Sociology* 35(2): 237–264.
Connell, R., F. Collyer, and J. Maia (2017). Toward a Global Sociology of Knowledge: Post-Colonial Realities and Intellectual Practices. *International Sociology* 32(1): 21–37.
Gilpin, R. (1968). *France in the Age of the Scientific State*. Princeton, NJ: Princeton University Press.
Gilpin, R. (1981). *War and Change in World Politics*. Cambridge: Cambridge University Press.
Hartmann, E. (2015). The Educational Dimension of Global Hegemony. *Millennium: Journal of International Studies* 44(1): 89–108.
Lake, D. (2013). Theory is Dead, Long Live Theory: The End of the Great Debates and the Rise of Eclecticism in International Relations. *European Journal of International Relations* 19(3): 567–587.
Sil, R. and P.J. Katzenstein (2010). *Beyond Paradigms: Analytic Eclecticism in the Study of World Politics*. London: Palgrave Macmillan.
Strange, S. (1994). *States and Markets*. 2nd edn. London: Continuum.
Takayama, K., A. Sriprakash, and R. Connell (2015). Rethinking Knowledge Production and Circulation in Comparative and International Education: Southern Theory, Postcolonial Perspectives, and Alternative Epistemologies. *Comparative Education Review* 59(1): v–viii.

Wojciuk, A. (2010). *Dylemat potęgi: Praktyczna teoria stosunków międzynarodowych.* [*The Power Dilemma: A Practical Theory of International Relations*]. Warsaw: Wydawnictwa Uniwersytetu Warszawskiego.

Wojciuk, A. (2014). International Power Dimensions of Higher Education in the Age of Knowledge. *Stosunki Międzynarodowe – International Relations* 1(49): 219–228.

Wojciuk, A., M. Michałek, and M. Stormowska (2015). Education as a Source and Tool of Soft Power in International Relations. *European Political Science* 14(3): 298–317.

1 Historical background and the theoretical model

The first part of this chapter provides a description of historical examples of the use of education and science for improving the international position of states. Though they come from the early modern period pre-dating industrialisation, the claim I am arguing for in this work is that the education of societies and development of science only become consistent factors of a state's international position with the arrival of modern statehood and the Second Industrial Revolution. A detailed conceptualisation of their significance is provided in the second part of this chapter. The model proposed there is grounded in the broader context of debates in international relations theory.

From the Middle Ages until industrialisation

Many different societies at different times have played a leading role in technological innovation and economic growth: the Middle East under the Caliphate of Baghdad, Song China, Medieval Spain, Renaissance Italy, Golden Age Netherlands, and England during the Industrial Revolution. The modern period that began roughly in the sixteenth century brought a much more uneven development to different regions of the world, quickly establishing the supremacy of Europe and then the West.[1] Its dominance continues to this day, in spite of twentieth-century prophecies of its imminent decline – whether caused by the Soviet Union, Japan, or China.

In the Middle Ages, the potential for development was more evenly distributed, at least between the three great civilisations: Chinese, Arabic, and European. In many ways, the two major cultures of the East had advanced further than Europe by the fifteenth century, reaching an unmatched level of development in science, knowledge, and innovation. Because nature was often cruel – bringing ruinous floods and droughts – the Chinese and other Asian peoples developed a variety of technologies to diversify their economies and to control essential water supplies. For many centuries before 1500, the East outperformed the West in development. It was a leader in the production of luxury textiles, such as silk and cotton, costly pigments, precious spices, gunpowder, and matches. It had also enjoyed major advantages in what we would now call materials engineering, especially bronze, iron, and ceramics, as well as in paper and woodblock printing. To Europeans, the most developed societies of Asia seemed fabulously wealthy (Goldstone 2009: 12–14). And yet, it was the Old Continent that won the clash of civilisations sparked by Europe's great geographical discoveries.

An undisputed explanation of the West's success in development in the sixteenth and seventeenth centuries is not necessary for the argument pursued in this book. However, since that is an important context for questions addressed in the following chapters, a short overview of the theories of the rise of the West may prove useful. The causes of the supremacy of the West have attracted speculation for at least 250 years, with various explanations being provided, neither of which constitutes a definite answer. Some scholars argue that material conditions, such as climate, topography or natural resources, virtually determined the ascent of the West. The temporal perspective drawn in this context can extend as far back as the conclusion of the ice age. Others refer to intangibles, such as culture, politics, and institutions (factors explored by a vast array of thinkers ranging from Karl Marx to Eric Jones, David Landes, Jared Diamond, and Daron Acemoglu), or religion (e.g. the thought of Max Weber and his various followers). Here, the long term reaches back just 1,000 years, to the Middle Ages, or 2,500 years, to the age of Socrates and Confucius. In general, scholars who favour long-term explanations agree that the success of the West resulted from a series of events set in motion millennia ago. Until 1950, the most popular long-term explanation pointed to cultural factors (Morris 2010: 11–14).

On the other hand, there is a group of scholars who support various short-term explanations which portray the success of the West as much more accidental. According to Andre Gunder Frank (1998), the East was actually better placed to succeed and achieve an industrial revolution than the West, and it would have taken the lead in economic terms were it not for a series of economic and political crises in the seventeenth century. Jack Goldstone (2009: 170–171) argues that until the early seventeenth century, the East and the West were equally likely to succeed. A large number of specific events had to occur in a particular order for a new approach to knowledge to emerge and spread. Goldstone's short-term explanation puts much stress on the act of defiance that Reformation was, which unleashed Europe's intellectual potential, freeing the continent from archaic ideology and sending the West down the path of industrial revolution. However, in his view, the development of modern society in Great Britain was a contingent process that might not have taken place at all. For Kenneth Pomeranz (2001), the Industrial Revolution was a 'gigantic fluke'. By mid-eighteenth century, both East and West were close to an ecological catastrophe, with excessive population growth putting a strain on technological capacities. The centuries that followed were likely to bring recession and a decrease in population. With the accidental discovery of America, Great Britain chanced upon an extraordinary opportunity of developing a complex trading system, which provided incentives for industrialisation. However, even this development would not have ensured the eventual revolution if Britain, again largely by chance, did not discover the rich and conveniently accessible coalfields. All theories, both long and short term, highlighting determinism or chance as key for the success of the West, agree that modernisation and the Industrial Revolution was a turning point for the West. They were, in turn, inherently related to the new role of education and science as political factors, rendering adherence to either of the theories irrelevant to the argument pursued in this book.

Given the complexity involved in identifying the sources of the success of the West, it is much more fruitful for our purposes to explore theories which refer to intellectual factors. Long-term cultural explanations traditionally stress the significance of the peculiar intellectual attitude espoused by Europeans. Among the specific intellectual conditions of the so-called European exception, David Landes (1998) names the characteristic features of the Judaeo-Christian tradition which contributed to the rise of the West. The first of those is respect for independent work and individual agency. The second feature characteristic for European civilisation is the pursuit of mastery over nature, supposedly a radical distinction between Judaeo-Christianity and other civilisations, particularly those based on pantheist religions which find divinity in every part of nature and consequently approach it with much greater respect. The attitude of Judaeo-Christian cultures is symbolised by God's injunction for man to subdue the earth. Third, it is often highlighted that this tradition was shaped by the linear concept of time, while other societies perceived time to be cyclical, returning to the beginning and starting anew. This linearity is also a part of the Judaeo-Christian tradition and it is indelibly linked to ideas of progress and regression, the sense of advancing towards something better or loss of something that used to be perfect. As a result, Western civilisation is often identified as the source of the idea of progress, which brought on the notion of modernisation and defined humanity's role in achieving it. Lastly, the fourth feature is that Western civilisation is distinguished from its Arabic and Chinese counterparts by the market (Landes 1998: 58).

The roots of the expanding intellectual autonomy of the Europeans have been traced as far back as the Medieval conflict between the Papacy and the Empire, when the intellectual monopoly dating back to Antiquity was challenged, which led to the emergence of two competing definitions of worldliness that the contemporaneous elites were now forced to choose from. Medieval philosophy, at that time coextensive with theology, debated the relationship between faith and reason. Abundant controversies led to the formulation of the doctrine of St. Thomas, which shaped the later intellectual development of the Church – the powerful claim that reason is not contrary, but rather complementary to faith. With this gesture, Christianity opened up to rational thought.

For Jack Goldstone (2009: 47–51), the success of a given polity depended on favourable intellectual conditions for social and technological innovation; unlike scholars from the past, however, he did not ascribe them exclusively to Europe. Goldstone argues that success is not connected to any particular religion or culture, but rather to the existence of many religions under conditions of pluralism and tolerance. He provides numerous examples from various places and times of vibrant intellectual environments generating rich cultures, formidable scientific achievements and wealth. Such was the case with the Arabic empire before the twelfth century, a vessel for the potent mixture of advanced Islam and older Jewish, Christian and Zoroastrian traditions, as well as Greek philosophy. The decline of science and technology in Mesopotamia coincided with intellectual closure and an exclusive focus on the Islamic tradition. China achieved the highest level of prosperity and technological development in the twelfth century, under the Song dynasty which oversaw the emergence of an intellectual climate influenced by the spread of Buddhism from India, Islam from Central Asia, and strains of Christianity and Judaism, flourishing side by side with Confucianism and Taoism. The decline of China under the Manchus coincided with the promotion of a rigid Confucian ideology. In seventeenth-century Europe, likewise, the practice of religious toleration declined and rulers began to enforce increasingly rigid orthodoxies and treat religious dissent as a threat to their authority. This led to a stagnation and even the loss of knowledge. Meanwhile, in Great Britain and the Netherlands, where a modicum of religious tolerance was maintained in spite of the political turmoil, innovations accelerated at the turn of the seventeenth century. Goldstone (2009: 128, 151) asserts that industrialisation drew on resources provided by advances in education and training of workers, the use of financial innovations and capital to fund new industries, and new legal and corporate forms of business entities. The breadth of innovation in Great Britain resulted from the scientific revolution of the seventeenth century. Joel Mokyr (2002: 29, 2005: 291–292) also points to intellectual conditions and argues that the increasingly common acceptance of Francis Bacon's belief in harnessing nature for material progress propelled an industrial Enlightenment, inspiring key thinkers of the period and shaping new elites. Bacon was the most influential figure among those who perceived knowledge as the object of constant growth and continuous expansion. The cultural beliefs that began to dominate the elites of the West created modern attitudes, institutions, and mechanisms by which new useful knowledge was created, diffused, and applied.

These factors were key to the formation in Europe of a peculiar intellectual climate which fostered the development of science, knowledge, and inventiveness, helping the societies to not only keep up with the times, but even to dictate the pace and direction of development over the following three to four centuries. At times, this would allow the West to help other cultures achieve progress and a higher standard of living, but oftentimes, the advantage was used to exploit the less cunning and advanced in areas of significance in a given period (Cipolla 1965).

The modern period also saw shifts among the European powers: though the South continued to enjoy supremacy in the fifteenth and sixteenth centuries, the centre of power gradually moved towards the North. Aside from other aspects of its impact, this process also involved a change in mentality. Declining interest in the world and intellectual isolation accompanied the swift decay of Portugal's standing in late sixteenth and seventeenth centuries. As a result, the nation ceded primacy in areas in which it used to reign supreme, such as navigation (Landes 1998: 135). It was the Portuguese who were the first to adopt a scientific approach to exploration of seas and oceans and education of naval officers. In 1484, King João II created a commission of experts in mathematics to work out a method of establishing the location of naval vessels based on the observation of the Sun. This was one of the first instances in the modern era of a European state employing a team of scholars to devise a practical solution to a burning problem on the basis of theoretical findings.

In the early sixteenth century, Portugal and Spain established schools for the specific purpose of training navigators, which went on to produce such figures as Amerigo Vespucci or Sebastiano Caboto. Great Britain openly courted Caboto's services. A paradigmatic case of buying the services of a specialist with advanced technological insight necessary for the expansion of a foreign state, the transaction allowed Great Britain to put Caboto's abilities to great use. In the early fifteenth century, Portugal educated sailors from other countries, including the Netherlands and Great Britain; within a century, it was reduced to employing foreigners for navigating the traditional routes of its own merchant fleet.

Though Max Weber's *Protestant Ethic and the Spirit of Capitalism* has been the object of many a critique since its publication and contemporary social sciences harbour plentiful doubts over the use of religion for explaining the relative success of capitalist development in some countries as opposed to others, the work highlights the peculiarity of the form of education in states where Reformed Christianity achieved supremacy. Protestantism was typified by the stress it laid on learning, especially acquiring literacy, and without gender distinctions. The significance of literacy derived from the demand that good Protestants read the Bible independently. Though Catholics received catechesis, they were unlikely to read Scripture on their own. As a result, on average Protestant youth were more likely to receive advanced education than Catholics. As contemporary research affirms, literacy among women also played a part by radically increasing the likelihood of educational attainment among their children. Already in the Middle Ages, the ability to read and write was common among the Jews, putting them at the forefront of intellectual life. The expulsion of Jews from the Iberian Peninsula had an impact on the intellectual life of Europe. A significant proportion of them moved to the North, many to the most liberal and tolerant region of the continent at the time – the Netherlands.

The onset of Reformation, involving the negation of widely held, universal Christian view of the world and of the role of religion in social life, sowed the seeds of scepticism and dissidence, inspiring new ways of thinking. In reaction to these changes, the Counter-Reformation created institutions that tackled the new challenges head-on while retaining the contours of the Catholic intellectual formation. One such institution was the Jesuit order, which educated many enlightened scholars of the modern era, such as Descartes. In the vast majority of cases, however, the Counter-Reformation led to a closing of the minds and a censoring of the knowledge which was perceived as a threat. In extreme cases, freedom of ideas was repressed with physical violence: Galileo ended up under house arrest, and his works were proscribed; the price Giordano Bruno paid for his convictions was his life.

14 *History and the theoretical model*

In 1558, the death penalty was introduced in the Habsburg empire as punishment for the unsanctioned importation of foreign books. A year later, Spain instituted a ban on studying abroad except in such 'safe havens' as Rome, Naples, or Bologna. The universities in Southern Europe, the finest places of higher learning in Italy and Spain, were transformed from intellectual hubs of the continent into centres for indoctrination. This trend in the intellectual history of Europe follows the pattern of growth and decline of major powers – in the same period, Spain, Portugal, and Italy slowly began to recede in the international arena, giving way to the much more open-minded Great Britain and relatively free-thinking Netherlands, later to be joined by Germany.

Though small in terms of territorial extent and population, the Netherlands became the richest region of the world at the time and instantly established a colonial empire of astounding proportions. The country received the Jews expelled from the Iberian Peninsula, including, for instance, the ancestors of the famous philosopher Baruch de Spinoza. It was also the chosen homeland for Descartes, who received the elite Jesuit education and kept faith with Catholicism until the very end, but sought intellectual freedom. Last but not least, it was in the Netherlands that Thomas Hobbes, a resident of the British Isles, published his *Leviathan*.

States beyond the Old Continent also failed to keep abreast of the innovations and scientific advancement achieved by European giants such as Great Britain and the Netherlands, which proved to have a detrimental effect on their potential. At the dawning of the modern era, China possessed a great fleet and advanced technology superior to European achievements (Goldstone 2009: 12), but could not disseminate knowledge and science. While the most dynamic states of Europe democratised knowledge, the Chinese restricted access to it to a narrow elite. In spite of the existence of an educated class of mandarins, its sense of superiority, distaste for expanding knowledge, and belief that anything foreign was by definition worse, prevented the Middle Kingdom from exploiting the opportunities provided by contact with other cultures. The unwillingness to adapt the achievements of foreign technology finds an apt illustration in an anecdote about the clocks that the Jesuits brought to Macau. In Europe, the clock quickly revolutionised the organisation of labour, leading to increased efficiency; in China, it became a piece of decoration or a plaything (Landes 1983). Though Jesuits brought not only clocks, but also the latest findings of science to China, these remained locked up in Beijing and thus could not bring about the kind of social change that had taken place in Europe.

China also lacked institutions for the systematic development and transmission of knowledge; there were no academies, scientific societies, or scholarly journals. Knowledge and science remained exclusive in contemporary China, recorded in a complex, oblique language, and largely bereft of any means of verification. The clear-cut separation between science, philosophy, and poetry that arrived in Europe with modernity did not occur in China. While the transmission of knowledge used to occur in one direction only in the past (Europe learning from the Middle Kingdom), by the colonial period, and even more vividly in the early industrial era, it was the West that possessed knowledge and technology that China would find to be of use (Cipolla 1970). By then, however, it was not prepared to engage in this kind of an exchange. As a result, it did not partake in the Industrial Revolution, paying the heavy price of developmental delay and, indirectly, loss of the status of a world power in the modern era (Landes 1998: 340–347).

Japan's response to contact with European civilisation differed from that of China. While it resisted Christianity in order to protect its social structure, it numbered among the few states which learned to produce the newly encountered goods. The Chinese exhibited European clocks at the imperial court; the Japanese began to mass-produce them. However, it was only in the nineteenth century that Japan underwent the changes that transformed it into a world power.

Already in the nineteenth century, Japan had sought to abandon the role of imitator and become a leader of technological advancement, quickly making up for lost time. Japan was not satisfied with producing consumer goods; it wanted to produce motors and machines, ships and engines, build highways, ports, and shipyards. Its strategy was based on the importation of knowledge, achieved both by sending native specialists abroad to obtain the necessary qualifications, and by inviting experts from abroad and learning from them. What typified this strategy in its Japanese variety, however, was the willingness to go beyond mere eavesdropping and imitation and their attempt to independently improve foreign patents. From the beginning, the goal was to increase one's own abilities and technological insight. The unprecedented success of this transformation remained for decades a favoured example in debates on varieties of developmental models (Vogel 1980). Aside from the determination, dedication, peculiar work culture, and smooth technological transfers, much has been made of the role high-level universal education and a large number of properly trained engineers played in the transition (Kennedy 1987: 538).

Like China, Arab and Muslim civilisations proved unable to adapt in time to the new economic conditions brought on by capitalism and the first wave of globalisation prompted by geographical discoveries. Aside from a failed attempt at industrialisation in nineteenth-century Egypt, Muslim states did not partake in technological advances or share in the modern concept of education and knowledge. Blighted by adverse conditions, particularly the lack of economic capital, they retained local – even tribal – cultures until the twentieth century, incapable of adapting new technologies or producing suitably trained personnel for the professionalising bureaucracy, army, and occupations. The elites of Arab countries often maintained their distrust of knowledge and technology from the West. The durability of feudal structures diminished the significance of a person's insight and abilities for their chances of social advancement, and the continued determination of social standing by birth, combined with the absence of sufficient institutional and infrastructural backdrop, limited the viability of investing one's time and energy into learning. These states continued to suffer from high rates of illiteracy – up to 100 per cent among women – even during the twentieth century. Arab science led the way during the Middle Ages (its golden age), but the modern era saw it lapse into increasing developmental delay in relation to Europe (Landes 1998: 410).

In the early stages of colonisation, South America boasted greater resources than North America. Rich deposits of gold and other minerals aside, it also offered better opportunities for agriculture. Spaniards perceived the British gains in the Western hemisphere as far less valuable than their own. The British and Spanish colonies followed different paths of development. South America was far less welcoming to immigrants from outside of the Iberian Peninsula, particularly non-Catholics; the dominant impulse was one of conservation and continuation. Meanwhile, North America benefitted from a constant influx of manpower, including those of exceptional ability, the well-educated and enterprising, as well as a wealth of knowledge from across Europe; furthermore, it exhibited a greater open-mindedness and a spirit of discovery. The United States adopted a peculiar, separate model of development, defined by near-unlimited natural resources, but relatively narrow labour power. The resulting system depended on standardisation to ensure higher labour efficiency. Work activities were organised to require only the most basic abilities: the same factories produced whole series of elements and assembled them.

It was only the Second Industrial Revolution that brought on economic development at an unprecedented rate, maintained for a very long time. The scope of the changes can be illustrated by comparing the incomes of the industrialising Western Europe and Eastern Europe, whose transformation was more gradual. In 1750, the difference between the former (not counting Great Britain) and the latter in terms of per capita earnings amounted to 15 per cent; in 1800, it grew to some 20 per cent; by 1860, it reached 64 per cent; and in 1900 – nearly 90 per cent (Bairoch and Lévy-Leboyer 1981; Aldcroft 2006).

In seventeenth and eighteenth centuries, Europe became clearly divided into the centre and the peripheries. At the onset of the eighteenth century, Great Britain – the initiator of the First Industrial Revolution that began when the steam engine elevated the country to the rank of top producer of textiles, iron, and energy – was already at the heart of economic development and exploitation of fossil fuels. The Second Industrial Revolution, symbolised by the introduction of electricity, began with the invention of steel production technology, and went on to give birth to the chemical and automobile industry, followed by other major branches of mass-scale production. The second wave of industrialisation benefitted from significant support from public policy and state bureaucracies, particularly in such states as Germany and Japan – less so in the USA, which was typified by an enormous internal market that did not require state intervention (Cerny 1995: 604–605).

Already at the onset of industrialisation, European peripheries were highly differentiated. For instance, in the eighteenth century, Scandinavia suffered from high poverty, but experienced a dynamic development in terms of knowledge, education, and political institutionalisation. Though industrialisation began late in that region, the delay was quickly made up for. The developmental leap Scandinavian states made in the nineteenth century can be attributed to the good preparation of the local societies in intellectual and scientific terms, high level of literacy, and high quality of university education.

In terms of education and knowledge, Russia was beset by contradictions, unable to plug the increasing gap dividing it from the West with sufficient speed, efficiency, and extensiveness. Though certain cosmopolitan intellectual milieus kept abreast of advancements in the world of science, the general population of Russia attained low levels of education. Like in Scandinavia, industrialisation arrived late to the country; unlike in Scandinavia, massive developmental delays in popular education, including high illiteracy rates persisting until the Bolshevik revolution, hindered progress. In the absence of universal education, the viability of socio-economic transformations that typified the modern era became drastically limited. Generally low level and elite character of education also affected the industrialisation drives initiated towards the end of the nineteenth century. Compared to the United States or Germany, Russian workforce was uneducated and under-qualified; engineers, scientists, and specialists capable of managing the ever-more complex processes of production were scarce. Bureaucracy and army, too, remained far less organised and efficient, due to lack of professional cadres. Only in the Soviet Union would millions of workers gain access to education on a mass scale. For this purpose, factory schools, technical high schools, and polytechnics were established, and the number of students rose (Kennedy 1987: 417). In 1898, the Russian economy possessed only 47,000 engineers; by 1941, that number increased to nearly 290,000 (Nove 1969: 232; McCauley 1981: 85–87).

Despite the name, the Industrial Revolution occurred in stages, across entire centuries. The social changes it wrought run deep, elevating technology to an increasingly significant status (Mokyr 2005: 286). Machines took over work previously performed by humans, making certain abilities redundant and limiting the amount of physical labour necessary to produce goods. Vast amounts of energy were unleashed, breaking the limits imposed by animal labour. Its production, in turn, required significant exploitation of resources (Smil 2006). The Industrial Revolution revised the list of human abilities and knowledge that men needed to work and states to expand economically. Mokyr (2005: 286) claims that the West is so much richer today than it was two centuries ago because societies 'know' more. This transformation was not just 'a matter of degree', bringing qualitative difference to the economy. Ernest Gellner (1964: 179), too, argues that an industrial society is one in which knowledge – and a new kind of knowledge – plays a highly different role than in previous forms of human organisation. The form of knowledge peculiar to industrial societies is modern science which, in turn, is unthinkable without an industrialised society. Traditional belief systems were stable and provided their followers with convincing and morally acceptable interpretations of the world; they also included justifications for the social order, including the distribution of power and privilege peculiar to it. Modern science seeks to dismantle these characteristics, offering no guarantees, respecting no hierarchies, and presenting itself as morally neutral.

Economic historians of the so-called European exception which accounted for the geographic placement of the Industrial Revolution highlight the significance of technological advantage. Progress alone does not suffice; new technologies demanded more advanced competencies, impossible to teach at the workplace, between the master and the apprentice, or to develop in the peace of the home of an ingenious philosopher-inventor. What was needed were formal systems of production and the dissemination of knowledge. Looking for an answer to the question, why the Industrial Revolution did not take place earlier, Mokyr (2002: 31–32) identifies the narrow epistemic base of technology as the main root of diminishing returns. Between 1400 and 1750 new techniques in ship design, metallurgy, medicine, printing, and energy, even revolutionary ones, typically crystallised quickly at a new technological plateau and failed to bring about a stream of cumulative micro-inventions. The main reason for that was the shortage of knowledge on how and why the techniques worked. Exploitable regularities provided the most common type of knowledge used in production. They worked despite lack of clarity concerning the principles that made them work. This led many inventors down the path of exhaustive exploration of dead ends, the most well known of which were perpetual-motion and the philosopher's stone. Knowledge about the natural principles at work substantially narrows the range of potential experimentation, making success more plausible and limiting resource losses. Of particular significance was the invention of experimentation, which required in-depth considerations over proper research strategies and the construction of instruments for use in observation and measurement. The concept of the experimental method as we know it today dates back only as far as Galileo in the sixteenth century.

The arrival of modernity also led to the formation of a community of researchers and scholars from various countries interested in common topics, the universalisation of knowledge, and a supranational structure of disciplines. News of scientific discoveries spread with increasing speed, allowing scholars to build on the findings of others. The first regularly convening scientific societies were formed, and the first scientific journals established. They soon became fore for cooperation as well as a stage for the combat for fame and primacy. The spoils of prestige and splendour belonged to the inventor. The desire for primacy often led to conflicts, such as the one between Gottfried Wilhelm Leibniz and Isaac Newton, both of whom claimed to have invented the differential equation. The controversy between the two mathematicians achieved international proportions, extending beyond the philosophical or scientific circles and dividing contemporaneous elites between those who sided with the Englishman and those who sided with the German.

Modern Europe was rich not only in scientific debates, but also in implementations, which very quickly began to transform work and increase its efficiency. Until the end of the nineteenth century, the Old Continent had a virtually absolute monopoly on scientific knowledge and a practically complete control over application, which translated into an unmatched productivity. The political and economic benefits of an educated population continued to expand at least since the late eighteenth century. Much of the tacit crafts-based knowledge spread by way of the continuous movement of skilled workers from one area to another, and 'industrial espionage' remained an important means of access to technology (Mokyr 2002: 57).

Before states and businesses could use them, new technological abilities and advances in the labour market required increasingly institutionalised forms of disseminating knowledge and conducting scientific research. This was particularly significant for governments of states that sought to catch up with Great Britain. In their bid to make up for developmental delays – first, in terms of the contours of the modern state, and only then in relation to the economy – France and Germany devised specific institutions tasked with disseminating knowledge and skills: the first technical schools, polytechnics, and research institutes. Already by the second half of the nineteenth century, this new, more strictly organised manner of discovering and transmitting knowledge proved particularly beneficial to those states, enabling relative gains in power in the Second Industrial Revolution.

The purpose of this brief historical introduction was to provide a context for and describe the intellectual climate that accompanied the First and Second Industrial Revolution in Europe, and then distinguished it – and later the West – from other parts of the world. The themes addressed here are explored at greater length in Chapters 2 and 3. This general view of the subject of the work sets the stage for the theoretical schema that provides the basis for the conceptualisation of education and science as factors of a state's international power.

The theoretical model

The following section is devoted to a description of the theoretical model, which identifies education as a factor of a state's international power. It derives from the conceptualisation of power in international relations by Stefano Guzzini. In his view, while there is merit to the concentration on the potential and strategic interactions between international actors that dominates mainstream theories, this perspective overlooks one crucial aspect of power – its structural aspect. In his conceptualisation, Guzzini (1993: 443) divides it into the agential dimension, entailing analysis from the perspective of the actor, and the structural (intersubjective) dimension, defined as governance, which is not determined directly by any specific agent or group of agents. I will discuss the agential aspect of power in international relations first, then its structural aspect, and finally attempt to analyse the emergence of social facts in the shape of interactions between agents and structures.

Agential power is easier to define – it entails an actor's ability to affect other actors and cause them to act differently than they would otherwise. Studies in international relations are clearly marked by a tradition of analysis of the power of state as an agent in terms of its resources. While this tradition yields easily adaptable prescriptions for studies of international politics, it has come under criticism from many sides owing to the irreconcilable paradoxes that it engenders. The causal relationship between a state's resources and its ability to affect other participants in international relations is not easy to grasp and explain.

However, scholars agree that various resources are necessary to enable states to exert an influence (Wojciuk 2010: 10, 35–40). Among the resources most commonly mentioned in this context are such material resources as geographical and demographic determinations, natural resources, industrial potential, military superiority, as well as non-material resources such as national culture, morale, or the quality of the government. While different approaches and paradigms assign priorities differently, orthodox materialism typifies only a handful of structural realists and some Marxists. Most theoreticians of international relations assign a role to non-material factors. These gain particular significance in constructivist approaches, in which even material resources owe their influence to a particular way of understanding and assignation of meaning. Thus, the non-material component inevitably affects the resources that define a state's power. A resource is relatively easy to operationalise – especially if it is material; therefore, while the weaknesses of this approach to state power should not be disregarded, it remains useful for comparisons and evaluations of international power. Such is the context in which it will figure in this work.

Conceptualisations of a state's power in terms of its resources is problematic primarily because the causal chain between specific resources and other actors in the system is not readily apparent (Wojciuk 2010: 63–68). A logical analysis in relation to the conditions of possibility of a state's activity and agency in the international arena might shed light on the matter from another angle. In this case, a society's education level and accumulated knowledge would count among the conditions of a state's agency. The question immediately arises, what sort of conditions could those be?

Studies of the nature of causal relations refer to necessary and sufficient conditions. It seems that an educated society is not a necessary condition of a state's power in international relations – after all, many states traditionally named among the great powers are not known for having a highly educated citizenry. Such cases exist even today, though modernisation and technological advancement make them less common. Does that mean that education and scientific knowledge are sufficient conditions of a state's power? Here, too, the claim seems debatable – one can easily imagine a state with well-educated citizen and highly advanced science but without other factors that allow the people's abilities and knowledge to be used, their potential to be realized. Thus, though education and science are not necessary or sufficient conditions of a state's international position, this work claims that they still play a vital role. Logic permits the existence of such conditions of a process or event that are neither necessary, nor sufficient, and yet remain significant by increasing the probability of an outcome: these are described as the INUS conditions (Mahoney, Kimball, and Koivu 2009: 124–125; Brady 2008: 227).[2] The difficulties in identifying the causal links in social life, a major challenge not just for this work, but rather for the social sciences in general, also define the kinds of public policy recommendations that are formulated. In this view, the state can only create potentialities and favourable conditions, but cannot secure total control of effects – the final result depends on circumstances that are not defined by the state. Though social sciences can identify the factors that make success more likely at specific stages, they do not provide foolproof recipes for success.

Aside from the aforementioned agential aspect, the conceptualisation of power in international relations proposed by Guzzini (1993: 450, 2012: 3) also addresses its structural dimension, which he describes as governance. Among its component parts, he names indirect institutional power, non-intentional power, and impersonal empowering. Indirect institutional power consists in imposing control over the effects of processes by changing the conditions of competition rather than through direct confrontation. The norms and rules of the game evolve according to their own pace and institution-specific logics, being shaped by all actors even if those who exert dominance within a system have more influence than other participants do. Changes in transnational governance in various issue-areas modify the context of actions performed by the agents, in the process ascribing various degrees of significance to different resources to affect the potential of the participants in a given game. As governance evolves, various resources gain or lose significance from the perspective of power; in other words, as factors of state power they play a historically contingent role.

Another component of governance, non-intentional power, is a notion borrowed from Susan Strange (1985: 15). It emerges with the increasing diffusion of power in international relations in terms of its effects as well as sources (a product of the transnationalisation of non-territorial networks). Like the sources of power, actors who shape the structures of governance become increasingly dispersed and heterogeneous, affecting the functioning of international political economy and creating a fragmented governance. In global terms, structures of governance are therefore a function of mutual interactions, conscious and unconscious influences resulting from decisions (or absence thereof) on the part of states as agents and various types of non-state actors (Guzzini 2012: 20). The centre of this system is not easy to locate because the network itself extends beyond the territories of even the most influential states. As a result, actors only have a limited ability to control the effects of their own actions, and their decisions often unintentionally, and even unconsciously force others to adapt. Analyses of international relations focused solely on the participants in specific games involving an interplay between their intentional actions often overlook the structural aspect of power. In contrast to studies that follow rational-choice approach, the concept of structural power deployed here accepts the existence and significance of unintended, uncontrolled, and somewhat implicit consequences of actions performed by particular participants for the institutional form and functioning of the structures of governance.

Impersonal empowering, the third component of Guzzini's formulation of structures of governance, refers, in turn, to power derived from a specific intersubjectivity involving, on the one hand, the privileging of individual actors within existing structures, and on the other hand, the entire area of discursive power. This aspect of structural power is inspired primarily by Antonio Gramsci's theory of hegemony, which indicates that, in international relations, power does not derive solely from the potential of agents, but also from the recognition and at least partial legitimation of their authority by other participants in a given game. It also refers to the theories of Michel Foucault, who found social control to be the most captivating aspect of power. To fulfil its potential within existing structures, agent-centred power must be at least partially accepted by other actors. This acceptance can be more or less conscious, which is why impersonal empowering often involves the engagement of specific, often hegemonic, discourses, routines, practices, and regimes. Thanks to their symbolic power, structures empower or 'subject' individuals to their authority and draw power from their actions in return. Thus understood, structures of governance deploy impersonal empowering explicitly, by extending special privileges to certain actors expressly deemed to be of more importance than others, or implicitly, by offering unconventional and symbolic appreciation based on discourse, practices, and routine to some participants in the game.

Within governance, impersonal empowering occurs in a certain specific intersubjectivity that naturalises arbitrary relations of dominance, making them so obvious as to be invisible. This most unconventional aspect of analysis of structures of governance involves the entire region between knowledge and power, the object of the research programme of governmentality. At the same time, the goal of knowledge-power is not reducible solely to social control and oversight: the government can, after all, pursue not only power as such, but also the welfare of the population, improved living conditions, increased wealth, improved healthiness, lifespan, and quality of life broadly understood (Foucault 2009). These actions, however, lead to the appearance of ever-more complex systems of management, monitoring, and surveillance of individuals. The weakness of analyses of governmentality is that once relations of power are deemed ever-present, the act of exposing them is no longer as critical. It is therefore crucial to identify the normative aspect of knowledge/power: whether its goal is to find 'the best practices', promoting freedom and emancipation, and offering solutions individuals can apply for their own benefit, or whether it deals in the discourse of threat and risk, strengthening the management and limiting freedom.

According to this tripartite formulation, governance can be defined as the potential of intersubjective practices to create effects, which involves both the conventional, social construction of options for various actors, and the less conventional symbolic structures of power. The structural approach to power thus highlights the informal side of governance rather than the agency of particular actors, and defines the political order in terms of its effects rather than sources. The analysis begins not with agents who establish the order, but with the constitutive elements of governance, and reflects upon the rules of the game without assuming the inevitability of intentionality or control. In other words, it takes into account unforeseen consequences and structural effects unrelated to the agency of any specific actor (Guzzini 2012: 5).

Power results both from the interaction involved in relations between agents and systematised norms and rules constituted through their actions. The actions of the subjects create a horizon of that which is conceivable and doable. Structures of governance, on the other hand, define and redefine the identities of the actors. The power of agents in international relations and governance are related, and neither is reducible to the other. Though every interpretation of governance implies an understanding of power and vice versa, governance is not reducible to power nor is power reducible to governance.

The first two chapters of this work put a greater stress on agential power, though not without addressing the structural side of the matter. The focus is, first, on the role of education and science in state-building processes (Chapter 2), and second, on their significance for economic development (Chapter 3). Chapter 2 attempts to describe the causal mechanism that involves education and science in building the modern state, both in terms of securing professional cadres for the state bureaucracy and in relation to the state's involvement in forming the society and ensuring its loyalty and identification with the state.

Chapter 3, in turn, analyses the economical mechanisms through which the level of education and science is translated into state power. Using writings in economics and economic policies addressing the questions of human capital, growth theory, competitive advantages, and national systems of innovation, it shows how skills contribute to wealth and prosperity. From this perspective, education and science number among the conditions of possibility for the economic welfare of a state, and thus define its influence on the international arena. Economic theories provide states with varied political recommendations in this regard – some restrict the government's prerogatives solely to the provision of minimal universal education and financial support for basic research; others postulate a much deeper involvement of the authorities in these fields. Here, I address the main public controversies and disputes between proponents of various approaches. These variations will define the ramifications of key political choices that today often meet with resistance among certain social groups.

The proposed analysis approaches the problem genealogically, as a process, since it took time for education and science to gain politico-economic significance for states in the international context. The static approach that characterises some social theories, including theories of international relations, is

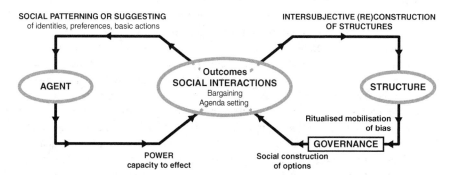

Figure 1.1 Schematic representation of Stefano Guzzini's concept of power in international relations.

Source: own elaboration on the basis of Guzzini 1993: 473.

ill-suited to this mobility and change. As a result, the pages of this book are filled with historical examples. By reflecting on the origins of institutions, one may perceive them in less obvious terms – not simply as an indelible part of the known reality – and thus better capture the role they play today. In this perspective, education and science cannot be assumed to have developed intentionally, according to some pre-determined, all-encompassing idea or plan for harnessing them to the state. The assumption that I followed comes from Norbert Elias (1994), who observed that social processes are fairly autonomous from human expectations and goals and that they are partially self-regulated. Similarly, the degree of top-down control was not consistent across all countries mentioned in this study. Yet even in the most authoritarian cases, institutions were shaped by many interacting factors and conflicts of interest among various social groups. Thus, one cannot say that the overall result was simply the realisation of an all-encompassing concept imposed centrally by the government.

Similarly, in responding to the question of the role education and science played in the Second Industrial Revolution, this work does not endorse the claim that school systems were purposely installed in the service of industrialisation (Hallinan 2000: 171) – a claim that is still accepted today among certain Marxist scholars. The development of school systems and science at times outpaced industrialisation, and if states intervened explicitly in this regard, this occurred primarily during the aforementioned centralisation efforts of absolutist rulers who sought to establish modern states and then to make up for delays in political and economic modernisation in relation to Great Britain, where these processes had occurred previously in a bottom-up, unpremeditated fashion. Nonetheless, education and science proved to have been of major value to industrialisation, especially since the Second Industrial Revolution. Introducing different rules, this revolution paved the way to economic, and then political, success for new players; among the spectacular examples of states that rose to top ranks in the process of making up for lost time were Germany and Japan. Their instant economic and then political rise, owed partly to education, science, and their adaptations for emerging branches of industry, quickly led to apprehension among established international powers of the modern era, who observed the advance of the former pariahs with a mixture of awe and anxiety.

Chapters 2 and 3 remain focused primarily, but not exclusively (since total separation is impossible here), on the agential level, offering a detailed account of mechanisms through which education and science affected the power of a state within the framework of analysis of processes of state-building and economic development. Chapter 4 returns to the analysis of an agent's power through resources – a more static approach, but still focused on actors rather than structures. This part includes a kind of international balance sheet in education and science. It also presents case studies describing the most characteristic strategies employed by the great powers as well as the most efficient of their lesser counterparts in developing educational and scientific resources and applying them in the economy. In every case, these considerations take into account the peculiar conditions of the various models of capitalism that have historically emerged in these states. Though I reflect on the structural aspect of governance in all parts of the work, Chapter 5 is particularly focused on them. It addresses the latest transformations of international governance in education and science, which involve an increase in significance of international comparisons for establishing the political options available to agents. Those changes impose normative choices while mobilising the resistance of a section of the public.

The historical processes that universalised education and altered its character were a part of much broader structural transformation often described in shorthand as modernisation, Industrial Revolution, or the transition from feudal structures to nation-states and markets, followed by globalisation. Though the theory of power applied here convincingly distinguishes (for analytic purposes) between agential and structural power, it is much harder to consistently discuss agency and structure in separation owing to the strict ties between them in political practice. The agent side is easier to capture because it is more attuned to the dominant social scientific paradigm and to the intuitive 'discourse' on politics. My deliberate focus on states, in turn, drastically limits the range of agents whose actions are described. A more detailed selection of various kinds of participants in the game, such as business ventures or even universities, would in itself make the 'actors' side far too complex and difficult to describe.

However, it is primarily the structure that exhibits the greatest complexity in this perspective, involving such general macro-level characteristics as the stage of industrialisation, formal institutions and organisations, informal regimes based on implicit rules, as well as various discourses – both global and highly local. These structural layers are established by various agents with the involvement of different (and increasingly diffuse) non-state actors, and the evolution of governance they effect is an uncontrollable process. This work does not propose to reflect systematically on all of these spheres, which in itself may not be possible at all. Yet, it is written with the forceful theoretical assumption that power is dual – agential and structural; and this assumption provides the guiding principle for the structure of the book.

My analysis of education and science as sources of state power in international relations yields the following main claims pursued in subsequent chapters:

1   Education and science were factors in the emergence of modern states, affecting their power in international relations. In this context, the causal mechanisms primarily involved:

   a   the establishment of state bureaucracy based on meritocratic criteria and independent from church hierarchy;
   b   the development of technical knowledge necessary for the implementation of major public works, also in infrastructure, requiring technical and engineering competencies – including those applicable in the art of war and military engineering;
   c   the formation of a national identity of the citizen and their loyalty towards the state.

2. In the process of industrialisation, scientific-technical knowledge became an asset to the state, particularly since the Second Industrial Revolution. From that point on, it provided a space for competition in the world economy, highlighting another aspect of differentiation in the centre-periphery system. Historically, several institutional models have emerged in the political economy of education and science, peculiar to the more liberal and more strictly coordinated models of market economy.
3. Modernisation and industrialisation, key factors in the transformation from feudalism to a mature capitalism, significantly modified the rules of the international game, promoting other kinds of resources and organisational forms of political agents. Due to these structural changes, education and science gained in significance compared to previous eras.
4. The political and economic success of the Western organisational model for the state led to its widespread adoption. Without debating whether this model was implemented freely or due to the hegemonic domination, the schema was applied to the construction of public institutions across the world, but not to identical effect.
5. The fact that economic sciences have proved the significance of human capital and scientific-technical knowledge for economic development contributes to the claim that education and science affect the economy. Another structural change, this time concerning the structure of scholarly knowledge, led to the modification of the actions of agents, now exhibiting an even more strategic understanding of these fields in the context of economic welfare. On the other hand, this highly normative change sparked a resistance among milieus opposed to the economisation of learning.
6. The latest shifts on the level of governance in education and science are typified by the pursuit of the best practices with a particularly strong focus on regimes based in international comparisons. These informal and implicit structures of governance partly modify the strategies of actors seeking effective, tested solutions. International governance in education and science sparks axiological controversies, mostly concerning the understanding of common welfare and of the proportions between economic priorities and other values. Various discourses clash on these grounds due to divergent interpretations of the degrees of harmony or conflict between the aforementioned aims, as well as adherence to divergent paths to the achievement of these priorities.

The purpose of Chapter 1 was to, first, provide an outline of the empirical problematic – as described in the brief historical sketch. In the theoretical part, I began by presenting the conceptualisation of power in international relations, which combines conventional and non-conventional constructivism, and then described my own model of education and science as factors of a state's international power.

Notes

1 Here, the 'West' includes Europe, the United States, and Canada; in using the term, I recognise its controversial nature as well as its divergent interpretations (Morris 2010).
2 In set theory, the concept of INUS condition draws on the distinction between necessary and sufficient conditions in terms of causal relations. Many causal factors combine to create particular effects. Individual causal factors are neither necessary, nor sufficient, but rather a part of a broader combination that is only sufficient for a given effect when taken as a whole. In itself, an INUS cause is neither necessary, nor sufficient. Instead, it belongs to a broader combination that is sufficient (but not necessary) for an effect. The acronym INUS comes from philosopher John Leslie Mackie, who defined such conditions as 'insufficient but non-redundant parts of a condition which is itself unnecessary but sufficient for the occurrence of the effect' (Mackie 1965: 246, 1980). Mackie's concept is one of many attempts to capture the complexity of causal relations.

References

Aldcroft, D.H. (2006). *Europe's Third World: The European Periphery in the Interwar Years*. Aldershot: Ashgate.
Bairoch, P. and M. Lévy-Leboyer (eds) (1981). *Disparities in Economic Development Since the Industrial Revolution*. Basingstoke: Palgrave Macmillan.
Brady, H. (2008). Causation and Explanation in Social Science. In J.M. Box-Steffensmeier, H. Brady, and D. Collier (eds), *The Oxford Handbook of Political Methodology*. Oxford: Oxford University Press.
Cerny, P.G. (1995). Globalization and the Changing Logic of Collective Action. *International Organization* 49(4): 595–625.
Cipolla, C.M. (1965). *Guns, Sails and Empires: Technological Innovation and the Early Phases of European Expansion 1400–1700*. New York: Pantheon.
Cipolla, C.M. (1970). *The Economic Decline of Empires*. London: Methuen.
Elias, N. (1994). *What is Sociology?*. New York: Columbia University Press.
Foucault, M. (2009). *Security, Territory, Population: Lectures at the Collège de France 1977–1978*. New York: Picador.
Frank, A.G. (1998). *ReORIENT: Global Economy in the Asian Age*. Berkeley, CA: University of California Press.
Gellner, E. (1964). *Thought and Change*. Chicago, IL: University of Chicago Press.
Goldstone, J.A. (2009). *Why Europe?: The Rise of the West in World History, 1500–1850*. New York: McGraw-Hill.
Guzzini, S. (1993). Structural Power: The Limits of Neorealist Power Analysis. *International Organization Archer* 47(3): 443–478.
Guzzini, S. (2012). The Ambivalent 'Diffusion of Power' in Global Governance. In S. Guzzini and I. Neumann (eds), *Diffusion of Power in Global Governance: International Political Economy Meets Foucault*. Basingstoke: Palgrave Macmillan.
Hallinan, M.T. (ed.) (2000). *Handbook of the Sociology of Education*. New York: Springer.
Harris, J.R. (1992). The First British Measures Against Industrial Espionage. In I. Blanchard, A. Goodman, and J. Newman (eds), *Industry and Finance in Early Modern History*. Stuttgart: Franz Steiner.
Kennedy, P. (1987). *The Rise and Fall of Great Powers*. New York: Vintage Books.
Landes, D.S. (1983). *Revolution in Time: Clocks and the Making of the Modern World*. Cambridge, MA: Harvard University Press.

Landes, D.S. (1998). *The Wealth and Poverty of Nations: Why Some are So Rich and Some So Poor?*. New York: W.W. Norton & Co.
McCauley, M. (1981). *The Soviet Union Since 1917*. London: Longman.
Mackie, J.L. (1965). Causes and Conditions. *American Philosophical Quarterly* 2(4): 245–255.
Mackie, J.L. (1980). *The Cement of Universe: A Study of Causation*. Oxford: Clarendon Press.
Mahoney, J., E. Kimball, and K.L Koivu (2009). The Logic of Historical Explanation in the Social Sciences. *Comparative Political Studies* 42(1): 114–146.
Mokyr, J. (2002). *The Gifts of Athena: Historical Origins of the Knowledge Economy*, Princeton, NJ: Princeton University Press.
Mokyr, J. (2005). The Intellectual Origins of Modern Economic Growth. *The Journal of Economic History* 65(2): 285–351.
Morris, I. (2010). *Why the West Rules – for Now: The Patterns of History, and What They Reveal About the Future*. New York: Farrar, Straus and Giroux.
Nove, A. (1969). *An Economic History of the USSR*. Harmondsworth: Penguin.
Pomeranz, K. (2001). *The Great Divergence: China, Europe, and the Making of the Modern World Economy*. Princeton, NJ: Princeton University Press.
Smil, V. (2006). *Transforming the Twentieth Century*, vol. 2: *Technical Innovations and Their Consequences*. Oxford: Oxford University Press.
Strange, S. (1985). International Political Economy: The Story So Far and The Way Ahead. In W.L. Hollist and F. LaMond Tullis (eds), *An International Political Economy*. Boulder, CO: Westview Press.
Vogel, E.F. (1980). *Japan as Number One: Lessons for America*. New York: Harper Colphon Books.
Wojciuk, A. (2010). *Dylemat potęgi: Praktyczna teoria stosunków międzynarodowych*. [*The Power Dilemma: A Practical Theory of International Relations*] Warsaw: Wydawnictwa Uniwersytetu Warszawskiego.

2 The role of education and science in the state-building process

The development of education systems was a part of the state-building processes that led to the formation of modern political entities. These processes involved not only the creation of a political and administrative apparatus along with various government agencies, but also the formation of ideologies and common convictions that legitimised the government and provided the foundations for such concepts as 'nation' and 'national character'. In Europe, these processes reached their greatest intensity in the eighteenth and nineteenth centuries, but, in spite of numerous similarities between particular states, the course they followed was not identical in every case.

During the transformation from feudalism to capitalism, states – which had thus far served only limited socio-economic functions – became deeply engaged in social, economic, and political questions, mostly for the purpose of stabilising the social order, promoting a national culture, and establishing and defending far more exact borders. Economic activity also came under more intense regulation concurrently with the development and entrenchment of a legal system securing the rights stemming from contracts and ensuring property laws. While these processes were accompanied by an increasing social demand for democracy and constitutionalism, states had meanwhile erected efficient and often authoritarian bureaucracies tasked with fulfilling the new functions. As a result, internal hierarchical power and external competitiveness became their characteristic features. Such was the emergence of the sovereign, unitary actors of international relations so typical of modern Europe, far more homogeneous in structure than their late feudal and early capitalist predecessors (Cerny 1995: 603–604).

Education was an indelible part of these processes, subsumed under the state apparatus, with schools turned into a locus of contact between the state and its population as well as an instrument of influencing it (Mitter 2004). The establishment of state education systems in the nineteenth century led to a radical enlargement of the number of persons included in the systems on the one hand, and to the dissolution of various educational subsystems controlled by corporations, cities, churches, guilds, or families on the other. These institutions introduced a sense of universalism to the relations between the government and the people, derived from the belief that a common model of education would suit different social groups and serve the state as well as the populace. The degree of centralisation and homogenisation was not uniform in all states, but each sought a common denominator for educating members of different estates and classes. Education thus became an institution of the state developed from the top down.

The initial model for the state education system was developed in eighteenth-century absolute monarchies as a part of a larger structure that also included, among others, bureaucracy, a standing army, and a tax system. The new institutions responded to the demand for an educated bureaucracy, but also for engineers and professional military officers, that is, occupations which lay at the heart of the modern rational state. As the demand for technological innovation increased – particularly with regard to shipbuilding, metalwork, and military engineering – so did the need for specialists equipped with the necessary competencies. For contemporary theoreticians of the state and absolute monarchs, education seemed to offer a solution for fulfilling the mercantile goals of the sovereign.

The development of education facilitated the propagation of national cultures and identities along with attendant national ideologies and nationalisms, which gained particular prominence during the nineteenth century (Hallinan 2000: 189). Incidentally, the nationalism of the eighteenth and early nineteenth century differed from its twentieth century variation, not being as tightly bound to xenophobia and strict attachment to ethnic criteria or the concept of community of blood that were mostly a product of the Romantic period (Hobsbawm 1990). The significance of schooling increased as national identities took shape and identification with the state superseded local, class, and religious identities. Education displaced traditional communities: in the nineteenth century, it gradually took over the function of moral, cultural, and political formation, thus far the preserve of the churches. It facilitated the integration of immigrants and ethnic minorities, promoted the dominant religious views and standardised national languages. It also disseminated the rules of rational calculation and economy, promoted patriotism, enforced moral discipline, and popularised a political and economic vision of the world, usually consonant with the views of dominant groups or classes. Education was at the centre of a veritable cultural revolution that accompanied the erection of states (Corrigan and Sayer 1985). From an ideological perspective, states sought to form a coherent entity from the feudal estates and the emerging social classes. At the discursive level, a common narrative was pursued that would operate across existing divisions.

At their inception in the eighteenth century, education systems were primarily associated with state-building processes rather than the rising of industrialisation (Hallinan 2000: 171). The first Industrial Revolution did not require special competencies and consequently yielded no immediate rise in levels of enrolment. Its onset, in fact, saw illiteracy rates in Great Britain increase. The basic competencies necessary for industrialisation were already found in societies and disseminated in a decentralised manner, independently of state structures. Religious institutions played a primary role in this regard, and the degree of education, though conducive to industrialisation, were irrelevant to it (Cipolla 1969: 102). Only in the second phase of the industrial revolution would skills and education seriously affect future development. Eric Hobsbawm claims (1969: 174) that results of technological progress only became a correlative of the input of a scientifically trained workforce, equipment, and research expenses at an advanced phase of industrialisation.

The idea of a national education systems dates back as far as the Reformation. Designs were put forward during the seventeenth century, and the eighteenth saw the first, very basic, attempts at establishing such systems by absolute monarchs: Frederick V in Denmark, Marie Therese in Austria, and Frederick the Great in Prussia. Funds allocated for the purpose at the time were too low to achieve any ambitious goals, but the efforts laid the foundation for later changes, implemented at a more significant cost and reinforced by the introduction of compulsory schooling. After the French Revolution, the fledgling national education systems were consolidated and institutionalised, first in Prussia and France, and then in lesser states on the continent: Switzerland and the Low Countries. Between 1796 and 1882 compulsory education was introduced in Ontario, British Columbia, and Manitoba in Canada, fourteen states in the United States of America, four regions in Australia, New Zealand, Scotland, and almost all regions of Austro-Hungary, the Netherlands, Switzerland, France, and England (Miller 1989: 123). The changes that were implemented at the time shared several similarities: the establishment of a universal form of teaching, the rationalisation of the administrative and institutional structures, and the development of forms of public funding for education.

During the nineteenth century, states consolidated primary education as free and compulsory; meanwhile, high-school education underwent a dynamic rise, shedding its elite status. In response to the demands of industrialisation, vocational and technical schools multiplied. Subsequently, universities and scholarly institutions were strengthened. Education and science were subjected to increasing regulation by the state, eventually supervised by a special branch of bureaucracy, while instruction at different levels – both general and technical – became the province of specially trained personnel. Finally, common education programmes and requirements for graduation to subsequent levels of training were framed. Governments gained a decisive influence on the education of their peoples and proved ever more efficient in defining the direction and pace of scientific research. Towards the end of the nineteenth century, state control of education reached a fairly advanced level. In most Western states, it took the guise of decisions concerning funding, various forms of inspection and accreditation, recruitment, training and certifying teachers, and finally also establishment of national education curricula and examination systems. Schools and universities, whether public or regulated by public authority, became an indelible part of the modern state. Higher education achieved greater autonomy, having been placed under much more lenient state coordination. The process led to an almost complete elimination of previous, dispersed forms of educational organisation based on families, religious communities, or guilds, leading to the professionalisation of education. Education became a mass undertaking, a crucial component of social organisation in capitalist states of the West.

These processes were far more centralised in France and Germany than in Great Britain or the USA. Germany serves as an example of early homogenisation and top-down structuring of the education system; meanwhile, in Great Britain, parallel organisation of education for different social groups and particular purposes persisted for a far longer time. These bottom-up networks would eventually seek state support, gradually conceding autonomy and submitting to external control. The resulting singular education system thus came into existence without a design. To this day, the English system exhibits a much greater variety than its French or German counterparts, bearing traces of different historical structures that comprise it.

In all cases, however, the state took on a key role, either by erecting a central institutional structure, or by adapting it from various existing networks. Specialisation was an inherent feature of systems established through integration, which forced particular groups to concede their broad autonomy, gradually ceding to the state the responsibility for supervision and funding. Meanwhile, in centralised systems the state had to ensure the level of specialisation required by particular interest groups in order to maintain legitimacy of its educational policies. The state-centric, centralised model clearly dominated in nineteenth century Europe (Green 2013: 80–81). The British model of free integration remained a peculiarity. Having taken the lead in consolidation of modern state structures, Great Britain experienced many processes of institutionalisation differently than the powers in pursuit: France and Germany. States on the peripheries of Europe and beyond formed their educational institutions under their enormous influence. Given that the process of erecting new structures occurred under conditions that resembled those particular to the 'pursuing' powers rather than those specific to the 'leader', here, too, top-down consolidation was the norm, inspired by solutions previously applied where modernisation was successfully accomplished. One exception was the United States, where the process followed a peculiar course due to, on the one hand, marked British influences, and on the other, significant autonomy of particular states with regard to the federal government, whose competencies were strictly limited.

This chapter will discuss the agential dimension of the power of the state on the international arena. It will address the role of education and, in part, of science in the process of establishing the modern state. Education and science will thus be understood as factors of political power. First, I will review the major theories of development of state education systems. While all of the approaches in question highlight the state-building aspect of these processes, accents are distributed in widely divergent patterns and specific phenomena do not receive the same evaluation. The theoretical propositions discussed herein are not fundamental to the work at hand, but rather of an auxiliary value. They lend credence to the belief in the role education plays in the establishment of state structures, while locating this process in more liberal or leftist axiological contexts.

The subsequent part will offer an empirical account of state-building processes with regard to the development of education systems. I identify the following mechanisms by which education and science contribute to state power: first, the rivalry between secular and sacred structures and the gradual displacement of the latter; second, the establishment of the state bureaucracy; third, the professionalisation of other vocations, including those related to the military; and fourth, the development of ties between the state and the citizen and emergence of modern identities.

The last part of this chapter includes an overview of specific, characteristic instances of state-building with a particular focus on the role of education and science in these processes. I will analyse three cases illustrating the different paths of the state-building processes. France offers an example of centralised state-building, which was initiated early in the seventeenth century and developed further during subsequent centuries. In contrast, Great Britain demonstrates a decentralised, uncoordinated, largely spontaneous process of modern state formation marked by a different approach to education, which proved very effective in the early phases of the transformation from feudalism to capitalism, but came to pose problems in the later phases of industrialisation, starting in the late nineteenth century. The third case is Poland after 1918, when the country regained independence after 123 years. Education played an important role in this delayed state formation process, which additionally required the integration and construction of a common identity for a population hailing from three culturally and institutionally distinct partitions: Russian, Austro-Hungarian, and Prussian (German).

Education and state-building processes: political ideas and social theories

Political and sociological ideas and theories highlight the significance of education for state-building processes from various perspectives, reflecting the different normative approaches to the nation-state with its institutions and to capitalism as an economic system. The two most distinct and influential contemporary perspectives are represented on the one hand by liberals, and on the other – by representatives of various leftist currents. With their approval and acceptance of inequality among the people, explicitly conservative approaches to education enjoy less popularity today, while elitist conceptions of intellectual formation seem to draw inspiration from alternative and, by definition, marginal designs rather than systemic solutions. The significance of conservative conceptions diminished in the process of formation of nation-states, whose emergence automatically limited the influence of feudal patterns of organisation of social life. Furthermore, conservative approaches to education vary significantly, much like conservatism is inherently divided into many currents, each representing a longing for different periods and values from the past. The definition of conservatism also varies from person to person: for some, the conservative model of education involves the classical set of subjects rooted in ancient canons and aristocratic virtues; for others, the mass model of education implemented during state-building processes, as described in this chapter, is conservative. Another feature distinguishing conservatism from the more progressive ideologies is the approach to emancipation. Here, many state modernisation efforts that involve education can be considered quite conservative, because they usually expand state power and control over the society and do not pursue the emancipation of the underprivileged groups.

Liberals stress the significance of evolutionary democratisation of social life through enlightenment and universalisation of liberty. In their view, common access to education leads to the emancipation of subsequent social groups and – thanks to meritocracy – enables social advancement. As a result, a growing proportion of the society is capable of fulfilling its own potential. Individuals can apply their causativeness to the exploitation of opportunities education provides, developing their talents through toil. The liberal state should limit its interventions in the life of individuals to avoid restraining their activity and allow them to retain the freedom of choosing their own path to success and fulfilment, achieved in proportion to talent and effort.

Left-leaning thinkers, in turn, highlight the persistence of social inequalities, particularly in terms of economic and cultural capital. In their view, an individual's causative powers are far more constrained than the liberals believe them to be, and the future success or failure, rather than being a correlative of individual effort, depends strictly on the context of a person's development. They stress the role education may play in the reproduction of social inequality, consider the different patterns by which the latter is inherited, and highlight the disparity in educational opportunities from the perspective of the organisation of school systems. In this context, though thinkers of a social-democratic persuasion tend more towards a defence of the state as a potential means to social justice through equating opportunities and establishing school systems geared towards fighting inherited inequalities, Marxist currents firmly stress that institutions of the nation-state are themselves inevitably embroiled in supporting the dominant classes. From this perspective, state education systems become a tool for symbolic, and at times even literal, social control. Leftist thinkers and scholars uncover the social conflict, fought primarily along the lines of social distinctions, within extant institutions and rules of the game, including those by which the state itself is governed. Subsumed under the state, education loses its emancipatory potential; thus, the proponents of these currents advocate resistance against the nation-state's monopoly on intervention in education as well as engagement in efforts to establish alternative schools teaching subsequent generations to think critically on the current socio-economic situation.

Émile Durkheim (1926) proposed one of the first sociological theories of the function of education in state-building processes. In his view, education had played a crucial part in societies even before the emergence of the modern state, and its guiding idea evolved through time. After all, it is society that defines its ideal of humanity, its intellectual, moral, and physical contours. To an extent, this ideal applies to all citizen: education plays a crucial part in forming homogeneous societies by disseminating supra-individual norms, rules, duties, and ways of acting. In Durkheim's opinion, society cannot exist without a minimal degree of cohesion. Education contributes to the formation of this homogeneity and reinforces it by imposing similarities among the youth from the very beginning (Durkheim 1926: 119). It fosters social integration through cultural transmission and imposes norms without which social cohesion is unattainable. This new form of integration emerged in the wake of the dissolution of traditional communities, the weakening of ties of tradition and morality. Meanwhile, the state took on the task of strengthening new identifications. Though the creation of the community of ideas and sentiments binding the members of societies to the new political entity was not its achievement, in effect it consecrated and maintained that community after the fact. The state became involved in the transmission of the values of modernisation to individuals and in the establishment of a sense of belonging to new, large social groups, attached directly to the state. Education's key function was thus the methodical socialisation of the young generation by its adult counterparts.

On the other hand, the French sociologist also noted the need for individuality and diversity without which the potential of cooperation that binds the society together would not be fulfilled. In Durkheim's view, this beneficial diversity is ensured, for instance, through training for different occupations. This aspect of education proved necessary during the process of industrialisation, when a diversity of abilities reflected the division of labour. Thus, not only did education impose the common ideas which Durkheim described as *culture générale*, but it also served to divide the members of a society according to their abilities.

Education plays a special role in states that do not enjoy consistently peaceful relations with neighbours – in such circumstances, it inculcates the society more forcibly with a national spirit; meanwhile, lasting international peace and cooperation contributes to the humanisation of learning (Durkheim 1926: 48–49). Durkheim believes that the role of education is not limited to forming individuals by developing their potential in the spirit of individualism, as some of the authors of the liberal pedagogy would have it, but also serves various social and national roles. By highlighting the task of education in state-building processes, this approach fails to reconcile the conflictual aspects of social life. As Steven Lukes observes (1985), Durkheim does not realise that the supposed 'goals of the whole society as an entity' may only be determined by specific social groups, legitimising their own position through the enforcement of a hegemonic understanding of common interest, and at the same time limiting the existential capabilities of the members of other groups. He fails to see that, while fostering community, education can also constitute and replicate social divisions.

These final features unexpectedly couple Durkheim with American functionalists, who focused primarily on the relationship between education and work, ascribing to the former a key role in establishing a meritocratic, modern society. Kingsley Davis and Wilbert Moore (1945) believed that by verifying the capabilities of the members of the society, schools perform the task of ascribing to individuals status befitting their potential. This stratification is perceived as vital for the state and society to function properly, as it provides a meritocratic indicator of an individual's potential.

Stein Rokkan claims that the emergence of the modern state was bound up with the use of state apparatuses by the centre to secure control over the entire country. This involved the elimination of resistance in provinces that failed to comply (Lipset and Rokkan 1967; Rokkan 1980). A significant component of the process was the subjugation of culture and religion by way of, among others, standardisation of language and broadening of the Church's reliance on secular authorities. Aside from 'enclosing' the populace within a limited territory, reformation and enlightenment in Europe brought about the homogenisation of culture and its subsumption under politics, which led to the politicisation and socialisation of the populations (Zarycki 2009: 29–30). For the purposes of this cultural policy aimed at standardisation and unification, states employed education systems, as well (Lipset and Rokkan 1967: 12; Rokkan 1980: 182–183). Curricula took on a national or universal orientation and rarely referred to the knowledge of local societies and cultures, even though massive numbers of students continued to live within such local structures. Local dialects disappeared at a high rate (Cha 1991; de Swaan 1993). With a successfully homogenised population, the chances that a state might be established and maintained as an autonomous entity increased – a loyal people would resist foreign invasion and was unlikely to act against its own government (Rokkan 1970: 101). Finally, a homogeneous people is easier to govern, with less energy and personnel required (Tilly 1975: 43–44, 79). Therefore, internal diversity of peoples decreased, while external differences increased.

Foucault (2009), in turn, observes that the same period saw the development of a peculiarly rational government with a special interest in the population. A sort of triangular relationship emerged between the government, the people, and the political economy. In a similar context, Charles Tilly (1975: 32) described a triangle between the government, the population, and routine relations between the two. Since the eighteenth century, the population was perceived as one of three attributes of the sovereign, next to territory and treasury, but its role had gradually expanded. On the one hand, it is the population, rather than individuals and groups, that becomes the key focus (and object) of the policies of the government which defines the rules to which that population is subject. On the other, the state comes to expect of the population (as a subject of politics) that it will act in a certain predetermined way. The state penetrates more and more areas of social life. Tilly (1975: 22) notes that the so-called normal people constituted the most numerous group resisting state-building efforts, which effectively took the guise of forcing the populace to give up a part of their crops, their work, goods, wealth, loyalty, and even land to the government.

According to the mercantilist doctrine, the population constituted a key factor defining the dynamic of development of the strength of a state, affecting all other factors of prosperity. It was the source of the labour force in fields and workshops, effectively the cause of competition on the labour market, which, in turn, brought on declining wages. The lower the wages, the lower the price of goods; as the potential for export increased, so did the strength of the state. A well-managed population was thus crucial to the achievement of prosperity and power. Consequently, the government apparatus exhibited an increasing interest in deciding how, where, and on what the population should work. From a mercantilist perspective, it constituted a productive force in the strict sense of the term (Foucault 2009).

Further on, Foucault observes that the special attention the enlightenment devoted to the complexity of social processes led it to exhibit increased scepticism towards the possibility of instituting strict control over the population. Instead of the enforcement of subordination to the state, attention turned to the discovery of techniques and methods of interaction with the government in various areas of social life. The process of government became more decentralised, and stability gradually gained primacy over enforced submission to the law – the government would only resort to the use of force against the people in exceptional circumstances. Knowledge-based policies became a key instrument of this transformation, knowing how to manage the population being preferred to using violence against it (Foucault 2009: 111–118). Statistics provided bureaucrats with an insight into the regularities of social life and feedback about the effects (including economic) of the sovereign's policies. This approach contributed to a peculiar rationality undergirding the modern state and its bureaucracy.

At the same time, the government encroached upon ever new aspects of social life, previously reserved for the family or traditional communities, now weakened by the ongoing transformation brought on by the advance of capitalism (Polanyi [1944]2001). As secularisation advanced, the state began to claim a part of the churches' responsibility for morality and the sphere of values. Such were the sources of, for instance, modern pedagogy and discussions over the formation of individuals simultaneously capable of self-reliance and being useful for the state. Foucault (2009: 316, 326) shows how efficient management of internal matters through influencing the attitudes of the population became an important basis for the state's international standing, decreasing the relative value of territorial acquisition.

The size of the population was not the only significant factor. Its welfare gained increasing prominence, too, particularly in pioneer-states of modernity. The well-being and happiness of the citizen, and everything beyond the bare necessaries of life, would be designed to suit the interest of the state. The people's welfare, Foucault contends (2009: 332), turned into yet another factor determining the strength of the state. Incidentally, in his view, the development of various mechanisms facilitating the advancement of states was the result of processes that were neither necessary, nor intentional – pursuing precisely the goal that was eventually achieved.

According to Marxist scholars, nineteenth-century schools served primarily as a tool for social control, displacing traditional mechanisms that withered in the wake of the transformation from feudalism to capitalism. The old methods became impractical as earlier types of social ties deteriorated and physical migration to the cities gained pace, resulting in the disintegration of traditional communities – at times reaching as far as the family. These processes were accompanied by various pathologies – in altered conditions, school became a tool of subjection, disciplining, and inculcating morality (Bowles and Gintis 1976: 178–179; Cubberley 1934: 149).

Pierre Bourdieu (1989), too, perceives a strict correlation between education and the rise of the modern state. Concurrently with the transformation from feudalism to capitalism, schools gained the privilege of sanctioning social divisions – next to economic capital, cultural capital defined a person's right to power and life opportunities, and shaped the social structure. In Bourdieu's view, ceremonies accompanying the conferring of academic degrees at elite schools serve as a rite of passage granting access to prestigious social functions. In fact, his theory questions the liberal faith in meritocracy, aiming to describe the hereditary transmission of social status by way of cultural capital – a process Pierre Bourdieu and Jean-Claude Passeron (1970) named reproduction. Bourdieu (1987) highlights the subtle mechanisms of exclusion that persist in spite of the quantitative expansion of education. Though divisions and boundaries are less obvious today than used to be the case, children from families of a lower socio-economic status remain over-represented in schools and university departments of lesser prestige and have narrower prospects. While former school systems, with their clearly marked boundaries, explicitly enforced distinctions corresponding to social divisions, contemporary systems, marked by opaque methods of organisation, force students to adjust their aspirations to 'school barriers' in less obvious manners than, say, through ruthless competition. To a degree, some agents may receive a devalued, incomplete education solely due to misconceptions. By overestimating the possibilities offered by education and diplomas, they achieve their own exclusion. However, this exclusion is not as brutal as in the past.

Antonio Gramsci (1971: 40–43), on the other hand, devotes less attention to direct control and disciplining of the lower classes, focusing rather on the more subtle mechanisms of discursive hegemony they live under. In light of his theory, the state is composed of numerous practical and theoretical activities that not only justify and maintain the dominance of the dominant class, but also allow it to gain approval for the rules it imposes on other classes. The state is thus equipped with a central legislative and executive apparatus along with the entire oppressive machine of the military and the police, as well as institutions of a moral and ideological character. Courts, schools, and churches are the outlets through which state intellectuals actively promote a vision of the world and rules of the game that organise the civic society and permit the subordinate classes to feel at home in an order designed to benefit the dominant class. For this purpose, all class interests are reconstructed and reformulated in a new, more universal language. In Gramsci's view, though the formation of states was bound up with the ideas of citizenship and formal equality, in fact the process led to the establishment of a hegemony of the dominant social groups. The state supported the formation of the new type or degree of civilization by providing the citizen with the education necessary to adjust to the modern relations of production. In Gramsci's theory of hegemony, the state is endowed with an 'educative' and moral function.

Gramsci notes that education, rather than being only a tool of social control and reproduction, can also become an emancipatory force; thus, it is ascribed a dual, Janus-like character. The two perspectives alternate constantly throughout the *Selections from the Prison Notebooks* (1971: 10, 323). Far from endorsing the materialism of Karl Marx and Friedrich Engels, Gramsci attaches great importance to ideas in the belief that it is primarily in the ideological sphere – in clashes between competing worldviews – that class struggle takes place. Ideas are the foundation of human communities, providing the ground on which people can move, gain consciousness of their own position, and possibly understand the struggle. Against static Marxists, who described schools as an unequivocal tool of class reproduction, Gramsci combines two perspectives in his analysis: that of reproduction and that of emancipation. In his view, schools are the field of a conflict between various actors, and the result of this struggle for hegemony is undetermined – emancipatory potential may yet win over reproduction.

In her studies of the processes of establishment of educational systems, Margaret Archer (2013) diverges from both functionalists and Marxists by highlighting the different routes of development of state education systems in particular countries, which reflect differences in the conditions and progress of the process itself. She criticises functionalism for reducing the goals of the development of education to a common mean and overlooking the conflictual aspect of social processes, which prevents it from explicating the emergence of these systems in states where economical development did not follow the same course as in countries of the nineteenth-century centre. Though Archer concedes that Marxism is more correct insofar as it allows for class conflict, it is burdened by economical determinism, which downplays political factors that achieved major significance in certain important instances, including France and Prussia. She rejects single-factor theories of the development of education and hypotheses of universal causes of its expansion, including theories of human capital, modernisation, political integration, social control, and ideological diffusion. Her own analyses focus instead on group interaction. In her view, the structure of educational systems reflects the ever-evolving goals of the groups in control. The groups themselves, however, are also limited by structural factors, including human agency. It is interaction, not determinism of particular factors, that defines the contours of the systems. While the interaction is determined by specific conditions and occurs under the influence of various factors, its result is not predefined. The shape of the changes depends on the social forces involved.

Archer (2013: 54) defines the state education system as a national, internally varied network of institutions devoted to formal education, operating under at least partial control and oversight of the government, with mutually interrelated parts and processes. She also points out that the emergence of the state was accompanied by the integration of education with the political centre and a broader institutional backdrop developed as part of that process (Archer 2013: 145). The French example is particularly indicative of the ways in which educational institutions at the primary, secondary, and university levels contributed to different institutional elements of the state. Such a return justified substantial state expenses needed for the establishment of universal education. Archer contends (Archer 2013: 153–154) that the development of educational systems allowed the emergent states to create efficient bureaucracies, foster political loyalty, enhance military strength, and ensure economic expansion. For many governments, education was also a tool for managing rapid social changes during the nineteenth century.

Though education served the state, the development of particular systems took place among a struggle between various influences and concepts as well as values and interests propagated by particular social groups; in fact, the process was not under complete control of the centre. In practice, the powerful ruling elite often sought to create an education system that suited its various needs. During subsequent phases, networks composed of members of other groups that pursued different goals were incorporated into the process through mediation and compromises (Archer 2013: 161). As a result, in spite of certain common isomorphic elements, there are marked divergences between education systems. Their internal variety stems from the integration of various networks serving interests that differed from those of the groups that founded the systems.

As subsequent, higher levels of education were integrated into the state systems, their internal variety decreased through standardisation. While the influence of powerful groups beyond the central, ruling stratum sufficed to ensure the maintenance of previous or appearance of alternative forms, the range and freedom of innovation was limited. Unification and systematisation went hand in hand with state control over education; variety and specialisation, in turn, reflected the necessity of integration with different social institutions. Education became unified as a result of subordination and enforcement of a universal administrative framing, which to some extent affected even federal states. The degree of unification depended not only on its range, but also on the intensity of control exerted by the central authorities; in other words, its nature was both quantitative and qualitative.

In practice, unification did not necessarily connote centralisation. A centralised system is characterised by the fact that one element or subsystem exerts a major or dominant role within the whole structure. That element can be said to govern or organise the system. Even a minor alteration in this central element will consequently reflect upon the entire system, causing an obvious change. However, while a centralised system constitutes a special case of a unified system, not all unified systems are centralised.

Systematisation constituted another characteristic feature of the emerging state education systems. It strengthened existing relations between its parts and developed new bonds between previously unconnected elements. Though from an analytical standpoint unification and systematisation are separate processes, empirically speaking, they were inextricably linked. The major contribution of systematisation consisted in developing a hierarchical structure that reflected a growing need for coordination stemming from the diversity of aims put before the institutions and from the pressure exerted by the interested groups to enforce the implementation of commonly accepted goals. The internal differentiation of the education system, on the other hand, is the result of competition between groups as well as political conflicts.

Furthermore, during the evolution of extant systems, groups which gained an influence on institutional solutions could solicit approval for and effectively implement new, more or less novel approaches. Specialisation was a result of the inevitable differentiation within systems designed to serve various purposes and various group interests. The extent of specialisation depended, for instance, on the range, variety, and complementarity of the features the system was expected to offer. On the other hand, it was also affected by the relative force of different pressure groups that managed to exert an influence on the shape of the system. Cohesive elites often instilled greater homogeneity and vice versa.

Thus, the form of integration of a given system was a product of social interactions that did not follow a predetermined design or submit to complete external control. Different alterations and reforms need not have been consistent and complementary with one another; in extreme instances, internal contradictions could become a persistent feature of such systems. The degree of integration depended on the extent to which peculiar forms of unification, systematisation, differentiation, and specialisation were mutually complementary or at odds with one another (Archer 2013: 174).

The major theories describing the significance of education for state-building processes outlined above serve a supplementary purpose in this study, providing justification for the claim that educational and scientific institutions constituted an important building block of modern political structures. By the same token, they became factors of the agential power of the state on the international arena. These theories – whether leaning towards liberalism or rooted in a more leftist axiological sphere – highlight numerous crucial characteristics of nation-states which will be discussed later in this chapter on the basis of empirical material.

The history of state education systems: from reformation to modernity

The following part discusses the process of establishment of state education systems in the context of the most significant phases of consolidation of modern states. If it faced few impediments, this was due in part to the development of specific social groups which pushed for changes. Other aspects under analysis include the struggle for power between secular and sacred hierarchies, the development of an efficient bureaucratic and military apparatus, and the consolidation of professions of key importance for modernity (including those peculiar to the military), as well as the moulding of the citizen by way of ensuring their loyalty to and identification with the state. All these mechanisms translated into the power of the state as an agent.

Reformation: State versus Church

In primordial societies, knowledge spread through family members and elders of the tribe. Formal education, initially the purview of priests and secular scribes, arrived together with scripture and the necessity for dissemination of writing and reading skills. However, the elites aside, schooling still followed patterns established in primordial communities. Prototypical primary, secondary, and tertiary schools developed between the fourth and second century BC in Greece, also creating the concept of education tied to a particular notion of the state and of the citizen. With the Middle Ages, the Church claimed complete responsibility for instruction (Butts 1955: 1–18).

In Europe, the dominance of religious institutions in this sphere lasted until the early modern era and was accepted by the political elites in spite of their simultaneous investment in strengthening the state – first by way of absolutism, and then the nation-state. The relatively long-lasting toleration of Church control over education on the part of secular authorities can be explained, in part, by the fact that, in the late feudal and early post-feudal period, only a narrow group of people was involved in this marginal activity which had little impact on the operation of major political institutions of the day. Though secular townsfolk organised their own education structures by way of the guilds, these endeavours had a limited scope and lacked the aspiration to expand beyond the strictly defined area of operations of the particular guilds.

During the formative period of the modern state, the alliance with the churches flourished – especially in Protestant states, where they became an element of the secular apparatus (Lipset and Rokkan 1967: 15). Owing to the initial conjunction of sacred and secular administration, clergymen and graduates of monastic schools proved of use in the development of bureaucracy. As a result, the penetration of villages and minor towns by the state – a time-consuming and costly process – was greatly facilitated, aiding their integration with the emerging administrative system. That clergymen served as quasi-bureaucrats was one reason why the state did not divest the churches of their role in education. On the contrary, during the early modern period, secular powers struck a balance between sacred institutions and religion on the one hand and the interest of the state on the other, at times even subordinating the former to the latter. Eventually, secular structures coalesced and asserted control over a growing list of functions formerly performed by the churches. In some cases, the states implemented the reforms with the approval of the sacred authorities; in others, the arrogation of merely a proportion of these competencies prompted resistance from religious institutions (Schilling 2010: 51–59).

The original impulse for the development of universal education, primarily involving reading and writing skills, came with the arrival of reformed religions, which expected their followers to be able to read sacred books on their own. For similar reasons, a sizeable proportion of Jews in early modern Europe was literate (Durkheim [1897]2005: 122). During Reformation, foundations were laid for state control over education, its organisation, aims, and programme. Initially,

Protestant states denied control over instruction to the Catholic Church and vested it in the national churches; later on, education became the purview of secular authorities (Butts 1955: 196).

At their inception, reformed religions played a significant part in the development of education due to the fact that, while the Catholic Church communicated with its followers through spoken word and painting, Protestantism proselytised with the written word. For this reason, Protestant countries of Northern Europe achieved primacy in education, at that time identified mostly with literacy. Already in the eighteenth century, Scandinavian and German states boasted significantly lower rates of illiteracy than the Catholic states of Europe (Boli 1989). By the end of the seventeenth century, illiteracy rates reached c.55–65 per cent in Protestant countries and 70–80 per cent in their Catholic counterparts. During the nineteenth century, this disparity found reflection in the growing advantage of Northern Europe over the Mediterranean South (Durkheim [1897]2005: 117; Cipolla 1969: 61).

Proponents of Reformation engaged in numerous efforts to expand access to education for the simple folk, laying the groundwork for a democratic education and advocating universal access thereto at primary level. Though Martin Luther called for access to learning to be provided to all children, including girls, such early advocacy of democratic education did not alter the fact that education divided into elite and common varieties. While Luther and John Calvin favoured the classical, Latin middle school, this proved inaccessible to the common man in the desired format. The rulers of England and France, on the other hand, reformed and modernised middle schools with a view to preventing expansion of access to education at this level. In spite of the increasing accessibility of education in Protestant countries, therefore, the dominant concept of instruction in Europe at the onset of modernity remained aristocratic.

Reformation achieved the practical universalisation of education by recognising learning in general as a good of common value. Protestantism brought about the demand for public control over instruction, the notion of a common education, the concept of compulsory education, and the idea of free instruction funded from the taxes. The Netherlands led the way in substituting church control over education with secular authority exercised by the state as well as particular townships. The country also boasted the highest enrolment rate of female pupils (Butts 1955: 205–230).

During Reformation, schools formed individuals willing to accept the social standing they were born into within a state closely tied to a national church. In Catholic states, the development of education became the prerogative of the Jesuits, who sought to replicate some of the advances made by the Protestants; as a result, school systems expanded dramatically in France, Rhineland, and Tirol. In Catholic Austria, Marie Therese put significant effort into developing education; meanwhile, in spite of Protestant dominance, Great Britain and the American South lagged behind. Under Reformation and Counter-Reformation, the political and religious aspects of education were strictly integrated. It was only with the Enlightenment that the idea of separation between church and state gained a clear shape and was expressed also in relation to education. The notion of a civic, strictly state-controlled instruction drew most of its impetus from the French Revolution and the thought of such figures as Louis-René Caradeuc de La Chalotais, Anne Robert Turgot, Denis Diderot, and Jean-Antoine de Condorcet.

Though Protestantism favoured advances in education, the construction of a national education system constituted a separate process. The network of church and confessional schools established in Protestant states was not identical with the rise of state systems of schooling, defined by their separation from ecclesiastical authorities. Thus, while religion offers a partial explanation for the divergent levels of education in different societies at an earlier stage of modernity, it does not account for the development of public schooling – a qualitatively distinct process bound up with the arrival of the modern state, which required a more or less brutal withdrawal from the tradition of confessional schools. Public education systems were geared towards universalism and sought to respond to the secular needs of the state and the people. Enlightenment initiated numerous debates on the emancipatory function of the school; radical reformers claimed that people are shaped by their environment and, as a consequence, are susceptible to education. From this perspective, biological differences mattered less than social formation. Already in mid-eighteenth century, the Encyclopaedists postulated the complete control of the state over education, advocating for a universal, free, compulsory, and secular schooling. The postulates were then partly included among the ideas promulgated by the French Revolution. Marie Jean de Condorcet devised a conception of primary schooling extended to all children and subjected to the demands of the state, science, and democracy. He believed that primary schools should be located at walking distance from all attending children, with gymnasiums operating in all medium-size towns, and middle schools in the largest cities. Condorcet also envisioned nine 'lycaeums' providing higher and vocational education. At the top of the pyramid, he placed the National Association of Sciences and Arts. Though this plan was not implemented, it provided inspiration for changes introduced during the French Revolution and the Napoleonic Era (Butts 1955: 276–277).

However, a disconnect emerged between the emancipatory, egalitarian ideas of the philosophers and their practical application, particularly at the most broadly accessible level of primary education, often marked by strong religious overtones and an authoritarian organisation (Ramirez and Boli 1987). In such circumstances, emancipatory goals could not be achieved. Education did not make nineteenth-century Europe democratic – in fact, the development and universalisation of education correlated positively with authoritarianism (Landes 1969). As Andy Green demonstrates (2013: 36–40), nineteenth-century advances in instruction did not arise as an effect of the democratic inclusion of new social groups into public life. It was the absolutist, strong state that stood behind public and common institutions of learning. Interestingly, in the 1880s, more democratic countries such as Great Britain, France, and the USA looked to the autocracies of Prussia, and then Germany, for paradigms for the development of education. The role of social movements was also drastically limited: their significance is incomparable to the impact of states, intellectually inspired by the nationalist and paternalistic ideas of Alexander von Humboldt or Karl von Altenstein.

According to Martin Lipset and Stein Rokkan (1967: 15), control over education played a fundamental role in the struggle between the state and the church. Disassociated from religious structures, education could develop and become universal. This was easily achieved in Prussia, where the church was subordinated to the monarch, but in Catholic France, for instance, where clergymen did not answer to secular authority, the non-religious education system defining the relationship between the citizen and the state clashed with the pre-existing model rooted in confessional schooling. Compulsory education at the primary level became a sphere of conflict between the central government and the diminishing religious institutions. In France, this struggle between the secular authorities and the Church has been taking place since the seventeenth century. Similar disputes emerged in such countries as England, Belgium, and the Netherlands, though there, the state faced a weaker opponent in the shape of the decentralised Protestant churches.

The establishment of state bureaucracy

The emergent modern states engaged in various activities unknown or uncommon to feudal monarchies, such as administration, tax collection, maintenance of a judiciary, formation of a standing, professional army, but also devoted their energies to military and civil engineering and public works. To fulfil this ever-growing list of increasingly complex tasks, the state required officers and specialists familiar with technologies – individuals capable of implementing the relevant policies. The power of the state as an actor depended on the efficiency of this process and of the new institutions. The essence of the modern form of government consisted in the exercise of rule through a bureaucratic administrative staff. In classic Weberian parlance, the state is that 'compulsory political organization' which controls a territorial area in which 'the administrative staff successfully upholds the claim to the monopoly of the legitimate use of physical force in the enforcement of its order' (Weber [1922]1978, I: 54). The modern state transformed personal rule and ad hoc justification of authority into depersonalised, public governance based on the rule of law. Professional administration is an indispensable component of the modern state, enabling it to achieve an immense capacity to mobilise and tap into societal resources and to wield coercive force (Collins 1986). What typified the official, claimed Max Weber ([1922]1978), were the relevant specialist qualifications, often certified with an exam and a diploma. Meanwhile, the fact that modern 'ministers' and 'presidents of state' are the only 'officials' of whom no qualifications are required, indicates, in Weber's view, that their power is formal rather than material. Rule by knowledge is indeed the essence of bureaucratic administration (Weber [1922]1978: 694).

The modern state, whose power was increasingly determined by the efficiency with which it managed its resources, established a new profession: bureaucracy. At the same time, the old institutions became increasingly dependent on knowledge. Tilly (1975: 6) contends that the formation of the technical personnel and bureaucracy was equally key for the formation of the states as the development of the army, the tax system, the police, and control over food supply. Wolfram Fischer and Peter Lundgreen (1975), who studied this problematic as members of Charles Tilly's team, also assert that the development of bureaucratic structures constituted an indelible part of the state-building process. The means applied differed, though, being defined by the particular conditions, context, resources, and often ambitions, as well. Yet, bureaucratic structures consistently developed according to Roman law and the administrative procedures of the medieval Church. The only predecessor of the bureaucratic structures of the state were the sacred and corporate hierarchies, primarily of civic character. In fifteenth- and sixteenth-century Europe, monarchs did not offer precise and fully articulated plans for establishing an independent administration. One available option was to attempt to appropriate the relevant extant structures from the Church. The problem with this solution, though, was the dual loyalty of ecclesiastical officials in the state's employ, which found a dramatic illustration in figures such as Thomas Becket – the twelfth-century Archbishop of Canterbury whose opposition to laws restricting the role of the Church within the state earned him banishment and then death – or Thomas More – the early sixteenth-century philosopher and politician beheaded for refusing to sign the Act of Supremacy. What was expected most of all of the royal-state bureaucracy was loyalty, and that could not be guaranteed in the long term if offices were handed out to magnates or ecclesiastics.

Foremost among the original tasks of the administration was the efficient extraction of resources for the king, the court, and the army. The expanding central structures, particularly the military, required expenses beyond the traditional capabilities of the royal domain or the monarch's fiefs. Financial administration would thus play a fundamental role in the development of the modern state. On the other hand, maintaining civic order, peace, and the law remained a crucial task. In other words, administration also involved exercising jurisdiction; these functions would only be divided later.

Great Britain, a trailblazer of the state-building processes, followed a path distinct from that chosen by its European competitors. There, bureaucracy in the strict sense only appeared in the late nineteenth century, well after the completion of the state-building process. Early on, in the days of the Tudors, Great Britain diverged from both France – which established schools of administration – and Prussia – which recruited officials directly from the army – by relying on the citizen to establish structures and 'do business' (Fischer and Lundgreen 1975: 481). The middle class, composed of landowners, entrepreneurs, professional lawyers, and administrators, united by similar interests and goals – stability, efficient implementation of the rule of law, including security of private property – remained allied to the king in the effort of raising the structures of the state. This group was so narrow that recruitment for state offices occurred outside of formal meritocratic procedures. No strict guidelines concerning the education of persons applying for offices were defined. Those elected to administrative posts usually had university education and possessed certain general competencies, primarily familiarity with foreign languages, law, accounting, or the art of war.

The system was efficient enough to meet the demands of an emerging modernity, while providing access to offices even to those who possessed only narrow competencies. In time though, when the continental states rationalised their operation, this model was proved comparatively inefficient. During the subsequent stages of development of modern states, administrations in France or Prussia would dominate not just in terms of size, but also professionalism. The British system was less formal – until the end of the nineteenth century, an office-holder in Great Britain was primarily defined by the social group to which he belonged, while French and Prussian civil service became a professional elite produced by a formalised system of education, adhering to a characteristic set of values, and exhibiting a peculiar *esprit de corps* (Fischer and Lundgreen 1975: 489).

The extent of the bureaucratic class in France was remarkable. In the sixteenth century, it numbered around 10,000 men; by the end of the eighteenth century, it grew to about 300,000, including $c.$50,000 high-ranking public officials. At the end of the *ancien régime*, there were as many as 629 categories of offices, each supplied from a different corps, indicating a highly specialised and professionalised administration designed to rebuff all attempts at returning to feudalism. In practice, though, offices proliferated because the state could sell them: in the seventeenth and eighteenth century, with the royal treasury constantly in need of new income, positions were continuously created and sold to increase revenue. Thus, the rich bourgeoisie received public offices in return for a part of its wealth (Fischer and Lundgreen 1975: 495).

Though under the *ancien régime* the king attempted to create an administration that would efficiently implement his policies, ground-level clashes between old, post-feudal structures of power and new networks – circumscribed by sinecures and far removed from meritocratic standards – could not lead to a professional administration. The state-building process involved both struggle and cooperation between the few major social groups: the king and aristocracy, old and new nobility, and bourgeoisie and gentry. It was only after the revolution that a modern administrative corps was established. The 1791 Declaration of Rights stipulated that virtue and talent should be the only factors taken into account when assessing candidacies for public offices. Though the establishment of the public officer corps in itself did not immediately dismantle the former system, meritocracy gained clear prominence, requiring that functionaries earn special qualifications and pass exams to qualify for a position. The French Revolution elevated the country's bourgeoisie to a position akin to that of its British counterpart. As a result, the rule of *la robe* ended, giving way to a meritocratic administration with a corps composed of graduates of *grandes écoles*.

48 *Education and the state-building process*

Thus, the system that had operated in pre-revolutionary France in relation to the technical professions was now applied to the administration.

Napoleon maintained the course of the changes, to some extent opening avenues of advancement in the public service for those outside of the upper stratum. At the time, enrolment in elite schools was drastically limited, and upward mobility was not a common occurrence. Napoleon sought to further dismantle feudal relations that typified the *ancien régime*. His reign saw the introduction of a standard programme of learning and a system of state exams, some of which qualified not only for education at higher levels, but also for public offices in the administration or the army. From this point on, promotions in public offices were centrally regulated, allowing for the emergence of a loyal and disciplined corps implementing state policies.

In Prussia, the establishment of administration became an even more important element of the state-building process due to not only to the political, but also the social and economic features of the Hohenzollern monarchy. Herman Finer wrote:

> in 1688 when the Great Elector died, his legacy was an army and a Civil Service; in 1688 when William of Orange ascended the English throne the English reward of a half-century's efforts was a sovereign Parliament. Thenceforward the cleverest young men in England passed (or did not pass) from the universities to the political parties and the House of Commons, while the clever young German ... passed through grade after grade of actual and diverse administrative service, to become a statesman.... Political science in England ... concerned itself principally with the question of political liberty and obligation. In Germany Cameralism, or the Art and Science of Government by Administrative Departments (*Kammer*), attracted the best minds of the seventeenth and eighteenth centuries.
>
> (Finer 1932: 1184)

Under the Hohenzollerns, the Prussian state-building process played out as a clash between the traditional state and territorial authorities of the provinces (*Ständestaat*) with their specific laws, and the *Polizeistaat*, that is, the authority of the public law, including administrative superiority over the territorial units and geared towards concentrating competencies in the hands of the monarch. Though the Prussian bureaucracy was typified by a high degree of militarisation, it was also the first to implement a competency-based system. Recruitment for all public offices, including the highest, occurred by way of exams. The system was watertight: the intellectual and professional qualifications required effectively limited nepotism and various forms of patronage (Fischer and Lundgreen 1975: 516).

Initially, to advance within the hierarchy of Prussian administration, officials needed to gain qualifications in their places of work. For instance, lawyers at the higher levels passed two exams – one at the university, the other in front of a state commission – spending the intervening several years as unwaged workers at state institutions, which ensured a breadth of practical insight. Among the competencies peculiar to this modern bureaucracy was the ability to assess costs and draw up budgets, reports, memoranda, or political recommendations. Aside from these abilities, bureaucrats would exhibit psychological predispositions, such as loyalty, a sense of duty, diligence, and submission. The model ensured a social mobility unparalleled in all of contemporary Europe and unmatched until the early twentieth century, providing routes of advancement for those of modest birth (Rosenberg 1958: 67). As a result of the Napoleonic wars, the army partly opened to social advancement, too. Since 1808 'knowledge and education' became the necessary conditions for gaining commission. In need of new cadres for its grand army in dangerous times, the state instituted meritocratic criteria, opening career paths for those lacking noble birth.

At the same time, however, meritocratic barriers to advancement to higher ranks served as an efficient tool of regulation: the bar was set so high that the potential for mobility on a scale that could threaten the social order was safely reduced. The meritocratic system did not threaten the dominant position of those of noble birth. Broader possibilities for advancement for the common man limited not only the cost of higher education, but also the viability of remnants of feudal standards of qualification for state offices. In other words, aristocratic privilege within the bureaucracy was maintained even as relations between classes loosened at the lower levels, with routes of advancement to low and middle ranks open. Thanks to a partial dismantling of these barriers, the system of administrative education also helped modernise the Junker class. While class divisions persisted, the state bureaucracy was professionalised (Fischer and Lundgreen: 1975: 527).

The politico-economic doctrine of mercantilist Germany was cameralism, which identified as the fundamental goal of the state the complete exploitation of its productive potential, including full employment, for the purpose of increasing the revenue for the ruler. Cameralism provided the political, economic, and legal basis for administration and public finances, as well as for the formation of officials. In 1727, Friedrich Wilhelm I established the first university departments devoted to the doctrine at the universities of Halle and Frankfurt am Oder. The course of study addressed the economy of the *Polizeistaat* and of private enterprises, including agriculture, as well as technological, statistical, and scientific knowledge. Since 1770, every official was expected to complete the course and pass the dual exam. The professionalisation of state structures began with lawyers to eventually extend over the entire broad category of administration employees. A standardised method of instruction for both legal and administration employees in public offices has been in place since the eighteenth century. With the advent of the nineteenth century, political sciences – that is, Prussian cameralism – ceded primacy for the benefit of legal studies. By that point, the state-building process had already reached an advanced stage, and increasing laissez-faire led to the reduction of administration and reinterpretation of the role of state structures as consisting primarily in the execution of the law rather than the management of state affairs (Fischer and Lundgreen: 1975: 519). When the impact of industrialisation became apparent, that is, towards the end of the nineteenth century, the significance of education of state officials increased again.

Though the establishment of modern bureaucracy in continental states began with absolutism, the process only achieved its proper dynamic in the nineteenth century. It involved the formation of administrative structures plugged into the central authority in order to push particularism out of the frame. Since public offices were traditionally the domain of the nobles, the elimination of the remaining feudal structures of power required an at least partial opening of the professions to those who did not belong to the former elites. Education, at first especially at the middle level, then also at the higher level, became a tool for social advancement and its relative openness or closure regulated the degree of vertical social mobility in the modernising states. A meritocratic bureaucracy proved to be a more efficient means of rule than the previous feudal structures of authority, contributing to the agential power of the states in which the aforementioned reforms were successfully implemented.

Professionalisation

The formation of a bureaucracy constituted a key stage of the professionalisation of state structures, now separate from ecclesiastical administration. However, for modern states to emerge in full effect, other professions had to develop, too. Increasing specialisation endowed the state with a much more effective military and the public infrastructure necessary for achieving modernisation itself. In this, too, Great Britain initially charted a path different from the one the continental powers would follow, only adjusting and professionalising its institutions at a later time. Yet, changes followed the same logic throughout Europe. Professionalisation of those occupations that contributed the most to the achievement of modernity helped establish the power of modern states as agents.

By analogy to the administrative structures discussed above, Britain's technical personnel was also recruited in a fairly informal manner – primarily through families which specialised in certain types of industry, in some cases to the extent of exercising monopoly. In spite of the absence of a formal qualification process, entrepreneurs sought out those with talent and competency, offering employment to the most skilled candidates, both from the British Isles and from the continent. 'Brain drain' has been a recognised strategy in Great Britain since the onset of modernity, more common there than in any other European country. Already in the fifteenth and sixteenth centuries, seeking to achieve technological advancement, the British state lured specialists in explosives from Italy, navigators from Spain, Portugal, and Italy, astronomers, chemists, and glass-workers from France, dyers, shipbuilders, and saltpetremen from Holland, printers and miners from Germany and Hungary, and ironmasters from Sweden (Fischer and Lundgreen 1975: 529). While the extent to which Britain's policy of mass-scale importation of trained specialists was premeditated is unclear, both the king and private entrepreneurs were able to actively seek out prospective employees on the continent and induce them to relocate for better pay. The British quickly learned from the foreigners, at times achieving greater skill in the span of a generation.

Great Britain secured its capabilities in navigation by acquiring the services of Sebastiano Caboto, a graduate of the most advanced schools of the time in Portugal and Spain. Up until the 1570s, Britain could not match Spain, Portugal, or even France in terms of navigation. Transatlantic expeditions required the enlistment of foreign officers. Yet, within just over a decade, Caboto's involvement yielded impressive results – Great Britain could boast navigators superior to those of the Netherlands, which now sought out British mariners for its own expeditions. British supremacy in the science of sailing began during the 1670s. It was in Britain that treatises and handbooks on the art of navigation were published (at the behest of private entrepreneurs). Mathematicians also became involved in the venture. The art of making navigation tools developed at the same time, contributing to the country's economic and technological advantage, which lasted for another two centuries. Rules of advanced cartography and hydrography were also developed at the time.

In none of these disciplines was development contingent upon tight state control. At most, the king supported talented men, such as Admiral John Hawkins, Francis Drake, or Martin Frobisher, and encouraged them to share their knowledge with younger generations. Apprentices were certified by trade corporations of the sailors. The king never interfered directly in the development of workshops nor attempted to manage them; the most strategically significant branches of early military and shipbuilding industry remained in the hands of prominent families. Across generations, technical knowledge accumulated in families of entrepreneurs and technicians in their employ.

In continental monarchies, professionalisation of the modern state followed a markedly different pattern. Absolutist administrations in France and Prussia engaged actively in supporting advances in science, technology, education, military technology, public works, manufacture, and trade. Development in these areas required extensive expert knowledge beyond the competencies of officials. Fischer and Lundgreen (1975: 545) point out that Britain's competitors in the struggle for supremacy could implement their strategies primarily thanks to the broad social outlook of their education systems. It was the mercantilist state of the early Enlightenment that created the institution of the expert, who gained his knowledge typically through education. At the outset, the organisation of the system of schools educating the experts was similar in France and in Prussia, though by the early nineteenth century, the two states embarked on divergent paths.

A similar degree of divergence can be observed in the processes of professionalisation of modern European armies. To defend the power of the king against rivals at home and abroad, armies and fleets required technical personnel. The army became professional during the early modern period; the process affected the leadership – still in the hands of nobles, though increasingly elevated on merit – to a lesser degree than the technological aspect of the military: for the first time, specialists possessed of expert knowledge became indispensable

(Cipolla 1965). Owing to the demands of colonial dominance and the continental balance of power, recruitment and training of gunners achieved key importance. Great Britain's advantage in the rivalry between the great modern powers was due to the supremacy of British navy and artillery. Military technology would later contribute to the rise of France, and then of Prussia.

In contrast to its continental counterparts, Great Britain did not develop formal institutions for military training. While the first artillery colleges appeared in Spain already in the late sixteenth century, the British monarchy left the development of new weaponry and military techniques in the hands of private entrepreneurs, mostly owners of ironworks. Only by the late Stuarts did monarchs make coordinated – though not institutional – efforts towards fostering cooperation between scientists, mechanics, and military engineers to achieve progress in military technology. Under Tudors and early Stuarts, the more technical aspects of the art of war were ceded to foreigners, mostly French and Dutch experts. Though scientists, practitioners, and strategists could cooperate at ease, their paucity in the country limited the exchange of experiences, while institutions for the coordination of integration of accumulated knowledge and its implementation in the art of war were lacking. It was only in the latter half of the seventeenth century that a system of instruction of military engineers was established (Fischer and Lundgreen 1975: 542).

France led the field in technical training of professional military cadres. Sébastien de Vauban, the great military engineer who personally conducted exams for all candidates for engineering posts in the French army since 1697, had been developing the necessary expertise already in the times of Jean-Baptiste Colbert and Louis XIV. The year 1748 saw the creation of the École du Génie, soon to gain high esteem across Europe, granting France the most in-depth expertise in artillery techniques and fortification. New developments in mathematics and natural sciences were used to further research and teaching. The school served as a predecessor to the famous École Polytechnique, established in 1795.

Universities maintained their status as the main institutions of higher learning since the Middle Ages, but during the seventeenth and, in part, eighteenth centuries, they gave precedence to theological studies and offered only classical education. In France, science in the modern sense of the term was organised through scientific associations, the Academy of Sciences (established in 1666) foremost among them. The idea of professionalised science paralleled the conceptions of Colbert, one of the creators of the French absolute monarchy. Since the establishment of the Academy, science – no longer the domain of private fraternities of scholars – became inscribed in institutions organised by the state. Colbert sought to use scientific knowledge to achieve practical improvements in navigation, the art of war, architecture, and engineering. Elements of this knowledge would also provide indicators for economic policies and the dissemination of technological insight (Hahn 1971).

The history of the Parisian Academy of Sciences foregrounds the close relationship between scholars and administrators in common pursuit of modernisation.

Academics acted as consultants both for the bureaucracy and state-owned factories (Hahn 1971: 68). Through the Academy, scientists came to play an important part in decision-making processes of the administration. As Robert Gilpin (1968: 95) notes, France was the first state to treat science as a profession and accept that highly qualified workers and experts contribute significantly to the strength of the state. The *ancien régime* implemented a policy of enlisting scholars and engineers as state functionaries. In the times of Colbert, France laid the groundwork for civil engineering. The year 1747 saw the establishment of the École des Ponts et Chaussées, created for the purpose of overseeing an immense state plan for a network of major roads. The school sought out persons with experience in engineering, requiring a very high level of familiarity with mathematics from its entrants (Fischer and Lundgreen 1975: 552). Both professional groups formed nationwide corps. However, the problem France faced was that the state and its administration absorbed so many graduates of these esteemed schools that too few remained available for employment in the private sector, which contributed to the delay in industrialisation in the early nineteenth century.

In 1700, following decades of planning and direct pressure from Gottfried Wilhelm Leibniz, the Royal Prussian Academy of Sciences was established in Berlin. The famous philosopher sought to combine *theoriam cum praxi* to achieve progress not only in science, but also for 'the state and the people' – in agriculture, production, and trade (Fischer and Lundgreen 1975: 548). Prussia's achievement in civil or military engineering during the eighteenth century could not match those of France, given the lower level of development of knowledge and technology, as well as a lesser degree of professionalisation, and the paucity of educational institutions. In this respect, Prussia may have begun its ascent at a later time, but it achieved parity with France already in the nineteenth century, and surpassed the Western rival in many areas by the turn of the century.

While the Prussian engineer corps was organised as early as 1729, the modern Prussian army could not match its French counterpart in terms of technological advancement. Berlin recognised this deficiency and even attempted (in 1775) to form a local equivalent of the École du Génie in the capital by acquiring the services of French engineers. The undertaking failed, and it was only with the arrival of the Bauakademie, formed in 1799, that the knowledge and professional standards of the local cadres were gradually increased. The technological delay was only overcome after the Napoleonic Wars. By the mid-nineteenth century, Prussia outpaced France in terms of training specialists for the developing industry. The year 1821 saw the establishment of the Gewerbeinstitut, an engineering school. Interestingly, its founders stipulated that the graduates could not be employed by the state. Instead, they were funnelled into the industry, providing a core of specialists who established the primary German fields of industrial production: textiles and metallurgy. They also contributed to the development of the railway system. In 1879, Bauakademie and Gewerbeinstitut joined to form the Technische Hochschule, a school of the highest pedigree in Europe at the time, which trained cadres for both administration and the industry.

It was in the same period that Germany gained an advantage over France in terms of technological advancement, technical education, and industrial progress. Even for British observers, Germans were unmatched in that regard (Artz 1966: 267). Many explanations are provided for this unprecedented achievement, among them the development of technical education at the regional level and in cooperation with the industry – while in France, most of the major areas of higher professional learning were served by singular institutions with only loose connections to enterprises. At the outset, schools in Germany were inferior to leading French scholarly institutions, but more accessible; the training they provided was devised in cooperation with the industry in order for their graduates to find employment there. By the nineteenth century, Prussia boasted the highest percentage of trained engineers in the general population.

Next to the ability to establish an efficient administration, the professionalisation of vocations related to technological advancement, in both civil and military aspects, became a marker of the power of the modern state, binding its politics to its economy. The onset of the process roughly coincided with the establishment of the state bureaucratic apparatus, enabling major powers to implement ambitious political projects, including colonial expansion, and programmes for development, particularly in the infrastructure. In the modern era, thanks to advances in technology, war also became increasingly an object of professionalisation and an object of knowledge, rather than a reflection of crude numerical relations. Professionalisation and its relationship with technology carried serious economic implications, which are discussed in more detail in a subsequent chapter.

Education and the citizen

By engaging in the organisation of education, the state not only established a modern administration, securing the technical competencies necessary for its own development, but also ensured its own legitimacy, moulding the citizen and creating a symbolic bond with the individual (Russell and Bajaj 2015: 95–97). For modern states to exist, those who inhabit them must identify as their citizen. New means of legitimising power and authority are also necessary. Nascent political elites in early modern states either displaced or sought to control kinship structures, ethnic ties, and religious authority and forge new identities based on the authority of the state and public official (Anderson 1983). That is why modern states recast and channelled individual loyalties, greatly affecting individual lives.

Martha Finnemore (1996: 335) observes that educational policies generally fall outside of the purview of scholars of international relations, which creates a serious gap, given that the area serves as the meeting point between two central aspects of Western modernisation: the state and the individual. Though the mechanism of assuming identity as a citizen is unobvious, it is clearly not a birthright, an unambiguous and simple given. States put effort into distinguishing citizenship from countless identities, for instance through schooling (Raciborski 2011: 178–179). The process of claiming control over education by the state usually involved legal sanctioning of compulsory schooling, often with specific definitions of the age at which learning is to begin and of the length of the process of education. The role of the government in defining school programmes and aims, and in monitoring the effects and operation of the system also steadily increased. Here, too, differences between particular states did not preclude the similarity of the pattern of development of education; with centralisation came a gradual standardisation. The earliest stages centred on primary education, elimination of illiteracy, and teaching numeracy. Incidentally, that middle schooling expanded did not necessarily mean it became more common. In many African and South American states, secondary education remains inaccessible for persons of a lower socio-economic status even today. In Europe before World War II, it was also quite exclusive; access thereto only broadened in the 1950s, in a new political climate marked by the rise of the welfare state.

Prior to the nationalist Romantics, Adam Smith, for instance, advocated an investment in the state as approximate to civic duty – promoting opposition to foreign enemies and safeguarding against internal enemies potentially threatening the state's constitution. Smith (1977: 1048) believed that, unable to properly exercise their intellectual faculties, men become deformed and crippled, which adversely affects the entire society. The state turns to universal education because increased education levels among the members of the popular classes correlate with decreased susceptibility 'to the delusions of enthusiasm and superstition, which, among ignorant nations, frequently occasion the most dreadful disorders' (Smith 1977: 1048). In Smith's view, educated, intelligent men are always superior to ignoramuses and fools in terms of morality and orderliness. They see themselves as deserving of respect, and indeed, they do deserve respect from their superiors. More inclined to independent analysis and the formation of individual opinions, they are harder to manipulation by rebels or clueless opponents of the government's policies. In free states, where security of the government depends to a large degree on the favourable opinion of the citizen, it is extremely important that people refrain from premature and impulsive judgement (Smith 1977: 1049). Thus, Smith believes that education allows the citizen to consciously evaluate the work of the government, contributing to the stability of the state and of its institutions. Education transforms people into agents, providing them with the tools for decision-making that are vital for maintaining democracy, while also ensuring security from any threats posed by the state (McDonough and Feinberg 2003). After all, liberals perceive the latter as a guarantor of individual freedom only insofar as it defends the law; as soon as the balance is lost and control of the government put to question, the state may become a threat to the very same values. In Smith's liberal perspective, education is a factor of the strength of a state and not an instrument of any nationalist ideology.

For decades, education was addressed as a crucial element in the transformation of the state. Debates raged over whether decreasing illiteracy would limit the viability of populist propaganda, or whether schooling curbed social insubordination (Jones 1938). Under feudalism, many subalterns were shielded from sudden ill fortune by tradition and patronage; with the arrival of the modern state, persons of low status could no longer rely on outside support in their struggle with various adversities. Initially, formal equality in the face of the law was not upheld by any instruments ensuring enforcement of newly granted privileges. Thus, the expansion of civic equality was accompanied by an increase in class inequalities (Bendix 1964: 77).

The pursuit of formal, universal education provided a basis for the inclusion of lower classes into political life. The ability to read and write became a condition of access to other civil rights. Schooling became not only beneficial, but also necessary as a condition of universal citizenship, while also establishing an immediate relationship between the central organs of power and the individual members of a community (Bendix 1964: 88).

In continental Europe, universal compulsory education first appeared in the enlightened absolutist state. In 1721 Fredrik II of Denmark became the first ruler to institute it, though only in the royal estates. His example was followed in Prussia, which created the necessary legal framework in 1737 with a conservative outlook: the object of learning was to strengthen the moral, religious, and patriotic spirit of the nation. In the Prussian monarchy, education became universal because the rulers and courtly circles believed it would increase the loyalty of the members of the society towards the sovereign.

Reinhard Bendix (1964: 89–93) contends that, as an aspect of the modernisation of the state, the development of education was in line with the convictions of various ideological camps of the day. Conservatives saw universal education as an instrument for ensuring loyalty towards the authorities and a means to imparting rules and mores and curbing what they identified as man's natural tendency to 'disorder'. Liberals believed that the state simply needed an educated population. Some even claimed that due to their contribution to the wealth of the nation, people have earned the right to basic achievements of civilisation.

The process of establishing the modern state should also be analysed from the perspective of the development of the category of the citizen, entailing the formal equality of all citizen before the law, regardless of the divergence of economic and cultural capital that renders their life chances unequal. Thus, the role of the state is to balance these factors to allow everyone access to at least a certain minimum. The expansion of universal education at the primary level provided a means to equalising opportunity, allowing those at the lower rungs of the social ladder to exercise their newly earned rights. Of note here is the fact that the equalisation of opportunities postulated by liberals was perceived as highly unsatisfactory by Marxists, who stressed that formal equality concealed the actual dominance exercised by the privileged, diverting attention from the reproduction of social inequalities.

Aside from an educated citizenry, the modern state also required for the citizen to be driven by a sense of loyalty embedded in a common identity (Czaputowicz 2013: 88–91). Universal state education systems provided the tools for forging this sense of unity over the various divisions and divergent interests (Tyack 1966; Grosvenor 2005: 283). In part, 'statal' values were successfully promoted through education because – differently than before – children from various social groups and classes received instruction according to similar programmes (Schlereth 1990: 15). The limiting of independent forms of instruction, for instance, organised by the church or privately devised, and enforcement of a certain common minimum in terms of the programme also contributed to this transformation. All programmes in national school systems devote significant attention to the culture of the country, its history, symbols, and the understanding of its place and role in the world and in relation to other countries. This ensures that schools remain an important tool for forging identity and transmitting values of special significance for the maintenance of the state and legitimation of the most fundamental beliefs concerning international policy (Inkeles and Smith 1974; Almond and Verba 1963). In comparison to other media, whose range is always limited, public education can reach every citizen on at least one level.

Benedict Anderson (1983: 80) argues that increased literacy made it easier to arouse popular support everywhere, with the masses discovering a new glory in the elevation of languages that they had humbly spoken all along through print. This proved especially important for 'new nationalisms'; for example, Anderson (Anderson 1983: 82) mentions the Hungarians, who needed to refer to a collectivity of all Hungarian speakers and readers in order to prove they deserved their own nation-state. According to Hobsbawm (1975: 120), schools became the most important tool the states could use for the creation of identities. They enabled the training of effective, patriotic, and efficient soldiers, while also disseminating nationalist aspirations and creating national identities and cultures (common for the entire nation rather than different between members of the higher classes and those from the popular classes, on the margins of the education system). The national cultures disseminated since the nineteenth century combined elitist notions with elements of popular culture – previously absent from institutions of formal education, but introduced to the mainstream by the Romantics. Among the indirect effects of these processes were such phenomena as the rise of nationalisms, wars of national liberation, and increased consciousness of national differences and distinctions. Anderson (1983: 71) provocatively quotes the famous dictum by Hobsbawm that 'the progress of schools and universities measures that of nationalism, just as schools and especially universities became its most conscious champions', at least in nineteenth-century Europe.

Education was especially important for those nineteenth-century states that used nationalism to achieve unity (Germany) or created a new, bourgeois model of the state to finally deal with feudal legacies (France). Its value was lower where modern statehood had already developed according to a different, less bureaucratic model, and the identity was already clearly distinguished, as in Great Britain. Though nationalism proved effective as a tool of nation-making, its political impact would be dramatic, leading to the exacerbation of international disputes and plunging Europe into two world wars. The first half of the twentieth century would indicate that the boundary between patriotic support for the state and nationalism threatening international peace and order could become blurred, and education could be used as an instrument in the service of ideologies.

Ernest Gellner (1964: 159) names the ability to read as the minimal condition of citizenship in a modern state and of participation in a modern community. Unless this condition is met, individuals cannot expect their rights to be recognised or attain the degree of affluence or the lifestyle reflecting contemporary notions of human dignity. In Gellner's view, only a national system of education can lead to the formation of this type of a citizen, given that it possesses sufficient resources to train and maintain the required amount of teachers and to establish an immense corps of specialists and intellectuals tasked with educating those teachers. As a result, it is state-like entities (and not tribes or townships) that become the minimal political units of the modern world, in which universal literacy is the norm. Access to universal education becomes the basic contemporary criterion of the emergence of a basic political unit. According to Gellner (1964: 160), universal literacy and limited mobility between various language areas combined to further the spread of nationalism as a form of political loyalty. Education accounts, in part, for why nationalism can and does move masses of people (Kohn 1946: 574; Calhoun 1997: 21).

Aside from enshrining a sense of identity and bond with the state and guaranteeing formal equality between the citizen, education was also meant to provide armies with loyal recruits capable of completing required tasks. Already during the Enlightenment figures such as Adam Smith – incidentally, an advocate for limited government – noted the impact of education on the strength of the state as a function of its military potential. He stipulated that such education should be provided to 'common people' even if by resort to public intervention. In his view, universal education and military service taken together contribute to the creation of a kind of 'pro-state spirit' in the society (Smith 1977: 1046). This is all the more interesting given the liberal character of Smith's outlook on education, quite removed from the statist/nationalist visions informing the French or Prussian models.

Schools played a special role for colonial states. School systems supervised by overseas governments were crucial in promoting colonial nationalism. Analysing the school system of the Netherlands and the colonial schools in Indochina, Anderson (1983: 119–140) concludes that overseas education was organised according to a highly rationalised, tightly centralised hierarchy, structurally analogous to the bureaucracy. It offered standardised curricula, handbooks, and instructional materials, as well as unified rules of graduation and identical templates of diplomas. Pupils and students from colonial schools of the same metropolis enjoyed similar formal learning experience, reading similar books and solving the same maths tasks.

The loyalty of the citizen, their security in the structures of the state, and a 'pro-state spirit' are the factors that define the strength of the state in international relations; education contributes to each. However, history frames it as a boundary area between the patriotism involved in democracy and the category of citizen as a conscious and considerate judge of the actions of the government on the one hand, and the nationalism bound up with a more authoritarian form of government and the category of nation as centred on community, following authorities rather than critically assessing their activities. This tension reflects the disparity between the liberal and republican understanding of citizenship – the latter, related since the nineteenth century to the Romantic idea of the nation, values community over the individual. Meanwhile, owing to factors such as globalisation, recent times are marked by the process of dissolution of the formerly strict bond between the state and the nation, which contributes to the denationalisation of citizenship but may also provoke resistance and reactionary identity-formation conducive of a strong national identification. The international implications of nationalism, and its tendency to generate conflict in particular, indicate that, though in certain conditions it may produce at times incomparably resilient identities, it does not result in positive relations with neighbours. In effect, as in the case of security dilemma, the rise of nationalism – much like the arms race – may paradoxically decrease the security of the state by rapidly increasing the power of the state as an agent in international relations. Rising nationalism in one state frequently provokes corresponding processes in other states, resulting in a more confrontational international climate in which the likelihood of conflict is heightened while the fear of losing the benefits of cooperation no longer drives political decisions.

Examples of the use of education and science in state-building processes

As the previous sections of this chapter have demonstrated, individual variety in the process of establishing the modern state with the use of education and science does not hide certain recurring patterns in this evolution. The identified mechanisms contribute to the reinforcement of the strength of the state as an agent of international politics.

The following section is devoted to a description of the institutional specificity of the British and French models, which often provided inspiration for reforms implemented in other countries. A separate fragment discusses the case of Poland, as well.

Great Britain – a success that became a burden

The history of the British education system stands in contrast to examples from both continental Europe and the United States. Scientific knowledge and education played a relatively small role in the early modern state-building processes and in the early Industrial Revolution. Most practical knowledge useful at the time was unsystematic and informal, often uncodified and passed on vertically from master to apprentice (Mokyr 2002: 30). The First Industrial Revolution needed little more than the mechanics that Galileo knew. However, gradually, that amount of knowledge became insufficient (Mokyr 2009: 21). Great Britain,

60 *Education and the state-building process*

the winner in the First Industrial Revolution, became a hostage of its own success and experienced difficulties in establishing mass education and modern science. Great Britain also led in the process of modern state-building, establishing crucial post-feudal political institutions early on. The institutional advantage achieved by Britain around the seventeenth century was so powerful that there was little urgency to reform it, unlike in the countries that were lagging behind the leader and experienced significant pressure to attempt institutional innovations in the state-building effort.

Techniques developed during the British Industrial Revolution were devised by 'hard heads and clever fingers'. They cannot be attributed to what we call science today, and during this period Britain imported at least as much knowledge as it exported to its political and economic competitors. Inventions were achieved by inspired and obsessive individuals, mostly working on their own (Mokyr 2009: 23, 35). Only during the seventeenth century did the modern type of knowledge begin to see development within what we now call Scottish Enlightenment, and the importance of practical applications of science and mathematics increased throughout the eighteenth century. In Scotland, the situation was different: unlike British universities, local institutions of higher learning did dedicate themselves to research into useful sciences such as medicine, chemistry, physics, and political economy. The choice of this path stemmed from the decisions of the patrons of the universities, powerful politicians who, inspired by the ideals of the Enlightenment, considered it to be the right course to take (Mokyr 2009: 54).

Francis Bacon was the first philosopher to propose a clear technological program for economic expansion. The Industrial Enlightenment spawned from the Baconian program, which consisted of three components. First, science should expand human knowledge and understanding of the universe by accelerating the pace of research into natural phenomena, which had attracted interest for a long time, armed with better equipment and the scientific method. Second, research should be directed to areas where the likelihood of solving practical problems was high – in medicine, manufacturing, navigation, and so on. Third, the costs of access to this knowledge should be made as low as possible, not only through dissemination but also through the organisation and classification of the known (Mokyr 2009: 40). The idea of science was the one of 'a rich storehouse, for the Glory of the Creator and relief of Man's estate' (Bacon 1996: 143).

Interestingly, the first state institutions that supported the expansion of useful knowledge in Britain were not technical schools or state-run associations of scholars, but intellectual property rights that protected inventors through the patents system. The proponents of patents argued that ideas were 'owned' and thus fell within the sanctity of private property, that the concept of natural justice demands that people who perform a service to society be rewarded, and that patents provided high-powered incentives for talented people to engage in research. Attempts to limit the diffusion of knowledge drew resistance from supporters of the Baconian approach, who argued that know-how should be shared and that its accumulation was a fundamentally cumulative endeavour. Knowledge was a public good, rather that a 'private property' (Mokyr 2009: 45).

The year 1660, saw the foundation of the Royal Society, which followed the Baconian concept of a 'House of Solomon', where specialists would congregate as at a research institute and cooperatively catalogue and experiment. Spontaneously organised by private interests, numerous 'philosophical' societies regularly attended lectures there and spent their meetings discussing practical and technical issues. At the beginning of eighteenth century, the Society lessened its interest in practical matters to concentrate on more abstract issues, but by that time, numerous minor associations had risen to prominence, including in smaller towns which would soon challenge London as centres of activity in technological advance. Such institutions were often located near important industrial centres, gathering local entrepreneurs, engineers, and sometimes natural philosophers. These communal entities disseminated useful knowledge with remarkable efficiency in the seventeenth and early eighteenth centuries, but in themselves, they did not practice scientific research according to the most advanced standards of the nineteenth century. During this period, a set of bridges were erected between intellectuals and producers. These channels of communication allowed 'culture' to affect technology and enabled economic progress in the long run.

Strikingly, the Baconian programme did not yield immediate success, dashing hopes for a quick technological pay-off to scientific research in the eighteenth century. At that time, scientific knowledge was much more capable of explaining why techniques worked, than of suggesting new ones. Still, the conviction that systematic knowledge and natural philosophy were the keys to economic growth persisted in spite of the early disappointments. Their value was only confirmed in the long run, at the turn of the eighteen century, when they helped achieve a sequence of improvements and adaptations, which later contributed heavily to a major increase in productivity. Mokyr (2009: 106–123) argues that the very advanced skills of British specialists were a crucial factor behind the British economic leadership. In the eighteenth century, British manufacturers not only led in some of the cutting edge technologies such as the use of coal, steam power, and the production of metals and textiles (lagging behind in chemical knowledge, glass and paper technologies, and luxury textile production), but also demonstrated an uncanny ability to recognise the discoveries of others and put them to work by eliminating faults and problems, and then deriving a profit. Those skills were transmitted from one generation to another without any formal institutional support, only through a private apprenticeship system. In 1803, French political economist Jean-Baptiste Say wrote enviously that:

> the enormous wealth of Britain is less owing to her own advances in scientific acquirements, high as she ranks in that department, as to the wonderful practical skills of her adventurers in the useful application of knowledge and the superiority of her workmen.
>
> (Say [1803]1821, vol. 1: 32–22)

The Swiss travel writer César-François de Saussure noted seventy-five years earlier that: 'English workmen are everywhere renowned, and justly. They work to perfection, and though not inventive, are capable of improving and of finishing most admirably what the French and Germans have invented' ([1726]1902: 218). The famous engineer John Farey wrote a century later that: 'the prevailing talent of English and Scotch people is to apply new ideas to use, and to bring such applications to perfection, but they do not imagine as much as foreigners' (Great Britain 1829: 153).

Great Britain benefitted from a class of skilled people more numerous than the workers of any other country, without whom it would not have become the workshop of the world. The difference between Britain and the continental states lie not only in the greater availability of technical skills, but also in their allocation. The continental states absorbed a large share of engineering talent into the military civil service, teaching, and administration. Meanwhile, the British state typically refrained from restricting the career paths of individuals endowed with such competencies, leaving them to seek employment in the private sector. Britain also possessed unique social, political, religious, and intellectual characteristics, supporting pluralism and individual liberty to a degree unmatched on the continent (Goldstone 2009: 172).

In spite of its economic power and leadership role in science, within one century, Great Britain fell back relative to the other major continental powers. If there was any virtue to the British education system of the eighteenth century, it was its status as a free-entry private enterprise. It was highly diversified, disorganised, competitive, under-regulated, and marked by high entry and exit rates. School curricula ranged from strictly conservative, religious instruction, to progressive programmes rooted in the ideas of Rousseau (Mokyr 2009: 232–234). Children from poor families enjoyed no schooling opportunities. Oxford and Cambridge admitted few students (in 1660, there were 460 freshmen; in the 1750s, the number fell to 200 a year) and the quality of instruction in science was low. Scottish universities represented a much better academic level.

In the nineteenth century, education in Great Britain remained voluntary, as subsequent governments rejected the notion of a top-down approach to the matter. This may suggest a similarity with the USA, where the system developed without any intrusion from the federal government, but the dynamic of grass-roots initiatives that typified the USA was absent in Great Britain. School reforms were blocked for most of the nineteenth century and the changes that were implemented concerned issues that had already been resolved elsewhere.

Until the mid-nineteenth century, the country had no state institutions for the supervision of education. The level of scholarisation was lower by half than in Prussia or the Netherlands. For those with limited means, it was typically restricted to the primary level and mostly provided by volunteers. Public support for these initiatives remained minimal, and the quality of instruction was low – not to mention the absence of a coherent programme. In spite of gradual reforms introduced by mid-century, in 1870 most primary schools remained in the hands of religious societies. The year 1833 saw the first public grant for universal primary schooling; over the following years, the outlay increased, turning the government into a populariser of primary education without actually imposing direct supervision. Throughout the nineteenth century, schools continued to depend on donations for funding and organise without input from the authorities (Green 2013: 263–278). The Education Act of 1870 would eventually lay the groundwork for a universal state education system at the primary level. In the early 1890s, education became free of charge, with school-leaving age set at eleven, soon rising to twelve. As a result, the enrolment rate among ten year olds increased from 40 per cent in 1870 to 100 per cent in 1900. The Education Act of 1902 led to a large expansion of resources and introduced grammar schools, which subsequently became the foundation for secondary education in Britain (Acemoglu and Robinson 2012: 358). Great Britain was one of the last major powers to introduce a public education system. The British case is puzzling – how could a state that boasted the lowest rate of illiteracy during Reformation become one of the least educated nations with a very high percentage of illiterate citizens by the Victorian era? Great Britain had all it needed to achieve a relatively high level of education among its populace. Already by the mid-nineteenth century, half of all Britons lived in urban areas – fifty years ahead of other leaders of this major demographic transformation. Politically, the state was also marked by relative openness and liberalism.

One of the most convincing explanations of the peculiarity of the British case points to its unsuccessful adaptation and delayed modernisation after the first Industrial Revolution. Though modern state-formation and industrialisation could initially advance by purely grass-roots initiatives, it eventually required increasing state coordination. The development of education was also delayed by major landowners with significant influence on subsequent governments, who favoured an elitist model of instruction (Nairn 1981). Hobsbawm (1969: 173) describes how the conditions that allowed the country to usher in the first wave of industrialisation prevented further advancement and modernisation in the second half of the nineteenth century. There was no impulse for reform nor a sufficiently influential interest group convinced of the necessity of universal education for achieving progress. The dominance of ideas of limited state and the British version of liberalism prevented effective top-down efforts in that direction (Gamble 1981).

Great Britain formed a cultural and national identity early on – already in the times of the Tudors – partly due to the geographical placement of the country and the consequent absence of foreign invaders. The Tudors quickly managed to impose English as the sole national language and centralise power. As with the Industrial Revolution, Great Britain acted as a pioneer in state-building too, as well as being the exception to the rule. Its bureaucracy did not achieve the extent it reached in France and then Germany. Employment in the public sector only began to open up in the 1860s, at first mostly in the less prestigious posts in colonial administration; recruitment based on merit necessitated reform in some of the middle schools.

The supremacy of laissez-faire also contributed to the poor condition of higher and technical education. While science developed outside of the institutions of formal learning, Great Britain still fell behind as competitors in continental Europe picked up speed. The classical model of instruction continued to hold sway in British schools, while continental states not only exhibited greater openness to scientific knowledge, but also fostered the creation of special universities devoted to the implementation of new discoveries. Analogous institutions only appeared on the British Isles towards the end of the nineteenth century.

This sense of lost primacy was already expressed at the time; for instance, in the 1884 report of the Samuelson Commission, consisting mostly of entrepreneurs, which includes a pertinent analysis of the relationship between the economy and education:

> during the first half of this century we enjoyed an unchallenged industrial supremacy, the result of many contributory causes. So conspicuous was the supremacy thus established that some among us came to regard it almost as part of the fixed order of Nature. Although conceivably we might improve ourselves, yet we were superior to other nations that improvement was hardly a thing of practical concern. Our neighbours, however, saw things more clearly. They were inferior to us in material resources and in natural ingenuity; but their inferiority in these respects forced upon their attention the value of thrift and of education. Whilst we have advanced, they have advanced faster still. The success of our rivals in not to be explained by reference to the low wages and long hours of work. It is mainly the sobriety and the intelligence of their workmen which gave them advantage. We must again and again repeat that neither elementary education nor technical education can be perfected apart from education in general. The strength of Germany lies in the culture of every class of Germans, in the real love of learning which animates the people and their rulers, in the patient, inquiring, and scientific spirit which has transformed almost every branch of human activity. This culture, this love of learning, this scientific spirit, are not rare among us, but neither are they diffused; they are the property of individuals and of small groups. In Germany the problem how to educate the whole nation as well as possible has for many years been constantly present to the minds of scholars and statesmen. In England, and still more in Ireland, it is less the education of the people than the advantage which parties can draw from controlling education that has fascinated journalists and members of Parliament.
>
> (The Samuelson Report 1884: 11–15)

France – the pros and cons of centralism

The French education system was established in the nineteenth century, as part of the process of erecting a post-revolutionary bourgeois state. However, like other institutions, the system owed its contours primarily to the previous attempts at centralisation, conducted under the auspices of the absolute monarchy. The peculiarity of the development of schooling in France reflects the character of the state-building process involved, which succeeded in establishing not only a fairly unified national community, but also a centralisation of power at a rather early stage. French became the official language of the state in 1539, suggesting a relatively high level of homogeneity among the population inhabiting the monarchy ruled from Paris. The French numbered among the first in Europe to achieve modern nationhood and statehood (Seton-Watson 1977: 42–46).

The situation of the peasantry in France was also unusual. Serfdom was abolished far earlier than in other countries of Europe and many peasants owned the land they tilled. Thus, they enjoyed greater privilege and freedom than their Prussian or Austrian counterparts. Even after the Revolution, French peasants resisted attempts to institute compulsory education; the push for universal education would only bear fruit in the long run, as the peasantry noted the resulting benefits. Eugen Weber (1976) describes how peasants were turned into Frenchmen in the span of just over a century after the French Revolution through military conscription army and public schools.

The French bureaucracy of the absolutist period was a product of venality – the selling of offices to the aristocrats – and heredity. At that stage, meritocratic criteria did not factor in, likely contributing to the limiting of middle schooling. It would only develop in the Napoleonic era, as recruitment into the administration became more competitive – the period was a veritable golden age of the high school (Artz 1966: 28).

A proponent of the mercantilist doctrine, Richelieu supported merchant and military schools. In his view, 'letters and weapons are equally useful to the creation and maintenance of grand empires: the former for regulating and civilising those within the state, the latter to extend and defend them' (quoted in Artz 1966: 43). The seventeenth century saw the establishment of the first state-controlled military academies, which enrolled as many as 4,275 cadets by 1684. In 1682, a naval college was established, providing a boost for trade as well as the navy. France led the way in development of the art of war and the relevant schools, which contributed to its military achievements in the early nineteenth century. The École Royale Militaire, established in 1753, enrolled over 500 cadets per year. There were specialised colleges of artillery, cavalry, and navy, as well as the naval university at Le Havre. By the early eighteenth century, the first schools of land engineering – École des Ponts et Chaussées and École du Corps Royal du Génie – had emerged, teaching practical applications of mathematics, physics, and chemistry for state-funded infrastructure projects. A mining school had operated already before the Revolution. The eighteenth century was a period of rapid development of merchant schools located in major cities.

The introduction of universal education in France was preceded by a heated debate over schooling between Enlightenment philosophers. Aside from Jean-Jacques Rousseau's famous treatise *Émile, or On Education*, the year 1763 saw the publication of the equally notable *Essai d'éducation nationale*, whose author, Louis-René de la Chalotais, claimed that:

to teach letters and sciences, we must have persons who make of them profession. The clergy cannot take it in bad part that we should not, generally speaking, include ecclesiastics in this class.... I claim the right to demand for the Nation an education that will depend upon the State alone; because it belongs essentially to it, because every nation has an inalienable and imprescriptible right to instruct its members, and finally because the children of the State should be educated by members of the State.

(Quoted in Bendix 1964: 110)

Even before the Revolution, numerous pamphlets demanded the establishment of a hierarchical education system involving all levels of education, from primary school up to the university, and completely centralised, with the University of Paris at the top of the structure.

The postulated meritocracy extended only to the bourgeoisie. For French Enlightenment thinkers, the social condition of peasants did not require more than primary education. It was also argued that members of all social classes should only receive schooling to the extent of the requirements of the duties assigned them (Archer and Vaughan 1971: 158). In the end, in spite of an animated debate and the presentation of multiple projects, no universal education system was implemented in *ancien régime* France.

Though it fostered emancipation and egalitarianism in schooling as well, the period of the Revolution also failed to bring about changes in the education system. On the other hand, the era saw an increase in vocational and technical schooling subservient to the state. The famous École Polytechnique was established in 1795, introducing a paradigmatic system of meritocratic, competitive entry exams organised in twenty-two French cities with the goal of identifying the 360 students who would spend three years exploring applied sciences and engineering under the aegis of the most elite cohort of scholars available at the time.

France only received a universal education system during the Napoleonic era. While middle schooling was defined by the rigour of secular lyceums, Napoleon allowed Jesuits to provide education on the primary level (Green 2013: 151). Even here, though, state control advanced further and further with every decade. The creation of the Université – an unprecedented institution tasked with oversight of secular education and under the direct control of the state as an expression of its monopoly in teaching – became the period's crowning achievement. The institution was characterised by a rigid hierarchy in which the highest level responded directly to the head of the state, while regional and local levels operated received no autonomy. All schools beyond the primary level – still dominated by Jesuits and only integrated into the system after several decades – found themselves under state control. The geographical and ideological unity of education thus ensured, the competencies gained in the schools were subject to review by the state by means of a system of central exams. Teachers were also subject to appropriate certification, which transformed the profession into a disciplined, pro-statist, quasi-officer corps.

Napoleonic middle schools applied a military-style discipline and a common programme implemented by teachers employed at the Université. The elite nature of the schools ensured that, even as some remained in private hands, the state exercised full control over this level of the education system (Green 2013: 131). Lyceums admitted only a highly select group of students (less than 0.02 per cent of all students of appropriate age in 1808). As a result, the Napoleonic system enabled advancement on merit, but only to a very narrow degree. Following a common programme, middle schools inculcated the middle class with loyalty to the state. At the same time, the characteristic Cartesian philosophical bent became a primary feature of the national programmes of education and a point of pride among the elite. François Guizot, the author of most of the education reforms of the first half of the nineteenth century, wrote:

> French schools distinguished themselves from those of most Europe by the teaching of philosophy to children.... To finish off their education, the elite of the nation were neither given responsibility as prefects, nor encouraged in athletic distractions, as were British children, but instead were offered a very peculiar intellectual training.
>
> (Quoted in Zeldin 1980: 150)

Though a liberal, he viewed education as a tool for regulating social divisions, but not for overcoming them (Anderson 1975: 40). Locating itself on the opposite side to the Baconian approach, Cartesianism loathed experimentation, valuing reason over empirical experience, and deduction over induction (Goldstone 2009: 152).

During Restoration, primary education became compulsory and free for the poor, but the requirement was not universally observed and the network of country schools was still in the process of development. Public financing of education increased until the mid-nineteenth century, and the number of schools grew, but universal access to primary education was not yet secured, as had happened in Prussia. The average number of years spent at school in France was six, meaning that both the extent and the universality of education in the country was far more advanced than in Great Britain.

In the field of science, the Great Revolution initially made a mark by disbanding the institutions that had contributed so significantly to developments in that area under the *ancien régime*, including the Academy of Sciences and the universities. However, the same period also saw the creation of the École Polytechnique. Later on, Napoleon partially restored the previous structure by establishing the École Normale Supérieure and the Conservatoire des Arts et Métiers. École Polytechnique and École Normale Supérieure represented a completely innovative model of organisation in contemporary Europe. During the first half of the nineteenth century, they drew the most renowned French scholars, particularly those dealing in hard science and mathematics. Along the way, these institutions also combined higher learning with research. The Paris Polytechnic possessed the most advanced laboratories in the world at the time.

The institutional organisation of higher learning in the late Napoleonic era survived in France until World War II. Like primary and secondary education, it was typified by an almost complete centralisation. The model consistent of fully independent networks of institutions dealing with scientific research, teaching natural sciences, and professional training in engineering and medicine. Problems with cooperation between the various segments of French higher education became apparent already by the middle of the nineteenth century. By the second half of the nineteenth century, this institutional fragmentation created a serious obstacle to the development of French science and technology, and academic circles successfully resisted all attempts at reform (Gilpin 1968: 86). Purely scientific institutions dealt in current, abstract knowledge without consideration for real-life applications. French engineering schools, on the other hand, retained the same quality levels, but did not keep abreast of scientific discoveries the way their German counterparts (Technische Hochschulen) did.

As Alexander von Humboldt himself claimed, France led the advance of scientific progress in Europe since the mid-eighteenth century, reaching an apex in the first half of the nineteenth century, when Paris rose to the rank of the capital of science. However, France's relative scholarly standing began to decline by about 1840, even as geniuses of the scale of Louis Pasteur or the Curies continued to emerge. Germany advanced at a greater pace. While physiology and chemistry were French inventions, it was German scientists that took the lead in these disciplines at mid-century.

Since the seventeenth century, the French had led the way in technical education and applications of scientific discovery in the industry. Throughout the nineteenth century, French engineers numbered among the finest in Europe, playing a key role in its industrialisation, with the Suez Canal serving for decades as a monument to their genius. Yet, by the 1880s, the French lost their impetus in this area, as well. Though ground-breaking discoveries in organic chemistry and electrical energy are attributed to French and British scientists, only in Germany were their findings fully exploited by industry. The pace of advancement in research and engineering declined for a variety of reasons stemming from different levels of social life, but the powerlessness of the government to reform the country's scholarly and technical institutions – cut to fit the Napoleonic era, but increasingly unsuited to the demands of modern scholarship and industry with every passing decade – was doubtless the direct cause. Resistance to change could largely be ascribed to the very same institutions. Meanwhile, their counterparts outside of France evolved swiftly (Gilpin 1968: 82–84). In the second half of the nineteenth century, the structure of higher education became the major barrier to advancement (Gilpin 1968: 112). Besides, the *grandes écoles*, which attracted the most gifted students, usually fed them into the administration, preventing their involvement in scholarly pursuits.

The French originated the central examination system which guaranteed uniform instruction at a considerable level. While this helped to secure the structures of the state, the Napoleonic education system would eventually prove to be a cul-de-sac. The exams focused entirely on verifying knowledge learned by rote, and the full submission of both primary and secondary schools to the standards of examination turned them into hostages to the system. Bureaucracy dominated the teacher profession, whose representatives exhibited an excessive tendency to embrace the ethos of Republican officials tasked with preparing their pupils for the state exams, while disregarding the significance of knowledge beyond the exam requirements, of stimulating curiosity and the pursuit of independent discoveries. The same applied to higher education, mostly aimed at training teachers for the school system. Universities soon gave in to this rigidity. As a result, in spite of the advance of knowledge and creation of new specialities around the world, France maintained the Napoleonic order of disciplines until the twentieth century (Gilpin 1968: 101–102).

While French scholars continued to act as public officials tasked with cultural transmission and preparing students for state exams, in Germany instruction focused on introducing theory through application, teaching was specialised, and particular discoveries were rewarded, even when achieved in narrow disciplines. The French wanted their professors to be intelligent and erudite, possessed of enormous, encyclopaedic knowledge. In addition, scholarly employees received no monetary incentives, as income brackets correlated strictly with specific levels in the hierarchy. Earnings were unaffected by the quality of one's achievements. Subsequent attempts to reform the pay structure at French universities failed due to the cadres' insistence on principles of equality. This organisational structure, in turn, motivated scholars to choose conventional, predictable problems rather than engaging in risky attempts to sail into uncharted waters.

Though the organisation of science in France and the country's education system had initially yielded remarkable results, its inadequacy to changing realities soon became apparent. By the second half of the nineteenth century, the inertia, rigidity, and successful resistance of the elites towards changes that would push them out of their comfort zone had become apparent. Meanwhile, the Germans reaped the fruits of a completely different model – at once astounding and frightening their contemporaries.

Poland – integrating the state through education

The key moment in the history of the development in Poland of a state education system on the model of contemporary European equivalents came with the initiatives of the Commission of National Education (Komisja Edukacji Narodowej, KEN) elaborated between 1773 and 1794. Stanisław Kot (1919) stresses that KEN broke with the tradition of learning popularised by a Jesuit, Father Stanisław Konarski, which assigned key role to the Church. According to Kot, the Commission was 'an adaptation of foreign examples', particularly from France, and diverged from previous Polish approaches, first, in the degree of state – or, more precisely, government – control over schooling; second, in the tendency towards secularisation; third, in the introduction of a unified school system; fourth, in the attempt to professionalise teaching; fifth, in the pursuit of universal education for the entire nation; and finally, in the attempt to implement similar rules of formation across the country in support of the state.

Mutually cohesive, these characteristics would promote an education system responsive to the demands of the state and supportive of the processes of modernisation. The universalisation of education played an especially significant role, particularly as it involved the stipulation that all estates should be included – the common folk, as well. French pursuit of state control even over private schools and over the contents of textbooks, including primers – a means to organisational as well as 'spiritual' centralisation – evoked admiration (Kot 1919: 1–4). Even though not all members of KEN supported centralised schooling – some proposing that distinctions between estates be retained – the conviction in the need for state education for all, whether secular or sacred, was universal (Kot 1928: 207).

Interestingly, Jean-Jacques Rousseau admired eighteenth-century Poland. Though aware of the unfavourable prospects of development (that soon lead to the collapse of the state) and astonished by the uncritical embrace of foreign fashions by the Polish elites, he revelled in Poland's political system, which offered its citizen a remarkably high degree of liberty for the times. His fondness of the Polish-Lithuanian Commonwealth led him to propose a reform and modernisation programme for the state, in which he assigned a major role to education. This education was to be rooted in an intimate knowledge and love of all aspects of the motherland. Rousseau suggested a national and secular education for all, without distinction for estate, rank or wealth, by teachers who must be Polish, married, possessive of integrity, enlightened intelligence, and common sense (Rousseau 1772: 435–441). Literacy was to be inculcated in children by way of readings on the home country; by the age of ten, pupils should know all major commodities produced in Poland, and by twelve – all of its provinces, communication routes, and cities. At fifteen, pupils would be expected to know the entire history of the country (and its laws at sixteen), so that no illustrious historical fact or personage was consigned to oblivion. Rousseau suggested that clergymen and foreigners be barred from teaching.

Rousseau's programme would not be implemented; within twenty-five years since its presentation, the Polish state ceased to exist – a traumatic event of vast proportions for its nation. As a result, the visionary idea of the French philosopher enjoys greater recognition in international scholarship on education than it is being remembered in Poland. After the partitions of Poland, the country's education system was developed and administered by Russia, Austro-Hungary, and Prussia, with each applying a different slant to the model. Schooling progressed the least in the Russian partition: its extent was low and illiteracy continued to hold sway over the popular classes. Teaching served as a tool for Russifying the society. While schools in the Prussian partition exhibited the highest degree of advancement, Germanisation gained pace particularly towards the end of the nineteenth century, with the arrival of Kulturkampf. Aside from recurring periods of repression, the Austrian partition was marked by leniency in the treatment of education, but its development did not match the standard established in Prussia. Prior to World War I universal education was introduced in Prussian and Austrian partitions; in the Russian partition, it was only extended to slightly more than half of the population. Prussia boasted a very diligently applied system of universal education in German up to the eighth grade. In Galicia, compulsory education lasted seven years in urban and six in rural areas since 1895, and instruction could be provided in Polish or Ukrainian. In the Russian partition, schooling was never universal and lasted for only three or four years. Russian was the primary language of instruction, though Polish was partially accepted in the central regions of the partition (Falski 1928: 66).

The establishment of a national education system in the Second Commonwealth after 1918 – that is, the first modern system of education in Poland – faced serious obstacles due to, first, the need to catch up with other European states (especially Germany with its massive advancements), and second, the challenge of post-partition divisions, consisting in the need to unify three completely different structures. The high esteem for the Prussian, and then German, education system was expressed not only by intellectuals and educational activists from Great Britain and the USA who had visited the country; it was also voiced by Polish intellectuals, and its role in ensuring internal cohesion and international recognition of the state was appreciated by such thinkers as Roman Dmowski (1908: 88–92). For the leader of the National Democrats, it was clear that Poland would not achieve statehood without inculcating loyalty among its populace, and the lack of education among the peasantry constituted one of the greatest obstacles to gaining independence. Dmowski believed that without education, a significant proportion of the society would not attain citizenship. The improvement of education among the peasants, on the other hand, would inevitably turn them into a political force, as has already been observed in the Prussian partition and in Galicia, where education became universal before the end of the nineteenth century. Devoting an entire chapter of his famous work from 1908 titled *Germany, Russia, and the Polish Question* (*Niemcy, Rosja a kwestia polska*; Dmowski 1908: 91) to education, Dmowski reinterpreted the struggle against anti-Polish policies in the Prussian partition and the Kingdom of Poland as not only a question of defining social policy, but also one of particular significance for the possibility of a future emergence of Poland in the international arena.

The emergence of a unified education system in the aftermath of the war, with limited resources to hand, proved a serious challenge. The reformers saw the Polonisation of schools in the former Prussian partition and the organisation of universal schooling in the former Russian partition – which comprised two-thirds of the territory of the Second Commonwealth inhabited by three fifths of its population – as key issues. The first step on the road to change, made already in 1919, involved the introduction of compulsory education in this area. To enable that, a network of schools had to be established, providing access to education on the primary level. Plans for the creation of this infrastructure were laid down by a socialist, Marian Falski (1925), more widely known for being the author of the first Polish primer; in his view, schools were obligated to support

72 Education and the state-building process

the public interest, and especially the overcoming of class barriers by way of opening educational opportunities to children from the 'lower strata'. These changes, aimed at unifying education across the partitions, eventually led to the lowering of its quality in the former Prussian partition, where students used to receive better instruction before the war.

Major changes in the school system were implemented at the turn of the 1920s, following the coup that established the rule of the co-called *Sanacja*: they included organisational, programmatic, and formational adjustments collectively dubbed as 'the Jędrzejewicz reform' (from the name of the Minister of Religious Denominations and Public Enlightenment and future Prime Minister, Janusz Jędrzejewicz).[1] The formational component of the reform clearly indicated its state-building ambitions. In 1927, Minister Gustaw Dobrucki, Jędrzejewicz's predecessor, issued circulars which implemented rules of formation as an element of state education. One of the documents stipulated that the main purpose of schools was to mould the young generation into socially conscious citizen endowed with a civic imagination. Civic education was designed to exploit the 'social tendencies' peculiar to the youth. According to this document, schools were to constitute a space for harmonious coexistence between pupils, regardless of national, religious, or social divisions and the economic status of one's parents (MWRiOP 1927). The circulars also stressed that teachers should refrain from taking sides in political disputes, focusing instead on the state as a whole. The ideals of civic education were promoted in school programmes through the use of such outlets as the magazine *Oświata i Wychowanie* (*Learning and Formation*), published by the Ministry, or the *Zrąb* (*Foundation*) quarterly. Jędrzejewicz gained the support of Józef Piłsudski for his position that education should be used to shape relations between the citizen and the state.

Special attention was devoted to the duties imparted upon all citizens by their national identity. In this connection, aside from the depoliticisation of schools, the role of the Church in teaching was drastically limited. The process of seizing an increasing array of structures from religious hierarchies by the state occurred with a significant delay. Subjects that had suffered particular neglect during the partitions would now receive greater prominence – this involved the celebration of Poland, its language, history, and culture. Describing his approach to the matter, Jędrzejewicz explained:

> since the conditions allowed the state to claim a leadership role in education, the state is now required to command it in a manner that will ensure that schools perform at the greatest intensity in the service of the state understood as the common good of all of its citizen. Such is the reason why I name state education, which is often called civic education, as foremost among all aspects of formation. It is my view that it was precisely common nationality that demanded universal and compulsory education, a unified school system, and the inculcation in the souls of youth on all levels of instruction of a certain generally acceptable relationship toward the state,

whose survival and security depend to such a great extent on the attitudes of the citizen and which finds the greatest support in the attitude and worth of its citizen.

(Quoted in Jędrzejewicz 1972: 128)

The state-building impact of the Jędrzejewicz reform can be gleaned from the statements of its opponents. Right-leaning critics claimed the reform enforced state formation at the expense of national formation and impinged upon the autonomous right of private schools to define their own programmes and organise. The Catholic Church was likewise opposed to the changes. In 1932, the cardinals August Hlond and Aleksander Kakowski lodged a complaint with the Prime Minister concerning the complete subordination of schools to the state. The government, however, defended this part of the reform in the conviction that the influence of the Church, as well as of the private school lobby, needed to be curbed. Jędrzejewicz claimed:

There is a factor that defines not only the condition of science, but also the degree and aims of formation in Poland. Formation is too significant an aspect of life in Poland to entertain the possibility of leaving it unattended. This major factor of responsibility is, of course, with the Government.

(Projekty szkolne na plenum Sejmu 1932)

Representatives of national minorities also expressed doubts about state formation due to concerns that the stripping of influence from local communities would lead to denationalisation. The Minister responded to these charges by stating that: 'minority schooling is and will be expected to foster not just outward loyalty, but even a positive attitude toward Polish statehood, and schools that fail to adequately represent this attitude will inevitably bear the unpleasant consequences of their actions' (Wbrew partiom opozycji 1933). The changes introduced to schools of all levels and types 'a frank and deep cult of the Polish statehood rooted in emotion and reason, as well as respect for and deference toward official power' (Wbrew partiom opozycji 1933).

School reforms in the Second Commonwealth garnered much opposition from the left, which believed they would entrench a firmly selective system preventing broader and less privileged social groups from gaining higher, and even middle education, while peasant children were condemned to incomplete instruction that corresponded in content to merely four grades. Critiques were also levelled at the insufficiently radical limitation of the influence of the Catholic Church. The character of the reforms also reflected the evolution of the Commonwealth towards the strengthening of the executive, including elements of authoritarianism, manifesting itself primarily in the 1930s.

The Second Commonwealth passed through an accelerated process of state-building by establishing its own administration. Due to the low quality of education in the Russian partition and Germanisation in the Prussian partition, the gist of public institutions was manned by officials from the Austrian partition, which, on the one hand, possessed Polish universities in Lviv and Cracow that dated back to before the partitions (as well as other Polish schools), and on the other, had a re-Polonised administration since the 1870s, which guaranteed a degree of practical experience in public service. The size of the challenge faced in this area can be illustrated by the fact that in 1923 only 15,000 out of a total of 120,000 state employees had higher education (Witkowski 2007: 373). By the 1930s, the state cadres were sufficiently developed to ensure most posts were occupied by persons who had passed the middle school final exam (*matura*) and finished studies in the Second Commonwealth. During the inter-war period, instead of establishing a special school for the formation of professional administrative cadres, the state relied on middle schools to provide mid-level administration officials and on universities for high-level cadres.

The case of Poland provides an illustration of state-building processes in a less economically developed state suffering from a delay of some 100 or even 150 years in political terms. Here, education was first applied to the work of establishing state structures already in the eighteenth century; the best proof of Poland's potential in that regard is the fact that it had attracted Rousseau's interest. Nevertheless, it was the weaknesses of the state that sealed its fate, soon leaving it prey to its neighbours. At the time of the regaining of independence in 1918, state institutions suffered not only due to relative delays in development in relation to the advances made in Western Europe, but also because of the necessity of integrating three distinct systems established during the nineteenth century by the beneficiaries of the partitions of Poland. Thus, educational institutions were both subjected to these processes and involved in the work of state-building, as in other states. The character of the resulting changes was not unmarked by the authoritarian spirit of the 1930s.

Conclusion

Chapter 2 discusses the role of education in state-building processes, offering detailed analyses of examples from selected states in Europe. One could argue that using Western states as the main reference point is a questionable practice; however, academic studies of modern state-building processes indicate that the model of political organisation developed in the Old World served, for god and for bad, as a universal touchstone. That particular conceptualisation of authority successfully displaced rival forms of political organisation in Europe and was then transplanted globally (Giddens 1987; Strang 1991; Herbst 2000). Hendrik Spruyt (1996) believes that imitation of some states by others or forced adoption of similar solutions constituted a key element in the 'culmination' of the system of sovereign states achieved through mutual interactions. While the process began in Europe, Europeans went on to spread it either by imposing it directly through colonial expansion or by forcing others to imitate it to successfully resist European domination, as in the case of Japan. State formation outside of Europe was greatly affected by external pressure, a vastly different international milieu (both in terms of security and economics), and a highly compressed time-frame.

It is this process that most clearly illustrates the development of a structural aspect of power in international relations, which perceives this method of sociopolitical organisation as simultaneously the most effective and effectively the only one applicable (Gilpin 1981: 117, 122).

John W. Meyer and Michael T. Hannan (1979) showed that the organisational models of state education systems were subject to diffusion in the same way as other state institutions. Bendix (1964: 1), too, contends that states emerging in the process of decolonisation inevitably passed through processes that bore at least a fleeting similarity to those experienced by European states in the eighteenth and nineteenth centuries. In spite of the commonality of the adopted models and similarities between the processes of development, the same stages do not necessarily follow the same evolutionary pattern of succession. 'Development' itself is also not a given: the adoption of institutional models as such does not allow the states that experience a 'delay' in relation to those that are in the lead to immediately achieve the same level of advancement. This is due to the fact that the institutions which play a part in achieving modernity are erected on structures that had operated in the societies for centuries. These foundations are sufficiently resilient to persist even as new institutions arrive. Though industrialisation and modernisation give birth to similar institutions and lead to significant social change, specific states and societies retain their distinctive traits. A similar structure can take on a variety of guises (Bendix 1964: 12–13). Meyer and Hannan (1979) call the implementation of patterns adapted to local conditions mimetic isomorphism, where isomorphism does not connote homogeneity.[2]

Among the cases discussed in this book, one may distinguish those that established clear paradigms for the construction of education systems; these certainly include France and Prussia/Germany (discussed in Chapter 3). Also addressed were examples of states which established their own structures at a somewhat later time and drew obvious inspiration from existing models. Thus, the Polish Commission of National Education sought to implement the French model of schooling, while the initiators of the Meiji Revolution in Japan copied institutional solutions from Prussia. Furthermore, once established, the Japanese system – with its rigour and discipline – resembled in many ways the manner of operation of the German schools. In both states, too, rapid modernisation had similar effects, lifting them to the status of world powers in surprisingly little time. Though their education policy was typified by efficiency, its normative aspect raises serious questions due to the services it rendered to nationalism, an ideology conducive of revisionist foreign policies. The subsequent aggressive posturing of these states led to military conflicts in Europe and the Far East. While the stress such educational policies laid on questions of identity had been consistently criticised, their efficiency made a vivid impression on foreign political officials. Japan's success shaped Asia's road to modernisation, providing a model for decision-makers in the Republic of Korea, Singapore, Taiwan, and recently also the People's Republic of China (described in Chapter 4). The mechanisms and principles observed in Western states may thus be – to an extent – extrapolated and applied more broadly.

The notion that education and science may serve state-building processes was already entertained by the mercantilist and cameralist doctrines that accompanied the consolidation of absolute monarchies. The contours of education systems were defined by the contemporaneous prescriptions for the absolutist state. The process coincided with the transition from a decentralised governance of the feudal state to the Weberian, rational model of administration. Aside from Prussia, where the process followed a different path, absolutist monarchs allied themselves with the emerging bourgeoisie against the aristocracy, supporting the development of cities, trade, and manufacture.

The state education systems of Prussia and France were devised before the two states truly embarked on the course of industrialisation. The purpose was not to provide superior conditions for economic development, even if such was, in part, the impact of changes in education. Initially, middle and technical schooling expanded in response to both states' demand for administrators. At the time, political and social questions, such as the maintenance of order and the shaping of values, virtues, morality, and citizenship, played a primary role. Economic arguments carried little weight in contemporary debates. Unsurprisingly, providing knowledge and abilities of immediate use for the industry and in response to demands from manufacturers figured quite low on the list of priorities for education. Furthermore, even as technological progress put ever-increasing demands on schools, education typically took time to adjust to these requirements (Green 2013: 55).

In his description of nation-making processes in the nineteenth century, Kennedy (1987) refers not only to positive examples, but also to cases where inadequacies in this sphere were not properly addressed, contributing to a dramatic decline. Russia is of particular interest in this regard, a state in which, as Kennedy (1987: 307–308) contends, lack of advancement in education not only postponed the socioeconomic transformation, but also impinged directly upon the country's military potential. Though the Tsar boasted a sizeable army, the low intellectual abilities among the peasants who comprised it rendered it increasingly ill-suited to the conditions of an industrial-era war. Kennedy also believes that the condition of education in Russia turned it into a weak state, bereft of an efficient bureaucracy and officer corps. In 1913, illiteracy in Russia exceeded levels found in mid-eighteenth-century Great Britain.

Education systems reached the furthest stage of development where governments implemented accelerated, top-down policies for establishing the structures of the state. This, in turn, coincided with nation-making processes, often sparked by an external military threat. In many cases, progress accelerated in response to a fundamental internal transformation. In these cases, a new social order had to be established. Another, related factor that promoted educational reforms consisted in the desire to make up for the supposed developmental delay in statehood and economy. Historically speaking, states that experienced a sense of delay or backwardness usually did not assume that the market or grass-roots initiatives would suffice to ensure change, and were more likely to claim responsibility for this aspect of social life, creating school systems and scholarly institutions, funding them, managing them, and defining the rules by which they operated.

The pursuit of territorial and cultural unity by the nation-states also often necessitated the creation of an efficient education system. Education played a particularly crucial role in those nineteenth-century states which, like Germany, pursued unity through nationalism or, like France, established a new, bourgeois model of the state on the remnants of feudalism – that is, states that created their identities from scratch. Educational reformers of the Second Commonwealth of Poland pursued similar goals. The same cannot be said of countries that had achieved modern statehood at an earlier time, on another, less bureaucratic model, such as Great Britain. Contemporary empirical research on a broader selection of states and data collected over the past 150 years corroborate these claims, proving that states facing military confrontation and threats from their neighbours statistically invested more in education than those that were not equally challenged (Aghion, Persson, and Rouzet 2012). In the long run, the identities designed by the proponents of a strong state did not uniformly translate into success on the international arena. Excessively antagonistic, conducive of nationalism and hatred of other countries, they often heralded a turn towards an aggressive, revisionist policy. Hans Kohn (1946) argues that states driven primarily by a sense of delay are much more prone to this kind of nationalism, instrumentalised for the purpose of achieving greater cohesion in a nation and rallying it around a common developmental goal.

Manuel Castells (1992) points out that, as a national project of development, the concept of developmental state includes a nationalist component. Aside from the aforementioned political goals, intensive and coordinated state-building efforts highlight the significance of economic development, mostly industry policies. On the other hand, in terms of ideas, they often lead to increase in nationalist sentiments, and in extreme cases to a fascist economy. This nationalism is not – and, aside from Germany and Japan, never was – necessarily radical or particularly xenophobic, expansionist, or conducive to aggression. Even in Germany and Japan, it initially took a defensive guise, concentrating on national security in the face of rapidly expanding political and economic competition. In the long run, however, the success of this developmental model enabled the transition to a more aggressive posture in the international arena. Furthermore, while early nineteenth-century nationalism was civic and liberal in scope, the latter half of the century saw the emergence of a far less open form thereof, rooted in ethnocultural and racial beliefs (Kohn 1946; Hobsbawm 1990). Education has served as a major tool for the establishment of a civic consciousness and a check on the government that helps to stabilise democracy; sometimes, however, it transformed into a means to authoritarian domination of societies.

In the wake of globalisation, education's role in forging national identities has been put to question by the global challenges necessitating a more universalist approach to loyalty and consciousness, extending beyond the limits of one's own state. Among modern political philosophers, Martha Nussbaum (1994) was one of those who stressed the need for a universal education, directing the civic loyalty of the young not only towards the state and its traditions, but also to universal commonalities highlighting the common humanity that transcends cultural differences. To what extent is it possible, though, to slowly build up fragments of a supra-national consciousness responsive to the demands of an era of complex and deep interdependence? Education programmes in some states treat global problems quite seriously, aiming at a civic consciousness that reaches beyond the canon put forward by newly created nation-states established during the nineteenth century. In this respect, one might think, for instance, of the European Union, which seeks to use education (to a limited degree) to foster bonds within the Community, breaking with the practice of employing schools for the transmission of a purely national civic loyalty.

The recent tensions between globalisation and the demand for strong states may stoke up nationalist tendencies that will affect school programmes. If education is seen as one of the factors defining the power of the state as an agent in international relations, the blurred line between patriotism and nationalism has to be reckoned with. As an element of a broader system, the prosperity of the state depends not only on its own potential, but also on the conditions of its environment. By analogy to the conclusions drawn from the security dilemma, one finds in this regard that, in spite of the at times immediate gains of some of the actions that strengthen the state – including those within the area of identity formation through education – the ultimate cost of degraded international relations and stifled international cooperation can outweigh the benefits. In most cases, in fact, it is impossible – even *ex ante* – to calculate precisely the potential costs of such a risky policy.

Once the complex interrelations typifying modern international relations are understood, the meaning of patriotism today and the sources of international security are up for debate. Though the genealogical approach to the role of education and science in modern state-building proposed in this chapter enables a deeper perspective on the significance of these areas for the power of the state in the international arena, contemporary recommendations diverge significantly from the recipes for success that had been of use since the nineteenth century until World War II. Studies in international relations have proved that in the twentieth century power was not coterminous with international security, and that these two values do not go hand in hand.

Notes

1 *Sanacja* was a political movement created by Józef Piłsudski prior to the 1926 *coup d'état*, which came to power in the wake of that *coup*. The movement persisted until Piłsudski's death in 1935 and then split into competing factions. The term *Sanacja* means 'healing'; its principles were applied to the Polish body politic after the chaotic early years of parliamentary rule, with seventeen different governments within mere eight years. The movement advocated authoritarian rule as opposed to parliamentary democracy; it subsequently curbed the activity of both Communist parties and the nationalist far-right subscribing to the tradition of Dmowski (Czaputowicz and Wojciuk 2017: 46–56).
2 The concept of mimetic isomorphism was also applied in organisation sociology by Paul J. DiMaggio and Walter W. Powell (1983).

References

Acemoglu, D. and J.A. Robinson (2012). *The Origins of Power, Prosperity, and Poverty.* New York: Crown Publishers.

Aghion, P., T. Persson and D. Rouzet (2012). Education and Military Rivalry. *NBER Working Paper*, No. 18049, doi: 10.3386/w18049, www.nber.org/papers/w18049 (accessed 9 December 2015).

Almond, G. and S. Verba (1963). *The Civic Culture: Political Attitudes and Democracy in Five Nations.* Princeton, NJ: Princeton University Press.

Anderson, B. (1983). *Imagined Communities: Reflections on the Origins and Spread of Nationalism.* London: Verso.

Anderson, R.D. (1975). *Education in France 1848–1870.* Oxford: Clarendon Press.

Archer, M.S. (2013). *Social Origins of Educational Systems.* London: Routledge.

Archer, M.S. and M. Vaughan (1971). *Social Conflict and Educational Change in England and France: 1789–1848.* Cambridge: Cambridge University Press.

Artz, F.D. (1966). *The Development of Technical Education in France, 1500–1850.* Boston, MA: MIT Press.

Bacon, F. (1996). *The Major Works, Wickers, B.* Oxford: Oxford University Press.

Bendix, R. (1964). *Nation-Building and Citizenship: Studies of our Changing Social Order.* New York: Wiley.

Boli, J. (1989). *New Citizenship for a New Society: The Institutional Origins of Mass Schooling in Sweden.* New York: Doubleday.

Bourdieu, P. ([1979]1984). *Distinction: A Social Critique of the Judgement of Taste.* Cambridge, MA: Harvard University Press.

Bourdieu, P. (1987). *Distinction: A Social Critique of the Judgement of Taste.* Cambridge, MA: Harvard University Press.

Bourdieu, P. (1989). *La Noblesse D'Etat: Grandes Ecoles et Esprit de Corps.* Paris: Les Editions de Minuit.

Bourdieu, P. and J.C. Passeron (1970). *La Reproduction: Élements pour une Théorie du Système D'Einsegnement.* Paris: Editions de Minuit.

Bowles, S. and H. Gintis (1976). *Schooling in Capitalist America: Educational Reform and the Contradictions of the Economic Life.* New York: Basic Books.

Butts, F.R. (1955). *A Cultural History of Western Education: Its Social and Intellectual Foundations.* New York: McGraw-Hill Book Compan.

Calhoun, C. (1997). *Nationalism.* Minneapolis, MN: University of Minnesota Press.

Castells, M. (1992). Four Asian Tigers with a Dragons' Head: A Comparative Analysis of the State, Economy and Society in the Asian Pacific Rim. In R. Appelbaum and J. Henderson (eds), *States and Development in the Asia Pacific Rim.* London: Sage.

Cerny, P.G. (1995). Globalization and the Changing Logic of Collective Action. *International Organization* 49(4): 595–625.

Cha, Y.-K. (1991). The Effect of the Global System on Language Instruction, 1850–1986. *Sociology of Education* 64: 19–32.

Cipolla, C.M. (1965). *Guns, Sails and Empires: Technological Innovation and the Early Phases of European Expansion 1400–1700.* New York: Pantheon.

Cipolla, C.M. (1969). *Literacy and Development in the West.* Baltimore, MD: Pelican.

Collins, R. 1986. *Weberian Sociological Theory.* Cambridge: Cambridge University Press.

Corrigan, P. and D. Sayer (1985). *The Great Arch: English State Formulation as Cultural Revolution.* Oxford: Basil Blackwell Ltd.

Cubberley, E.P. (1934). *Public Education in the United States: A Study and Interpretation of American Educational History*. Boston, MA: Houghton Mifflin.
Czaputowicz, J. (2013). *Suwerenność [Sovereignty]*. Warsaw: Polski Instytut Spraw Międzynarodowych.
Czaputowicz, J. and A. Wojciuk (2017). *International Relations in Poland: 25 Years After the Transition to Democracy*. London: Palgrave Macmillan.
Davis, K. and W.E. Moore (1945). Some Principles of Stratification. *American Sociological Review* 10(2): 242–249.
DiMaggio, P.J. and W.W. Powell (1983). 'The Iron Cage Revisited' – Institutional Isomorphism and Collective Rationality in Organizational Fields. *American Sociological Review* 48(2): 147–160.
Dmowski, R. (1908). *Niemcy, Rosja a kwestia polska [Germany, Russia, and the Polish Cause]*. Częstochowa: Wydawnictwo Antoni Gmachowski i S-ka.
Durkheim, É. ([1897]2005), *Suicide: A Study in Sociology*, translated by John A. Spaulding and George Simpson, London: Routledge.
Durkheim, É. (1926). *Education et Sociologie*, 2nd edn. Paris: Librairie Felix Alcan.
Falski, M. (1925). *Materjały Do Projektu Sieci Szkół Powszechnych Na Obszarze Województw: Warszawskiego, Łódzkiego, Kieleckiego, Lubelskiego i Białostockiego Oraz M. St. Warszawy*. Warszawa: Książnica Atlas, Zjednoczone Zakłady Kartograficzne i Wydawnicze Towarzystwa Nauczycieli Szkół Średnich i Wyższych – Sp. Akc.
Falski, M. (1928). *Wyniki spisu dzieci z czerwca 1926 w zastosowaniu do badania potrzeb szkolnictwa powszechnego*. Warszawa: Książnica Atlas, Zjednoczone Zakłady Kartograficzne i Wydawnicze Towarzystwa Nauczycieli Szkół Średnich i Wyższych – Sp. Akc.
Finer, H. (1932). *The Theory and Practice of Western Government*. London: Methuen & Co.
Finnemore, M. (1996). Norms, Culture, and World Politics: Insights from Sociology's Institutionalism. *International Organization* 50(2): 325–347.
Fischer, W. and P. Lundgreen (1975). The Recruitment and Training of Administrative and Technical Personnel. In Ch. Tilly (ed.), *The Formation of National States in Western Europe*. Princeton, NJ: Princeton University Press.
Foucault, M. (2009). *Security, Territory, Population. Lectures at the College De France, 1977–78*. London: Palgrave Macmillan.
Gamble, A. (1981). *Great Britain in Decline*. London: Macmillan.
Gellner, E. (1964). *Thought and Change*. Chicago, IL: University of Chicago Press.
Giddens, A. (1987). *The Nation-State and Violence*. Berkeley, CA: University of California Press.
Gilpin, R. (1968). *France in the Age of the Scientific State*. Princeton, NJ: Princeton University Press.
Gilpin, R. (1981). *War and Change in World Politics*. Cambridge: Cambridge University Press.
Goldstone, J.A. (2009). *Why Europe?: The Rise of the West in World History, 1500–1850*. New York: McGraw-Hill.
Gramsci, A. (1971). *Selections from the Prison Noteboooks*. New York: International Publishers.
Great Britain, B.P.P. (1829). vol. 3, No. 332 ('Select Committee on State of Law and Practice Relative to Granting of Patents for Inventions').
Green, A. (2013). *Education and State Formation: Europe, East Asia and the USA*. Basingstoke: Palgrave Macmillan.

Grosvenor, I. (2005). There is No Place Like Home. In G. McCulloch (ed.), *The Routledge Palmer Reader in History of Education.* London: Routledge.
Hahn, R. (1971). *The Anatomy of Scientific Institutions: The Paris Academy of Science 1666–1803.* Berkeley, CA: California University Press.
Hallinan, M.T. (ed.) (2000). *Handbook of the Sociology of Education.* New York: Springer.
Herbst, J. (2000). *States and Power in Africa.* Princeton, NJ: Princeton University Press.
Hobsbawm, E.J. (1969). *Industry and Empire.* Harmondsworth: Penguin.
Hobsbawm, E.J. (1975). *The Age of Capital 1848–1875.* New York: Charles Scribner's Sons.
Hobsbawm, E.J. (1990). *Nations and Nationalism since 1780: Programme, Myth,* Reality. Cambridge: Cambridge University Press.
Inkeles, A. and D. Smith (1974). *Becoming Modern: Individual Changes in Six Developing Countries.* Cambridge, MA: Harvard University Press.
Jędrzejewicz, J. (1972). *W służbie idei.* Londyn: Oficyna Poetów i Malarzy.
Jones, A.J. (1938). *The Education of Youth for Leadership.* New York: McGraw-Hill Book Co.
Katz, M. (1976). The Origins of Public Education: A Reassessment. *History of Education Quarterly* 16(4): 381–407.
Kennedy, P. (1987). *The Rise and Fall of Great Powers.* New York: Vintage Books.
Kohli, A. (2004). *State-Directed Development: Political Power and Industrialization in the Global Periphery.* Cambridge: Cambridge University Press.
Kohn, H. (1946). *The Idea of Nationalism. A Study in Its Origins and Background.* New York: Macmillan Company.
Kot, S. (1919). Geneza Komisji Edukacji Narodowej (odbitka ze sprawozdań Akademji Umiejętności z czerwca 1919 roku).
Kot, S. (1928). *Dzieje wychowania. Podręcznik dla seminarjów nauczycielskich,* wyd. 2. Warsaw: Gebethner i Wolff.
Landes, D.S. (1969). *The Unbound Prometheus: Technological Change and Industrial Development in Western Europe from 1750 to the Present.* New York: Cambridge University Press.
Lipset, M. and S. Rokkan (1967). *Party Systems and Voter Alignments: Cross-National Perspectives.* Toronto: The Free Press.
Lukes, S. (1985). *Emile Durkheim, His Life and Work: A Historical and Critical Study.* Stanford, CA: Stanford University Press.
McDonough, K. and W. Feinberg (eds) (2003). *Citizenship and Public Education in Liberal Democratic Societies: Teaching for Cultural Identity and Cosmopolitan Values.* Oxford: Oxford University Press.
Meyer, J.W. and M.T. Hannan (eds) (1979). *National Development and the World System.* Chicago, IL: University of Chicago.
Miller, P. (1989). Historiography of Compulsory Schooling: What is the Problem. *History of Education* 18(2): 123–144.
Mitter, W. (2004). Rise and Decline of Education Systems: A Contribution to the History of the Modern State. *Compare* 34(4): 351–369.
Mokyr, J. (2002). *The Gifts of Athena: Historical Origins of the Knowledge Economy.* Princeton, NJ: Princeton University Press.
Mokyr, J. (2009). *The Enlightened Economy: An Economic History of Britain 1700–1850.* New Haven, CT: Yale University Press.

MWRiOP (1927). Okólnik Ministra Wyznań Religijnych i Oświecenia Publicznego do Kuratoriów Okręgów Szkolnych, z dnia 29.08.1927 r. w sprawie regulaminu pracy wychowawczej w szkołach średnich, Dz. Urz. MWRiOP Nr 12, poz. 203.

Nairn, T. (1981). *The Break-Up of Britain*. London: Verso.

Nussbaum, M. (1994). Patriotism and Cosmopolitanism. *Boston Review* 19(5): 3–16.

Polanyi, K. ([1944]2001) *The Great Transformation: The Political and Economic Origins of Our Time*. Boston, MA: Beacon Press.

Projekty szkolne na plenum Sejmu w dniu 22 stycznia 1932 roku (1932). *Przegląd Pedagogiczny 3*: 71.

Raciborski, J. (2011). *Obywatelstwo w perspektywie socjologicznej*. Warsaw: Wydawnictwo Naukowe PWN.

Ramirez, F. and J. Boli (1987). The Political Construction of Mass Schooling: European Origins and Worldwide Institutionalization. *Sociology of Education 60*, 2–17.

Rokkan, S. (1970). *Citizens, Elections, Parties*. Oslo: Universitets Forlaget.

Rokkan, S. (1980). Territories, Centres, and Peripheries: Toward a geoethnic-Geoeconomic-Geopolitical Model of Differentiation within Western Europe. In J. Gottmann (ed.), *Centre and Periphery: Spatial Variation*. London: Sage.

Rosenberg, H. (1958). *Bureaucracy, Aristocracy and Autocracy: The Prussian Experience 1660–1815*. Cambridge: Cambridge University Press.

Rousseau, J.J. (1772). Considérations sur le gouvernement de Pologne. In *Collection complète des oeuvres* 1780–1789, vol. 1, in-4°, Genève: Peyrou-Moultou, 415–539.

Russell, S. and D.M. Bajaj (2015). Schools, Citizens and the Nation State. In T. McCowan and E. Unterhalter (eds), *Education and International Development*. London: Bloomsbury.

Saussure (de), C.-F. ([1726]1902). *A Foreign View of England in the Reigns of George I and George II: The Letters of Monsieur César de Saussure to his Family*. London: J. Murray.

Say, J.-B. ([1803]1821). *A Treatise on Political Economy*, 4th Edition, Boston: Wells and Lilly.

Schilling, H. (2010). *Konfesjonalizacja. Kościół i państwo w Europie doby przednowoczesnej*, trans. J. Kałążny. Wydawnictwo Poznańskie: Poznań.

Schlereth, T.J. (1990). *Cultural History and Material Culture*. Charlottesville, VA: University Press of Virginia.

Seton-Watson, H. (1977). *Nations and States: An Enquiry into the Origins of Nations and the Politics of Nationalism*. Boulder, CO: Westview Press.

Smith, A. (1977). *Inquiry into the Nature and Causes of the Wealth of Nations*. Chicago, IL: University of Chicago Press.

Spruyt, H. (1996). *The Sovereign State and Its Competitors: An Analysis of Systems Change*. Princeton, NJ: Princeton University Press.

Strang, D. (1991). Anomaly and Commonplace in European Political Expansion: Realist and Institutionalist Accounts. *International Organization* 45(2): 143–162.

Swaan (de), A. (ed.) (1993). The Emergent World Language System. *International Political Science Review* 14 (Special Issue).

The Samuelson Report (1884) Report of the Royal Commission on Technical Instruction (accessed 30 October 2017) https://babel.hathitrust.org/cgi/pt?id=coo1.ark:/13960/t13n2r088;view=1up;seq=5.

Tilly, Ch. (ed.) (1975). *The Formation of National States in Western Europe*. Princeton, NJ: Princeton University Press.

Tyack, D. (1966). Forming the National Character. *Harvard Education Review* 36(1): 29–41.

Wbrew partiom opozycji. Wczorajsza mowa ministra Janusza Jędrzejewicza w komisji budżetowej Sejmu (1933). *Gazeta Polska*, 24.

Weber, E. (1976). *Peasants into Frenchmen: The Modernization of Rural France, 1870–1914.* Stanford, CA: Stanford University Press.

Weber, M. ([1922]1978). *Economy and Society: An Outline of Interpretive Sociology*, 2 vols. Berkeley, CA: University of California Press.

Witkowski, W. (2007). *Historia administracji w Polsce 1764–1989*. Warsaw: Wydawnictwo Naukowe PWN.

Zarycki, T. (2009). *Peryferie. Nowe ujęcia zależności centro-peryferyjnych*. Warsaw: Wydawnictwo Naukowe Scholar.

Zeldin, T, (1980). *France, 1848–1945: Intellect and Pride*. Oxford: Oxford University Press.

3 Human capital and knowledge in economic theory

Joseph Grieco and John Ikenberry (2003: 9–10) observe that states have always ultimately depended for power on wealth and human productivity. Though the claim is debatable, and this work relies on a more complex model of power in international relations, the role of the economy in this regard is difficult to overstate. From a narrow economic perspective, then, one could agree with these writers that state leaders actively pursue economic development in the hope of using at least some of the material resources gained in the process for political purposes, including foreign policy. Based on an analysis of various models of development, Grieco and Ikenberry argue that contemporary economic policies focus on competitiveness, with governments investing in education, science, and research and development (R&D), increasingly with a view to securing progress in these areas, as well. The more competition exists between states, the more important it is for them to mobilise social resources and extract some of the wealth they produce; thus, economic power is directly involved in maintaining political status.

Douglas North and Robert Thomas (1973) share a similar perspective on the relationship between a state's competitiveness and its international standing. For them, states are engaged in a constant strategic rivalry, with success and security a historical privilege of those who prove themselves more adept at supporting economic development while ensuring that some of the generated wealth is extracted without hampering progress. Capitalists are mobile: they seek out the most advantageous and profitable locations for production and trade, while states compete to draw in and retain productive capital and companies. What they want is that a balance is struck between providing suitable conditions for investment and ensuring the extraction of some resources for continued operation.

One of the claims advanced in this work is that, with the arrival of the Third Industrial Revolution, education and science gained new significance for the state and its global competitiveness. This is not to say that these fields were irrelevant or overlooked during the previous stages of economic development; to the contrary, they played a significant part in the Second Industrial Revolution, acting as the condition of possibility for this period of industrialisation and enabling the rise of such states as Germany or Japan to the first order of world powers. On the other hand, the belief that the level of education and scientific development affects economic growth dates back at least to mercantilism (discussed more broadly in Chapter 2). It has been appreciated by the luminaries of economics in the eighteenth and nineteenth centuries, from the liberal Adam Smith to the statist Friedrich List. The history of contemporary human capital theory, like that of reflections on the significance of technological advances for economic development, dates back to the 1950s. These ideas, well recognised among specialists and debated by political decision-makers and experts in the employ of international organisations, gained particular popularity in view of the conviction that information and telecommunication technologies were sufficiently ground-breaking to achieve a deep socio-economic transformation worthy of the name of the Third Industrial Revolution. Today, this discourse gives new meanings to public policy and points it in new directions. The potential of education and science in a state thus becomes an increasingly significant feature for it from the perspective of international relations. Familiar categories of human capital, knowledge, and innovativeness attract increasing interest and inspire reforms, both those described by liberal axioms, strictly forbidding the state from extending beyond a specified, narrow purview, and those clearly marked by statism, expanding the role of the government in view of the economic challenges of globalisation. At the same time, firm resistance and protest brews among certain milieus that dispute the normative foundation of the categories in question and perceive reform as another element in the economisation of the state and its policies that brings harm on other values and areas of social life (Sedláček 2011).

This chapter is devoted primarily to the agential aspect of state power in the international arena but it also touches upon its structural dimension. From the agential side, it addresses the role of education and science in economic development. The mechanisms that allow these factors to further economic welfare are the particular subject of subsections on human capital theory, growth theory, competition state, and national innovation systems. The structural aspect is mostly explored in the analyses of the Third Industrial Revolution, the centre-periphery framework of the world economy, and global value chains. Within the applied model, this aspect of power is also involved in discourse, including the scientific expert input. The same follows for findings of the economic theory and other sources of political recommendation for the state; all of these ideas are treated as elements of structural power within the model. In accordance with the definition of the agential and structural aspects of power in international relations, they are treated as indivisible – which will be even more obvious here than in the previous part of the book.

The discourse that highlights the role of education and science in the economic development of a state is primarily rooted in economic thought, combining knowledge of various epistemological characters, with elements of academic knowledge and the perspectives of experts, consultants, and think-tanks. The theories that science proposes are presented in a hermetic language, in complex mathematical models that attempt to capture the complexity of relations between numerous variables, and provide an opening onto difficult, detailed disputes that can be hard to understand, particularly for a layperson. Meanwhile, experts and consultants – both independent and in the employ of prestigious international organisations, think-tanks, and private consultancy firms – offer analyses that are easier of access for those not in the know and give clear recommendations to governments.

This chapter also contains an analysis of two countries which achieved major economic success during the Second Industrial Revolution: Germany and Japan. The advances they made in material development astonished contemporary experts and continue to evoke admiration among economists. Both states used education and science to build up their power, reinforcing their efforts with an ideological investment in hard-line nationalism. From an international standpoint, their economic success was used to foster a revisionist, expansionist foreign policy.

Human capital, technological advancement, and economic growth

Though the concept of human capital became an instant hit at the turn of the twentieth and twenty-first centuries, it is, in fact, not a new idea. Similar concepts can be traced at least as far back as Adam Smith, who observed that the gaining of new abilities through education, studies, or practice involves on the one hand a real expense, while on the other provides a capital embodied by the person who possesses them.[1] Smith was the first to approach education as an investment. In his *Inquiry into the Nature and Causes of the Wealth of Nations*, he claimed that labour which requires greater qualifications commands better pay, allowing those who had invested in their own education to recoup the expenses. He also observes that, though the abilities gained by individuals through education, studies, or practice increase their own wealth, they also provide a means to advancement for the entire society. For this reason, an improvement to the skills of a worker may be treated in the manner of the acquisition of a machine which facilitates production – both require expenses, but can cover them and generate profits (Smith 1977: 368). Even though Smith accepted that education must be class-specific, with marked differences between the simple folk and the higher strata, he believed that even the former should be provided with universal access to literacy and numeracy prior to employment. Compulsory education on such a basic level could be introduced at a minor cost to the state treasury. Every community would be equipped with a school accessible to children from families of low status at a small cost, with the rest covered from private expenses. In Smith's view, the successful achievement of the aforementioned basic skills would become the necessary condition of gaining employment or of being granted the right to independent trading (Smith 1977: 929).

The actual notion of human capital was probably first referred to in 1897 by Irvin Fisher (Goldin 2014), but the term did not gain wider currency until the 1950s (Mincer 1958), earning broad recognition thanks to the microeconomic studies of Theodore W. Schultz (1960) and Gary Becker (1962, 1964), who are commonly associated with it (Herbst 2012: 21–30). Macroeconomic approaches to the impact of knowledge and skills of individuals on economic growth, on the other hand, derived from the attempts to study past economic growth. Moses Abramovitz and Robert Solow indicated that conventional measures of increase in financial and labour outlay cannot account for the entirety of economic growth in advanced industrial economies. It was assumed that the part of economic growth unexplainable by the increase of capital or labour (the so-called Solow residual) reflected an increase in productivity. The model did not specify the causes of increased labour efficiency, marking its sources as exogenous, and thus not a part of the model. Solow (1957) himself ascribed the effect to technological change, treating knowledge as a public good – non-rivalrous and non-excludable. This prevented him from accounting for the divergence in pace of development among various states and the absence of convergence between them, a major flaw of the exogenisation of technological development.

In response to Solow's research, numerous studies were conducted to find an explanation for the rise in productivity. Attempts were made to treat growth as endogenous, that is, to include it as a part of the model. One current sought to extend the understanding of capital to include human capital; another traced the mechanisms of production of knowledge (Chattopadhyay 2012: 62). In this perspective, technological progress was modelled as a result of endogenous processes involving, on the one hand, investments in human capital (development of education and training), and on the other, expenses on R&D (Herbst 2012: 30–33). The inclusion of human capital and technological advancement in the growth model turned them into a veritable engine of economic growth. As a result, the endogenous growth theory convinced many states to strategically invest in human capital and technological change (Mazzucato 2011: 33).

The definition of human capital comes from Schultz (1960), who suggested that education be treated as an investment in the individual and thus a form of capital. He noted that productivity is not uniform among individuals, and the quality of human effort can be improved by the application of specific knowledge or skills. As a result, employers are willing to pay more to persons endowed with higher competencies. Schultz's theory proposes a firm, direct causal relationship between education/experience and productivity. In his view, individuals and societies derive significant economic gain from investment in personal skills.

Schultz named four main categories of investment that result in an increase in human capital: formal education on three levels (primary, secondary, and tertiary), adult training programme, vocational training and apprenticeship at the workplace, and investment in healthcare (Chattopadhyay 2012: 23). In addition, he claimed that an improvement in abilities and knowledge affects not only work itself, but also physical capital, which becomes transformed through innovation, research, and new ideas. Human capital was thus tied to technological development. In this conception, education determines growth not only in the narrow sense, but also in the broader, national and social contexts, since its positive effects can be advantageous for public health, demographic growth control, general well-being, civic values, and participation in democratic and legal processes, as well as rational decision-making. Educational disparities, in turn, lead to divergent productivity, and thus unequal pay, giving rise to social inequality (Schultz 1961).

A breakthrough occurred in human capital theory with the microeconomic works by Becker (1964). Assuming that individuals are calculatingly rational, he proposed a theoretical and empirical analysis of the emergence of human capital, with a special focus on education. Becker agreed with Schultz that various forms of learning contribute to an individual's cognitive capacities, leading to increased productivity and income, which then provides a measure of human capital. Becker treated educational expenses as an investment yielding returns traceable both on the level of the individual and the society. He believed that rational individuals invest in their own capital, calculating gains from new abilities, and thus – if their resources allow – learn as long as economically viable. For Becker, human capital is a mean of production.

Today, human capital is defined as the set of abilities possessed by the labour force, and higher skill levels among the workers translate into higher productivity. In light of this theory, education and training makes individuals more productive. At the same time, since education and training require investment, they are treated as capital, just like any other investment that allows for the production of other kinds of capital. Expenses on human capital naturally increase when the returns exceed the cost. Within this theory, the return on the investment is primarily private, as increased human capital increases productivity, and thus earnings (Acemoglu 1998). However, an increasing number of studies confirms that the profit has a public character. Observable external effects include a general increase in productivity among the labour force by way of a spillover effect, with the overall rise exceeding the sum of individual improvements (Moretti 2004c), but the gains are not limited to efficiency. Public gains also include improvement in general health, internal safety, and the quality of civic involvement (Moretti 2004a, 2004b; Milligan, Moretti, and Oreopoulos 2004; Dee 2004). From a micro perspective, therefore, human capital theorists perceive education as an individual choice, whereas macro-level analyses treat it as a public matter. It should be noted in this context that the macro-level gains are not limited to the aforementioned external effects, but also bind human capital theory to technological development and growth theory.

For economists, conceptualising the relationship between human capital and economic growth has been a challenge. As Herbst (2012: 33) observes, even today, in spite of fifty years of research, one should tread particularly carefully when suggesting a clear and final proof of human capital's role in determining growth. For example, the positive correlation between average length of formal education and per capita income levels does not prove the existence of a causal relationship between these two variables – and even should such a relationship exist, it is unclear how it would operate. The wealth of a state and the strength of its economy contribute to investment in public education, producing an effect that may prove more significant than the impact of human capital on economic growth.

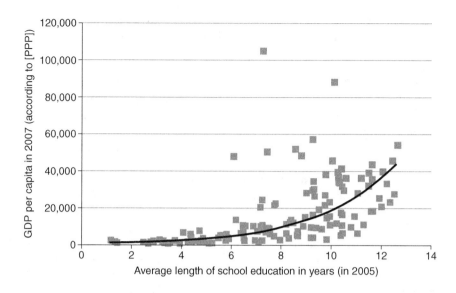

Figure 3.1 Correlation of mean education level and GDP per capita in national economies.

Source: own elaboration based on Barro and Lee 2010.

In the intervening years, however, many attempts were made to prove the existence of such a causal relationship and the role of human capital as a factor of economic growth. Early on in this research, Solow ascribed the part of growth that could not be explained by increased outlay in factors of production to advances in knowledge. Education and science, in turn, contribute to the production of knowledge, as well as its dissemination. Edward Denison (1962) proved empirically that about one-fourth of the rise in production in the USA between 1929 and 1957 could be ascribed to improvement in education levels among the labour force. In the 1980s, economists erected the so-called new growth model, which treated changes in levels of human capital and technology as endogenous. The accumulation of human capital and technological advancement was expected to account for the part of growth represented by the Solow residual (Lucas 1988).

Paul Romer (1990) believes that technological change is a result of conscious actions by individuals, including investment in human capital, as well as R&D. Within the endogenous growth theory, economic growth can be compared to preparing food. The process is always limited by the available ingredients, that is, material resources – though an increased amount of ingredients would yield more food, this is not the only road to progress. Thanks to knowledge, derived both from familiarity with good recipes and individual creativity, the same ingredients can produce better food. While Solow perceives an increase in knowledge about the ways of preparing food as external to the model, Romer contends that advances in knowledge are an effect of individual activity that can be made more likely, especially through investment in individual abilities of those who prepare food (human capital) and the pursuit of new recipes and techniques of preparing food (R&D) (Romer 2007). Technological change thus involves new, more effective ways of combining resources, developed by trial and error, experiment and research. However, new ideas contribute to growth not only through a reorganisation of material resources, but also through innovation in non-material areas, such as work organisation. As a result, physical and human capital are used more efficiently.

To understand how human capital and knowledge affect growth, it is crucial to recognise the relationship between these terms. When distinguishing between human capital and knowledge, one should note that the former, understood as the abilities and experience of the people, is a rivalrous good in consumption, which means that individuals can exercise their competencies only in one task at a time. In a given instant, the employer uses the knowledge and abilities of an employee exclusively. Knowledge, on the other hand, understood as 'ideas' or a certain recipe for action, is of its nature available for use by many individuals at any given time. This distinction is vital for understanding the process of growth (Chattopadhyay 2012: 66). Richard Nelson (1959) and Kenneth Arrow (1962) argue that knowledge resembles a public good. Using information is not competitive in consumption (the fact that a given agent uses them does not prevent others from doing the same). At the same time, the provider of the good cannot exclude others from consumption (unless special institutional arrangements are implemented, such as patents). Furthermore, while at first the production of the good generates costs, the price of subsequent use and reproduction is practically equal to zero. The cost of replicating ideas or specific instructions is minute, and they can be used repeatedly without limiting access to knowledge for others.

As knowledge is put to use, the practice becomes easier, with more and more people gaining the ability to engage in it; the likelihood of it being learned and extended independently into other, innovative, new knowledge likewise increases. This characteristic of knowledge as a public good implies that its production must be hampered by market failure, which is not capable of securing an optimal demand for it (Cimoli, Dosi, and Stiglitz 2009: 22).

In practice, however, the ability to replicate solutions is limited because it requires the involvement of individuals endowed with specific competencies. Meanwhile, as a rivalrous good, human capital is only available to one enterprise at a time and typically to one national economy. This is a real obstacle to the diffusion of knowledge, preventing it from functioning as a public good for all individuals, enterprises, and states, even if their access to knowledge is theoretically ensured. Furthermore, today, access to knowledge may be limited by factors other than available human capital. It can be regulated by law, such as intellectual property or patent laws. A debate is taking place today, concerning the merits of granting free access to knowledge to anyone capable of consuming it relative to the demand for limiting the right to knowledge. From the perspective of economic growth on a global scale, unhindered access to knowledge as an actual public good is the most efficient solution. However, were that the case, the market would be less likely to provide financial support for expanding knowledge. Even public financing raises the question of the distribution of cost and profit of R&D activity in the context of competitive rivalry between states. In practice, then, public knowledge versus exclusive access to knowledge is mostly a discussion about legal and practical issues.

As this summary of selected aspects of growth theory and human capital theory indicates, the two areas were perceived as related ever since scholars showed an interest in them. As far as detailed explications of this relationship and its peculiar conditions are concerned, however, a variety of answers were presented: it clearly was not obvious, proportional, or self-explanatory (Prettner 2012), and its occurrence is predicated on a number of contextual factors (Pritchett 2001). For instance, the newer endogenous growth model by Oded Galor and David Weil (2000), later expanded by Galor (2011: 147), identifies a causal relationship between human capital and technological advancement. At the outset, in the so-called Malthusian era, one saw low incomes, no education, and a very slow population increase. Gradually, with the expansion of the population and density, technology advanced, since – argue the two scholars – greater proximity between human settlements facilitated the creation and accumulation of knowledge in primal conditions. Technology, in turn, generated a demand for new abilities and amplified their effects, increasing the return on education, and education contributed to the pace of technological development. As the boundaries of technological knowledge shifted and new discoveries demanded greater professionalisation, the role of human capital increased. Technological development and the demand for human capital thus fed into one another (Galor 2011: 147).

One should stress, however, that no complete answer to the question of the causes of growth exists. Concepts that relate to knowledge and human capital provide merely possible or partial solutions (Bukowski 2015: 18). One is reminded in this context of the institutional theory, according to which growth hinged upon the appearance of specific institutional frameworks favourable for individual creative action (North 1990). It is vital that those institutions are inclusive, rather than exclusive. However, this concept cannot account, for instance, for the divergence in growth between states possessing similar institutional frameworks; this gap is filled with the theory of technological leap, which stipulates that in states that have passed through the Industrial Revolution, institutional foundations alone are not sufficient; it is also necessary to reallocate the labour force from the less productive agriculture, craft, and informal economy to more productive sectors (Rodrik 2014).

Regardless of the variety of approaches to human capital and knowledge in growth theory and other economic theories, as well as disputes between the proponents thereof, they all share the same problem of measuring the variables they use. Human capital is hard to measure; one has to decide whether to measure education by degree of participation, duration of participation, expenses, abilities, or perhaps only the abilities that are deemed important for the market, and so forth. Scholars of human capital also cannot agree on the means through which education creates the abilities that are vital for productivity. Some ascribe greater significance to cognitive (including interpersonal) abilities and those related to conduct, such as efficiency in action, grit, good work organisation, diligence, persistence, ability to work in a group, and initiative (Heckman, Stixrud, and Urzula 2006; Farkas 1996). Both types of competencies are acquired in the family, at school, and then at the workplace, as well as in the virtually untraceable process of socialisation.

Early research attached greater significance to quantitative measurements of participation in education; in time, focus shifted towards attempts at capturing qualitative differences in human capital, that is, real abilities of various societies. In one of their works, Eric Hanushek and Ludger Wössmann (2007) argue not only that the impact of actual abilities of employees (as measured by testing) on their income is greater than that of formal education, but even that the material value of actual knowledge increases with time, while the value of formal education decreases. Eric Hanushek and Denis Kimko (2000) provided more arguments for the discussion by claiming that the quality of education matters more than participation itself. There is no parity between six years of education in Saudi Arabia and Finland. If ideas and innovation are the engine of growth, the development of cognitive abilities that will go on to contribute to science, research, and implementation, is vital. The disparity between the abilities of students in various countries are not explained by participation and duration of

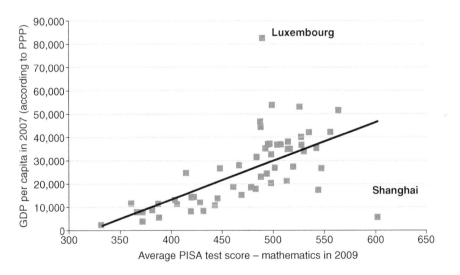

Figure 3.2 Correlation of educational attainment and GDP per capita.

Source: own elaboration.

schooling, or even by the financial outlay on education. Hanushek and Wössmann (2010) indicate that quality of education is best approximated through teaching outcomes. Only in comparative studies of states, based on measuring skills in mathematics, reading comprehension, and scientific reasoning, can one clearly observe a stable and strong correlation with economic growth. The ability to use the knowledge gained in the process of education, in turn, depends on the quality of said education. Hanushek's conclusion to his thirty years of research into the relationship between education and economic growth is that any education does not do – the decisive role is played by its quality, measured by the cognitive abilities it inculcates (Bukowski 2015: 39–43).

During the 1980s and 1990s, endogenous growth theory also motivated the conviction that increasing and sustained expenses on education, research, and development were the key to economic growth. The first decade of the twenty-first century, however, saw many a controversy emerge in relation to those models. Analysis of historical data, including those relating to the American economy, indicated that increased employment in the R&D sector did not translate into significant economic growth during the second half of the twentieth century; there was also no correlation between increased outlay on R&D and productivity after World War II. A survey of studies on innovation, expenses on R&D, productivity, and economic growth provides inconclusive answers, and a detailed discussion of the various aspects of this debate is beyond the scope of this work (Ha and Howitt 2006). The problem with identifying factors affecting economic growth is that the specific variables in question are not easily distinguishable in the empirical reality – on the contrary, they interrelate dynamically, forming a complex system (Smil 2006: 288–290). This accounts especially for the difficulty in unambiguous assessment of the impact of education, science, and development-related activities on economic growth.

Controversies over state policy recommendations for education and science: the market and the state

Tracing the debate over public policy recommendations in education, science, and the related fields of R&D and innovation, one notes the near-constant parallel recurrence of two clear currents. The first of those ties in with a broad understanding of the developmental state and conscious, strategic efforts by the government to achieve industrialisation or more extensive technological progress. The other looks to the tradition of neoclassical economics, with its careful limitation of the role of the state to those areas where its presence is indispensable, the rest being left to the market. In this sense, the state is less efficient as an economic actor than private entities. However, since markets have a tendency to fail, the state is allowed to exercise certain prerogatives in regulating economic activity. Among classical economic thinkers, proponents of the larger state often referred to Friedrich List, while liberals invoked Adam Smith and David Ricardo. Between those two positions, there is an entire continuum of views on the proper amount of state in the economy.

These views clash, with each side enjoying supremacy in turn. Thus, the 1960s were a period when the idea of an active state gained popularity, while the 1980s succumbed to a hegemony and frequently dogmatic applications of firm market solutions. The early twenty-first century, on the other hand, introduced the so-called Third Way, an attempt to combine capitalism and social democracy to the disappointment of both sides – the liberals believed it involved the state too extensively and inefficiently, while social democrats thought it gave in too much to the markets. Policy debates in education, science, and R&D reflect broader popularity trends. However, both sides agree that education and science are crucial for economic growth, and that the state has a role to play in this area.

From the perspective of liberalism and neoclassical economics, education fosters growth effectively when it provides the competencies that the market requires (Tilak 2002). Instruction should thus be adjusted to the labour market from the perspective of both the employers and the students and their parents. In this context, the education system is an efficient relay mechanism between these spheres, and the role of the state is limited to ensuring that it works effectively and adapts flexibly to the demands of the market. Individuals are expected to invest in their own education and, according to Becker's theory that perceives them as rational calculating actors, they will do so when the return on their investment covers the cost – or, when there is a market demand for higher qualifications. In light of the neoclassical approach, the state should not extend beyond providing an absolute minimum of education to the citizen, since it is neither as well equipped as the market to decide which abilities should be inculcated, nor capable of inculcating them more efficiently than market-based educational institutions. This model is perceived to be efficient regardless of the individual conditions of the state in question and, according to the proponents of neoclassical approaches, should be applied both in technologically advanced states and in those that are in the process of development. Here, the state is expected to impose fair rules of the game and implement them effectively, as well as to provide public infrastructure including basic human capital – the rest will be accounted for by the market. Proponents of liberal approaches also stress that the private character of gains from education indicates that its cost should be covered by individuals. Meanwhile, resource shortages preventing individuals from investing in their competencies should be addressed by a credit system rather than public financing.

The theory of building up growth-inducing capability, on the other hand, contends that, while states that develop successfully have consistently adapted capabilities to the labour market's demands, the process involved more state imposition than proponents of neoclassical economics would admit, ranging far beyond simple reactions to signs of market failure (Ashton, Green, James, and Sung 1999; Brown, Green, and Lauder 2001). Developmental states actively created demand for more advanced abilities as part of their public policy. Such an approach typified states that would later undergo modernisation, seeking to make up for time lost in relation to the leading countries. The development of education and knowledge systems, while aimed primarily at establishing the structures of the state (as illustrated in Chapter 2), proved particularly useful for industrialisation and capitalist development during the Second Industrial Revolution.

At later stages, the model was replicated and adjusted to the context of what Alexander Gerschenkron calls late development (Kohli 2004). His proponents recommend the model to contemporary political decision-makers, as well, in the belief that market coordination of the system of education and training leads to the maintenance of a gap in the quality of human capital between the centre and the peripheries, rather than the convergence that the neoclassical model anticipated (Cimoli *et al.* 2009). Gerschenkron (1962) studied the manner in which states that experienced late development (which in his analysis included all states other than Great Britain) reacted to difficulties that needed to be compensated for if the distance to the leader was to be shortened. Relative delay in development caused tensions to arise between expectations built up by the success of other states and the actually experienced stagnation. This tension motivated institutional innovations and promoted the pursuit of local substitutes for factors that had previously ensured the developmental success of the leaders. The greater the delay, the more effective the policy of guiding investment into specific branches of the emerging industry, and the more insistence on capital-intensive, rather than labour-intensive, production methods. The same approach also affected education: given the limited supply of reliable, stable, and disciplined labour force, the state was forced to create it. The means applied by states that were making up for the delay in relation to Great Britain, particularly France, Germany, Japan, and Russia, were more coordinated and concentrated than the instruments used in the liberal Britain, where industrialisation occurred in a bottom-up fashion, independently, and, at first, very slowly. To be effective, change must be applied along a 'broad front', beginning simultaneously at various different points to account for problems such as the complementarity and indivisibility of economic processes. Railways would have been impossible without mines, financial institutions controlling sufficient capital, and relevant advances in engineering; a successful transformation thus requires a whole set of policies.

On the other hand, scholars and experts who subscribe to neoclassical economics tend to stress that knowledge is a public good. Gregory Mankiw, Edmund Phelps, and Paul Romer (1995: 298) define knowledge as the sum of technical and scientific discoveries recorded in textbooks, scientific journals, and on websites, cumulated by higher education and transferred as a resource to individuals in the process of learning. Knowledge traverses the world with ease; even in the poorest countries, one can usually gain access to advanced publications. Even if a company establishes a monopoly in a specific innovation, this rarely lasts long. Within this theory, states thus enjoy unrestricted access to extant knowledge, but differ in their ability to use it, which depends primarily on human capital, and, in some cases, on infrastructure.

Opponents of this theory, meanwhile, claim that knowledge – particularly of an advanced type and capable of yielding ground-breaking technological applications – is not a public good of equal access; on the contrary, it is profoundly national. The belief that the findings of basic sciences are an international resource, rather than a good owned by particular states, may have been well founded in the past, the arrival of increasingly complex military and civilian technologies during the twentieth century removed that possibility. The proposition that a reading of a relevant scientific article would suffice for a scientist or engineer to create an effective implementation procedure is unrealistic today. The uses of science are much more subtle, requiring the understanding of research conducted within the discipline, and thus active participation in the research community. In this approach, basic research and a part of advanced applied science belong to the state as a resource yielding direct and indirect benefits (Gilpin 1968: 59).

Analyses of the involvement of the governments of world powers in the development of key technologies, primarily for military purposes, point out that some of those efforts produced crucial technologies. Had the R&D sector been motivated solely by the market demand driven by the civilian population, technologies that altered the universe of contemporary societies after World War II would have taken a far longer time to devise. It is primarily the general purpose technologies invented under government control, typified by prevalence (or presence in many sectors), capability to improve over time (meaning that their cost of use may decrease), and adaptability to invention and creation of new products and processes, that served as a driver of innovation in various areas (Mazzucato 2011: 54). Today, some think that only states can create a demand for the new energy technologies that the world requires due to climate change, and which are far to risky and costly to attract sufficient business interest without public support.

Where these diverse approaches agree is in positing that it is in the interest of the state at every level of advancement to possess human capital capable of absorbing the knowledge required at the subsequent level of growth. A significant proportion of experts also agrees that the major powers jockeying for position in international relations are particularly invested in owning a science and R&D sector capable of devising cutting edge scientific and technological discoveries. It is less certain, however, what role science and R&D play in states that are in the process of catching up and are currently at various stages of development. One could agree with proponents of neoclassical approaches, that a significant proportion of knowledge is indeed global in character and accessible for persons endowed with relevant competencies. Ground-breaking technological discoveries, in turn, require major investments, most of which will go to waste, since it is in the nature of innovation to be achieved after numerous failures.[2] Investments in applied research and innovation that are poorly executed and provided with insufficiently favourable conditions can result in losses for the state, as in cases where the state cannot act on a scale sufficient for the achievement of the minimal critical mass necessary to ensure success at a reasonable time and a satisfying return on the initial investment. Meanwhile, states that do not count themselves among world leaders, but possess the necessary human capital, can exploit the scientific findings of the leaders and 'free-ride' by applying them to their own implementations without bearing the cost of failed investments. Such a strategy may at times prove more effective than the costly and risky engagement in the race. For this latter approach, the state does not need a scientific cadre capable of pushing the boundaries of knowledge, but rather one sufficiently effective to keep up with the achievements of world science and be able to apply them.

After World War II, this strategy of maintaining sufficiently good cadres to apply the knowledge gained by the leaders without risking the loss of investment was deployed by Japan and most Western European states, and then by the Asian Tigers. One frequently used example is the invention of the transistor by American scientists. Already in 1959, more than half of transistor radios sold in the USA were imported. By acquiring a licence, the 'backward' Japanese could not only catch up with the American industry in the implementation of the invention, but even overtake it. At the time, it was said that the USA paid for R&D, while the Japanese managed to quickly claim the lion's share of profits (Cooper 1961: 110–111).

Obtaining the human capital necessary to absorb the indispensable technologies is a challenge in itself, particularly for less developed countries. In today's global science, every country that is not a major power can expect its most talented minds to emigrate. In this regard, proponents of the developmental state would recommend that governments provide special incentives to increase the likelihood of retaining scientists capable of keeping abreast of developments in science on their own (even when not being a part of the worldwide elite) as well as transmitting these competencies to their students. One would also need an industry capable of using the knowledge, which requires a management endowed with proper competencies and psychological and administrative predispositions peculiar to the business elite. Small wonder then, that the search for an answer to the question of the conditions of successful implementation has become a field of study in itself (this problematic is addressed more broadly in the section devoted to national innovation systems).

While discussions in the 1960s focused on state involvement in proactively developing education and science along with R&D, the 1980s saw a shift towards approaches inspired by neoclassical economics – often described as neoliberal – which tended to advocate a drastic limitation of the role of the state and dependence on the market as the most effective mechanism of coordination.[3]

Within this paradigm, the main purpose of the state is to foster a climate favourable for transnational investments. Aside from infrastructure, effective regulation, and efficient institutions ranked yearly by such outlets as *Doing Business*, the modern competitive state should provide human capital understood as abilities, education, an experienced labour force, and the infrastructure for R&D (Cerny 1995: 611). After all, capital seeks profits, and abilities number among the factors positively affecting the gains from an investment. Welfare states have applied recommendations provided by experts inspired by neoclassical economics to reforms devised to improve the adjustment to the conditions of international competition. This involved refraining from intervention, particularly on the macro level, with a limited degree of involvement on the micro level (e.g. creating incentives for entrepreneurs and consumers), which was more readily approved by the proponents of market solutions. States were expected to replace comparative advantages with competitive advantages (Zysman and d'Andrea Tyson 1983; Cerny 1997: 260).

In view of the limited means of coordination available to states in a globalised economy governed by the market and deregulation, education gains a special significance. Traditional welfare states could provide various kinds of support to those social groups that fared poorly or not at all under a capitalist system (Esping-Andersen 1990). The logic of a competition state is different – its primary focus is to ensure that the individuals themselves fare better on the labour market. Education serves as a primary means to that end. As a result, investments in education and training have partly replaced direct intervention in the labour market, worker security, and wage policies – instruments peculiar to the welfare state (Reich 1992). According to this approach, success in the global economy requires a well-educated labour force that can adapt easily to new challenges. A state's ability to establish an efficient system for education and training becomes an increasingly important element in the competition within the global economy – not only because of specific competencies, but increasingly also due to the need to adapt, as reflected in the idea of lifelong learning.

Today, education is also presented as a means to reducing social tensions resulting from inequalities generated by the capitalist economy, which most likely entail a transformation of the labour market – mostly a permanent dissolution of certain professions and the necessity to acquire new competencies relevant to the professions that will eventually emerge (Rifkin 1996: 207; Brynjolfsson and McAfee 2011). The continuing development of information and communication technologies that will make certain occupations redundant also raises the threat of structural unemployment. States are advised to serve much narrower purposes than in the past and with greater efficiency. Today, education counts among the few forms of public intervention which enable the achievement of equality of opportunity to enjoy support from the left as well as the right. The two sides differ, however, in their views on the scale and content of this engagement. Higher education and science generate far more controversies, much as direct involvement of the state in R&D.

Solutions now applied in various states in the fields of education, science, and R&D in most cases entail a combination of market-based instruments and those that condone a greater involvement of the public authorities. It is difficult not to agree that since the 1990s and even more so after the crisis of the 2000s, it was market-based thinking that provided the paradigms for changes in these areas. This results in increasing resistance from left-leaning milieus that highlight the detrimental effects of those activities.

National innovation systems and competitive advantages

In the early 1990s, several approaches challenged the mainstream policy dogma by claiming that neoclassical theories – still in their heyday at the time – went too far in limiting the role of the state. Most prominent among them were the alternative approaches advanced by Michael Porter (1990), Henry Etzkowitz and Loet Leydesdorff (1998, 2000), Michael Gibbons *et al.* (1994), and Christopher Freeman and Bengt-Åke Lundvall. These ideas exerted a major influence on state policies in science as well as R&D. Though they drew inspiration from human capital theory and growth theory, they were stated in simple terms, with clear recommendations reminiscent of studies on management rather than economics. Here, I will devote the most attention to the understanding of competitive advantages and the category of national innovation systems. These concepts were the most extensive, offering a systemic approach to the role of education and knowledge in economic development, in both temporal and spatial terms.

The concept of competitive advantages in education and science

During the early 1990s, Michael Porter (1990), a professor at the Harvard Business School, made the bestseller list with a work devoted to the idea of competitive advantages, which went on to enjoy significant popularity as the correct model for devising the strategy of the state during the era of globalisation. This approachable text, written in a popular scientific style, influenced political decision-makers. Porter himself was sometimes referred to as a 'competitiveness guru'. Rather than advocating a limitation of the role of the state, his recommendations assigned to it a crucial role in many areas, including education and knowledge. Porter favoured national economies, appreciating the value of their development potential. In his view, welfare is the end result of processes occurring in determinate geographical locations, and globalisation – far from nullifying the state – makes its policies all the more significant from the perspective of global competitiveness.

In the opening sentences of his famous work, Porter observes that:

> national prosperity is created, not inherited. It does not grow out of a country's natural endowments, its labor pool, its interest rates, or its currency's value, as classical economics insists. A nation's competitiveness depends on the capacity of its industry to innovate and upgrade.
>
> (Porter 1990: 73)

Globalised competition forces enterprises to innovate and seek more efficient solutions. The role of the state increases when the creation and application of knowledge gains in significance, since those processes are mostly local in nature and depend primarily on national values, culture, political and economic institutions, and history. States can win in global competition in areas in which they offer optimal conditions for development.

Thus, Porter opposed the views then espoused by the mainstream, which claimed that competitiveness derives from the costs of labour, interest rates, exchange rates, and the effects of scale. In his view, these factors have a short-term impact, and long-term thinking about competitiveness demands a focus on innovation understood as technological advancement as well as the establishment of new ways of producing goods. Porter uses the concept of competitive advantage that the state can establish, as opposed to comparative advantages conditioned by extant factors that typify classical economics. Locating himself on the opposite side of dependency theory, he claims that in contemporary economies, affluence and poverty are an effect of conscious policies of the state, which – no longer dependent on inherited resources – can actively develop competitiveness or refrain from it, allowing productivity to decrease and thus inviting poverty. Porter names the ascription of knowledge and abilities to a narrow group as a prime example of failed policies putting states on the road to poverty (Porter 1998: 146).

According to his theory, global competition makes questions of the size of the government and the scale of public intervention irrelevant, since the government's role is supposed to be minimal in some areas (trade barriers, prices), and very broad in others (such as ascertaining the high quality of education and training). Educated, healthy citizen working in safe conditions are the key to productivity. Such is also the function of schools and universities: to create conditions favourable for productivity (Porter 1998: 162–163, 587). In the twenty-first century, only those states will succeed which manage to create sufficiently attractive conditions to convince leaders in different trades to relocate their production.

Key factors of production in the economy of the late twentieth century are characterised by the need for systematic, substantial expenses and high specialisation. Cheap labour no longer suffices to attract the most profitable branches of the industry and services, while states such as Switzerland, Sweden, or Germany prosper in spite of high cost of labour and a history of periodic labour shortages. Indeed, Porter (1998: 636, 695) identifies continued competitiveness in spite of high wages as the goal of public policy. High productivity increases the national income, which translates into high tax profits that allows the state to bear the cost of public services, which increase the standard of living and define the power of the state in international relations. Porter also believes that high productivity allows enterprises to improve ethical standards, including labour conditions and employment equality, as well as to limit the negative impact on the environment.

The theory also leads to the conclusion that the welfare of the state and of the citizen depends on workplaces typified by high productivity. On the other hand, workplaces generated by low costs of employment are constantly threatened by the possibility that another state might offer even cheaper labour. In this context, delocalisation is simple, labour is replaceable, and technologies necessary for production are easily imitated. Competition based on labour cost in a globalised economy is thus very risky in the long term (Porter 1998: 1658).

Imitation allows competitors to appropriate technologies and, in time, to learn to produce goods of similar or identical quality without suffering the losses that inevitably result from the pursuit of new solutions, and eventually to offer the same product at a lower price. For this reason, leading states are pressed into a constant search for improvements and new products to retain their supremacy. Within this line of thinking, the only available option is to be ahead of the game. Discussing the role of the government, Porter recommends that it engage actively in creating an institutional environment and other conditions favourable to innovation. Education and science play a key part in this context because innovation requires long-term, sustained investment in research and human resources, as well as physical capital. It is far from enough to focus on primary and secondary schools, as the competencies they inculcate are insufficient to create a competitive advantage. Particular significance is attached to advanced and specialised undertakings, such as meticulously devised systems of practices, as well as the cooperation between universities and the industry.

Examples discussed in the work testify to the fact that states which invest the most in education achieve advantages in many branches of the industry and services that boil down to human resources.

While individual conditions in each country would decisively affect education reforms, Porter (1998: 11990–12005) did propose certain general recommendations. Due to the major impact his theory has had on the discourse on competitiveness and the various inspirations different states drew from it for their policies, these recommendations warrant consideration:

1 Educational standards should be high, with pupils and students encouraged to compete with one another; the loosening of requirements and withdrawal from grading, as applied in the 1970s in such states as the USA, Great Britain, Sweden, and Germany, yielded poor results from the perspective of their competitiveness; maintaining high standards in the entire system is difficult and requires state action.
2 The teaching profession should warrant admiration and carry prestige.
3 Instruction of most pupils and students should include elements of practice, and formal education should provide them with the ability to expand their abilities at their place of work; thus, it is vital that the programme also include elements of mathematics, computer use, natural sciences, and foreign languages, as well as writing skills. It is also a good idea to instruct some of the most talented students in hard sciences and engineering.
4 It is to be expected that well-respected and high-quality teaching methods outside of the university exist; economies thrive when they can depend on prestigious polytechnics and vocational schools, as illustrated by the examples of Germany, Japan, and Korea. High university enrolment rates do not necessarily indicate the presence of an optimal strategy for building human capital.
5 A strict relationship between educational institutions and employers should be established. The German and Swiss models, in particular, with their

extensive and universal system of apprenticeships, testify to the efficiency of this solution; on the higher level, it continues in the cooperation between universities and the industry.
6. Companies should invest in training, ensuring it maintains quality and is applied systematically. Japanese enterprises – where promotion is often partly conditional upon passing a knowledge test – are particularly effective at training their employees. Trade organisations offer courses that instruct in abilities useful for the development of the entire trade, allowing for a critical mass to be achieved even when the companies involved are minor.
7. Immigration policy should encourage mobility of persons endowed with specialised abilities.

In Porter's view, the government should also provide support for the development of science and technology. Due to the spillover effect, the benefits of this progress extend beyond any single firm – hence, control over investments cannot remain in private hands. This applies to basic research, in particular. In states that have competitive advantages, the government supports research in various ways, at times including direct financing of scientific laboratories or tax inducements for different entities to engage in scientific endeavours. Development in research is achieved primarily by an innovation policy, since supporting science and technology is in itself insufficient. According to Porter (1998: 12052–12097), good policies in this context are characterised by:

1. Connections between scientific and technological policies and competitive advantages of the industry in a given country, as well as adaptation to specific areas, their degree of development, and the capabilities of companies and universities.
2. Focus on research institutes rather than government laboratories, which will allow future generations to receive instruction in the most advanced findings of science.
3. Special attention devoted to technologies that can be applied in business; in this context, investments in defence industries are deemed less effective due to the fact that they do not generate as clear a spillover effect as civil trades.
4. Strong and beneficial ties between research institutions and the industry.
5. Encouragement of research activities at the level of individual companies. The government may support it with grants and subsidies for the industry, but these policies have led to controversies since the removal of risk leads companies to focus on failed ideas without sufficient consideration. Furthermore, they tend to use public funding for projects that they would have pursued anyway. Another, better approach is tax privilege for those entities that invest in R&D, accepting the risk involved on their own. However, some companies invest aggressively in R&D even without any clear material incentive from the state. In Porter's view, partial subsidies for research contracts between companies and research institutions yield the best results.

6   Increasing the pace of innovation is more important than delaying diffusion. Though patent security encourages investment in R&D, a balance must be struck to allow for technological competition between entities, a key to progress and new inventions. Long-term patent coverage obstructs new developments, while technological advantage is harder to maintain when resources are assigned exclusively to the maintenance of the right to past inventions.

Many international institutions, both public and private, concerned with economic development adopt a Porterian approach to education, knowledge, and innovation, as well as global competition. Since the early 1990s, this has contributed to the dissemination of a discourse describing science and education – both lower and higher – as major drivers of progress in that regard. For instance, the World Economic Forum in Davos publishes a yearly *Global Competitiveness Report*, in which it provides an assessment of the degree to which states are prepared for global economic competition. The definition of competitiveness applied by this milieu identifies it as a set of institutions, policies, and factors that determine a state's chances in global competition. Additionally, they believe that the competitiveness of a state is affected by many factors, such as institutions, infrastructure, macroeconomic conditions, health, technology, as well as lower and higher education (Schwab 2012: 4–7). Early education is treated here as a part of the fundamental conditions of competitiveness, while higher education and technological preparedness belong among the variables describing efficiency enhancers; meanwhile, innovations themselves provide a measure of the advancement of a system. The same organisation also publishes a far more extensive analysis in *The Human Capital Report* (World Economic Forum 2015: 4): a study that includes data for specific age groups, indexing such information as enrolment in education at all levels, quality of instruction, literacy rates, and on-the-job training.

The European Union's *Innovation Scoreboard* uses a broadly similar format, providing many variables from the areas in question. The indicators are divided among so-called enablers – variables describing the research system, financing, and economic impact. Under human resources, the report lists the number of doctoral students, percentage of people aged thirty to thirty-four with higher education, percentage of youth with at least middle education; under research systems, one finds such data as co-authorship of scientific publications by scholars from various states, the upper 10 per cent of cited publications, and the number of doctoral students from outside of the EU; the rubric for financing includes public and private outlay on R&D, and employment impacts include the employment rate in knowledge-intensive positions.

Porter's notion of competitive advantages as well as the reports and analyses of WEF and the EU provide good examples of the mainstream discourse on the impact of education, science, and R&D on the global competitiveness of a state. While these ideas are rooted in economic theory, particularly human capital theory and growth theory, they are sufficiently simplified in comparison to academic approaches to be able to provide useful political recommendations. Though some critics on the left have a highly negative view of them due to their attachment to the market, comparisons with neoclassical orthodoxy indicate that they allow for a much greater involvement of the state than the latter does.

National innovation systems

Aiming at the achievement of the goal identified by Porter – competitive advantage – the creators of the concept of national innovation systems (NIS) advocate an even greater expansion of the state. In their view, the government should not only provide the infrastructure for entrepreneurs, but also support some of the activities geared solely towards the achievement of technological advancement with conscious, strategic actions. Though the concept has been elaborated since the 1960s, it was brought to light concurrently with the idea of competitive advantages, during the final decade of the twentieth century. This strain of thought can be traced back to the nineteenth-century conceptions advanced by Friedrich List (1789–1846) and Alexander Hamilton (1755–1804), who had already identified the weakness of the classic liberal approaches to economic development devised by Smith and Ricardo.

As List and Hamilton observed, the state can and should use its policies to create the best possible conditions for its own development. To simply accept the existing comparative advantages is a luxury that only the most advanced states can afford, and only temporarily, at that. List and Hamilton argued that Ricardo's theory of comparative advantages does not account for qualitative differences between various types of economic activity. Due to the fact that this activity is not uniform in quality, even the most specialised and efficient producers of goods of low technological status may only earn a fraction of the proceeds of entities specialising in producing goods requiring high input of knowledge and technology. In his *Report on Manufactures* (1791), Hamilton claims that due to its specialisation in agriculture, the USA will have an unfavourable trade relation with Europe, necessitating public support for the development of the state's own productive sector. In its legislative efforts, however, the Congress did not follow the author's recommendations.

The same cannot be said of nineteenth-century Germany, where List's economic theories exerted a significant influence on the strategy of industrialisation adopted by the state. The notion of the so-called national systems of political economy emerged as an attempted response to the question of how Germany could surpass Great Britain economically. List advocated protection of emerging branches of industry and state involvement in creating potentials and accelerating the processes of industrialisation and economic growth. In a study from 1841, List charged Adam Smith that he:

> has merely taken the word capital in that sense in which it is necessarily taken by rentiers or merchants in their book-keeping and their balance sheets.... He has forgotten that he himself includes [in his definition of

capital] the intellectual and bodily abilities of the producers under this term. He wrongly maintains that the revenues of the nation are dependent only on the sum of its material capital.... The present state of nations is the result of the accumulation of all discoveries, inventions, improvements, perfections and exertions of all generations which have lived before us: they form the intellectual capital of the present human race, and every separate nation is productive only in the proportion in which it has known how to appropriate those attainments of former generations and to increase them by its own acquirements.

(List 1841: 183, 113)

In his view,

there scarcely exists a manufacturing business which has not relation to physics, mechanics, chemistry, mathematics or the art of design. No progress, no new discoveries and inventions can be made in these sciences by which a hundred industries and processes could not be improved or altered. In the manufacturing State, therefore, sciences and arts must necessarily become popular.

(List 1841: 162)

The views on the role of the state in the process of development espoused by List and his followers impacted contemporary politics, leading, for instance, to the development of the famous German system of technical education and training. In reality, however, its emergence was only partially due to strategic actions of the state geared towards economic goals; the gist of state activity remained focused on state-building, and the eventual shape of the system was decisively affected by the emergence of institutions created in the process of handling the impact of interest groups. In other words, it was a combination of grass-roots processes along with spontaneous and coordinated state policies aimed at establishing state structures and providing them with cadres, rather than a strategic pursuit of industrialisation, as List would have it (see Thelen 2004). According to economic historians, this system played a decisive role in Germany's lightning-fast development and the achievement of the state's most cherished goal: the overtaking of Great Britain (Landes 1969; Barnett 1988; Hobsbawm 1969). It also evoked admiration and jealousy among foreign observers, particularly British and French.

List stressed the importance of state coordination of development. His works reflect on the importance of educational institutions, training, science, technical institutes, and – more broadly – the accumulation of knowledge, as well as the promotion of strategic branches of industry. They also propose solutions understood today as interactive processes of learning between the producer and the user. List supported technological transfers, as well, which the nineteenth-century Germany endorsed, appropriating key machine technologies from the British and then advancing them to a degree beyond that achieved on the British Isles.

Popular among experts and political decision-makers, the concept of NIS saw the light of day in mid-1980s. Developed by Freeman and Lundvall, it drew significant inspiration from List's notion of national systems of political economy. Its other sources were Joseph Schumpeter's understanding of capitalism as a process of so-called creative destruction and Nikolai Kondratiev's observation of long-term cycles of prosperity driven by the same technological change Schumpeter reflected upon. However, though List represents a clearly statist attitude, Schumpeter and Kondratiev focused on spontaneous changes achieved without state intervention. Yet, proponents of NIS believe that it is precisely this process of elemental change disproportionately supportive of those who already enjoy an advantage that demands active engagement of the state in developing networks that foster innovations.

Invoking Marx, Schumpeter (1943) stressed that innovations are the source of the wealth of nations, and that capital alone cannot suffice to create prosperity in the long run. Like other critics of the classical model, he argued that it devotes too much attention to competition based on pricing. Reviewing the evolution of capitalism, he proclaimed that change is achieved not through competitive pricing, but through new products, new technologies, new sources of supply, and new types of organisation. Thus, competition based on qualitative advantages plays a key part here. Technological stagnation leads to a decline in profits among those who remain tied to specific technologies. One of the sources of the dynamic of capitalism, the advance of know-how also contributes to the increasing inequality between the rich and the poor. Innovation as the driving force of economic growth and social change, but also as the means of qualitative advance beyond older technologies, is a central component of Schumpeter's concept of the so-called creative destruction.

Knowledge and the creativity it entails need not derive from ground-breaking technological advances – most ideas that yield profit for entrepreneurs emerge from new applications or combinations of commonly accessible technologies. Schumpeter criticised the conceptualisation of R&D as a lottery of sorts, in which specific levels of R&D define the chances of success for determinate amounts of innovation. Innovations cannot be predicted by normal probability since they constitute instances of immeasurable risk (the so-called Knight's uncertainty) that cannot be calculated (Reinganum 1984). As a result, the 'systemic' component of technological progress and growth gains in significance. Schumpeter opposed the admission to mainstream economic thought of notions such as the behaviour of enterprises and price and quantity equilibrium, stressing that it is progress and change, not equilibrium, that constitutes the most significant feature of capitalism.

Like other scholars from their circle, Freeman and Lundvall drew inspiration from Schumpeter, among others, claiming that the assumption of stable equilibrium that typified the dominant theory during the 1980s prevents it from accounting for technological progress and aspects of innovation as empirically established. This is due to the fact that the neoclassical model expects participants to choose between well-defined alternatives, while every real innovation entails risk, which means its results are unknown by definition. Once classical economic models are updated with uncertainty, localised nature of learning processes, and limited rationality (instead of assumptions of perfect information and full rationality), it turns out that divergent conditions between states often translate into differences in the chosen paths to development.

Aside from nineteenth-century Germany, these claims drew empirical inspiration from the advances made by Japan, which, having implemented a conscious policy of supporting innovation, achieved a pace of development far superior to that of the Western states with their neoclassical policies (Johnson 1982). During the 1980s, in particular, the example of Japan's improvement astonished American and European scholars to a degree comparable only to the development of nineteenth-century Germany or contemporary China. Questions were asked over the source of those successes. In search of an answer, the significance Japan attached to actions geared towards long-term benefits for the industry were set against the short-term thinking of English-speaking countries, who limited themselves to exchange rate machinations or the exploitation of relative advantages in costs of factors of production. It was also noted that similar tendencies were exhibited in the industry policies of the Asian tigers, particularly the Republic of Korea. In spite of differences in the particular solutions applied, both countries achieved technological progress through networks of cooperating private and public entities, rather than a simple increase in expenses on R&D.

In 1963, Freeman co-authored the so-called Frascati handbook – the first attempt at defining the rules of measuring and collecting statistical data in R&D (OECD 2002). The handbook defined basic research, applied research, R&D, scientific employees, and even proposed a division of disciplines of science into main categories and subcategories. It finally achieved the dissemination of measurements of innovation proposed already in the post-war USA, where efforts were put into conceptualising the effects of the system founded on a combination of science and industry, recently created for the military. Also in the 1960s, with a view to the technology and arms race, OECD conducted the first, experimental attempt to compare the R&D potential of Europe, the USA, and the Soviet Union (Freeman and Young 1965). The resulting document was not limited to a statistical estimate concerning the particular indicators in R&D, but betrayed its authors' conviction that a state's potential in this area does not simply reflect its financial outlay. The object of the comparison between the aforementioned states was to identify recipes for supporting science and innovation with the greatest possible profit for state development. The report firmly underlined the significance of ties between science and both civilian and military industry. A review of the public policies of OECD states in these areas provided a systematic proof that reducing innovation policy to R&D is an error, as various other factors play a part, especially academic research, which had not received sufficient attention. During the 1970s and 1980s, knowledge was accumulated about innovative processes and their sources. Other conditions of successful state innovation policies were named, aside from R&D expenses, including, in particular, the importance of networks of internal relations and contacts with the world outside of business. The conclusions of contemporary documents indicate the need to invest in knowledge infrastructure and human capital, as well as to ensure closer ties between the industry and the universities, which were deemed crucial for the long-term functioning of the economies. Already at the time, Silicon Valley and Stanford University were brought up and analysed as an example of convergence between the two worlds (Lundvall 2015: 4).

In 1982, Freeman presented an approach to technological change inspired by List's ideas to a narrow audience inside the OECD, using the phrase 'innovation system' for the first time. The notion of NIS enjoyed wider currency towards the end of the 1980s, in the context of industrial policies in Europe. In spite of the hegemonic discourse of reduced government and the increasing popularity of the belief in the irrelevancy of nation-states in an era of globalisation, OECD experts and others pressed for innovation systems to be identified as 'national' (Sharif 2006: 753). It was also stressed that NIS were not limited to markets, but also included institutions and relations within these systems. Proponents of innovation systems approaches argue that it is not enough to programme the stimuli rightly for a general transformation to occur. A systemic approach involves numerous feedback loops while micro-level attitudes reflect macro-level conditions, and the system itself (macro level) is shaped through learning, innovation and competency-building at the micro level. OECD and other international organisations began to gradually adopt the notion and deploy it in their analytical schemata; it was then appropriated by academics and the world of politics (Sharif 2006: 745).

Innovation systems consist of networks of institutions from both private and public sector which act or interact to initiate, import, modify, and achieve the diffusion of new technologies. Participants in these networks as well as contextual factors exert an influence on the efficiency with which a given system creates knowledge for economic purposes. The role of the government is not limited to the creation of knowledge in universities and laboratories, but also includes the achievement of the necessary conditions for the diffusion of knowledge and innovation across different sectors. Aside from the traditional financing of basic research, the state imposes a vision of new areas and then invests in the early stages of research that the private sector is unwilling to engage in, either because it is too weak, or because of high-risk anxiety. It can also support the formation of networks between business, science, and the financial sector. Today, the most commonly referenced fields where such involvement takes place are renewable energy and nanotechnology.

The Organisation of Economic Cooperation and Development, often popularly associated with neoclassical economic solutions, played a key part in the dissemination of the notion of NIS, mediating between the worlds of academic experts, consultants for international organisations, and political decision-makers (Sharif 2006: 752). Divergences in innovativeness derive from institutional conditions and differences between the processes of technological change, which can be described qualitatively with some ease, but are not as easily quantifiable; in particular, they cannot be simply illustrated by the outlay on R&D. The latter approach is more akin to OECD's position, reflecting a greater interest in specific political recommendations than in theoretical rigour.

The first state to adopt the concept of NIS in its internal policies was Finland – this occurred already in 1992. The category lay at the core of the analyses of public policies conducted in 1993, 1996, and 2000 by the Science and Technology Policy Council. Nordic states are in the lead not only in research, but also in implementation of innovation-friendly policies. From their perspective, such policies are necessary for small economies that succeeded in staking out a good position in a globalised world because of the increased threat of asymmetry in the area of knowledge.

Knowledge in the era of the Third Industrial Revolution

At the foundation of the belief that subsequent industrial revolutions significantly altered the conditions under which societies operate lies the conviction that economic progress is evolutionary and can be divided into phases, waves, or eras. This argument has been advanced by, for example, Karl Marx, Nikolai Kondratiev, and Joseph Schumpeter. Industrial revolution and industrialisation are terms that cannot be reduced to technological change because they do not refer only to the economy, but also to social, political, and public relations phenomena, as well as various combinations thereof. Agriculture, demographics, technology, trade, or transportation should thus be seen as areas of synchronous change (Braudel 1984: 557). Every era is typified by a specific cluster of technologies whose gradual development induces economic growth. Incidentally, this argument does not require – and typically does not involve – a determinist perspective. Effective development of various technologies of key importance for a given phase demands relevant institutions and support structures. State institutions follow an internal logic and exhibit their own peculiar ordering, binding together technology, science, politics, and culture.

After a period of high returns due to the application of a new technology, the profits begin to dissipate, and the pace of growth declines. For development to continue, new know-how has to be implemented and institutional structures have to be reformed. As a rule, the evolutionary approach to economics is opposed to neoclassical approaches, with their concentration on overall balance and assumptions of long-term consistency of conditions (*caeteris paribus*). From the perspective of studies of irrevocable processes, *caeteris paribus* does not make sense. Instead of balance, one should rather speak of technological and social evolution or mutation.

Scholars disagree in their assessment of the number of major economic cycles. Inspired by Kondratiev's wave theory (though criticising the content of the Russian economist's theses and his excessive concentration on econometrics), Christopher Freeman and Francisco Louçã (2001) identify five such cycles: the First Industrial Revolution, basically limited to Great Britain and characterised by the production of cotton, iron, and water power (*c.*1780–1848); the Second Industrial Revolution, involving such achievements as railways, steam engine, and mechanisation (c.1848–1895); then, the development of steel-making technology, engineering, and electrification (c.1895–1940); then exploitation of oil with advances in motorisation and mass production (since c.1941), also known as Fordism or Taylorism; and finally, the Third Industrial Revolution, which is taking place today, typified by information and telecommunication technologies, as well as the transition to new energy technologies.

On the other hand, Freeman and Louçã (2001: 146) describe the development of subsequent technologies in the following terms:

1 Laboratory invention, prototypes, patents, small-scale trials, initial implementations. This stage can last a very long time, and its results are not readily visible.
2 Decisive demonstration of technical and commercial viability.
3 Dynamic development and growth, often leading to turbulences of economic as well as political nature, which result in the elaboration of new institutions.
4 Consistently high level of growth within the new system, now accepted by the society as transparent fact. The new technological regime applies to the leading economies; the technology is increasingly implemented, branching out into new areas of the industry and services.
5 A slowdown and erosion of profits as the system matures, facing the challenge of new technologies. This leads to another crisis requiring structural adjustments.
6 Maturity with potential for a limited 'renaissance' owing to coexistence with newer technologies; alternatively, gradual waning.

Prior to the Second Industrial Revolution, the thus-far poorly developed science affected the welfare of states and societies only to a limited degree, though the technologies of production of gunpowder, iron, and ships contributed to the colonial domination of Spain, France, or England even at that early stage. The First Industrial Revolution did not require scientific knowledge – to progress, it only needed the abilities that artisans transmitted to their apprentices and a certain creativity in combining well-known solutions, factors unrelated to the degree of advancement in science. In contrast to transformations during the nineteenth century, change occurred very slowly, affecting virtually just Manchester and the surrounding area over the first few decades, and then gradually spreading across Great Britain and the Netherlands. Other states did not experience industrialisation in its initial phase. Only in the second half of the nineteenth century would the scientific understanding of phenomena and technological innovation converge more consistently, providing an important characteristic of the so-called Second Industrial Revolution. This combination of science and technique with the economy occurred in nineteenth-century Germany. The shift in the logic of technological advancement was relatively unfavourable to Great Britain.

Though scientific research for industrial purposes had existed before, Germany was the first state to systematically apply the theoretical findings of science to developing technological innovations. It was here that the first transfer of the methodology of scientific experimentation from the university to the industry took place (Gilpin 1968: 20–22). The breakthrough occurred within German electric industry and organic chemistry. British philosopher, mathematician, and physicist Alfred N. Whitehead described this transition as the greatest achievement of the nineteenth century, 'the invention of the method of invention'. Though previously established methods of seeking new solutions for the industry were not abandoned completely, scientists now began to occupy an important position in the productive sector. Germany became the first world power in history to owe its lightning-fast rise in the international arena directly to its scientific potential and well-developed education system.

The development of the USA, another state to profit from these processes, also occurred during the Second Industrial Revolution, but followed a different model – one based on drawing in talented individuals from Europe (and other regions of the world) rather than investing in the state's own education and science after the German example. New inventions developed in the USA were also propelled by constant shortages of workforce, which distinguished the American conditions from those found in the overpopulated Europe. This problem was solved through mass production, which radically increased productivity per a single labourer. As part of the organisational innovations, the process was broken down into simple, repetitive actions. As a result, though work on new technologies required of their creators to gain advanced competencies and exhibit a creative approach, productive work itself was reduced to relatively straightforward activities. Fordism allowed many people of relatively low education level – compared to the artisans of yore with their advanced skills – to find employment. In its American guise, therefore, the Second Industrial Revolution is typified not by a general increase of competencies within the society concurrent with the advance of technology, but rather intensifying divergence of the necessary skills. On the one hand, new technological discoveries demanded advanced knowledge that was imported from Europe; on the other hand, mass production reduced the range of abilities necessary for the production of goods. This example cogently illustrates that, while human capital is necessary to absorb a technology in theory, the simplification of work achieved with its implementation may lead to a different result, not requiring the supply of advanced competencies.

During the twentieth century, the technological advancement involved in the Second Industrial Revolution effected a radical transformation of the labour force and enabled the achievement of an unprecedented pace of economic growth. Mechanisation and the development of chemical solutions caused employment levels in agriculture to fall down to barely 5 per cent in Western states, with employment in resource extraction, construction, and productive industries – which had reached its maximum level of 47 per cent in the USA after World War I – decreasing below 20 per cent by 2000 (Smil 2006: 282). In the past few decades, the value of human capital and innovativeness for the advancement of the state has gained additional publicity due to the belief that another major technological change is now taking place. Some scholars and experts give it the name of a Third Industrial Revolution.

Automation and robotisation of production, which the Third Industrial Revolution has introduced, will likely lead to further decrease in employment in the productive sector with far-reaching consequences given the significance attached to those workplaces as markers of the technological advancement of an economy. The impact of lowering employment levels in all other sectors is mitigated by the service sector, whose share increased from 31 per cent in 1900 to over 80 per cent in 2000 in the USA; for the EU, the share was 68 per cent in 2000, while in Japan, it was roughly 60 per cent (Smil 2006: 283). The service sector also requires better educated workers and greater investment per employee. In 1900, only 14 per cent of Americans had finished high school, and only 2 per cent graduated from a university; 100 years later, the numbers were 83 per cent and 25 per cent, respectively.

It is often said that the Third Industrial Revolution will further increase the significance of knowledge and abilities, raising their value to historic levels (Brynjolfsson and McAfee 2011: 8). Technological change increases the demand for advanced skills, limiting or eliminating the need for simple skills. As a result, income inequalities between qualified and unqualified workers increase (Acemoglu and Autor 2012). Additionally, subsequent branches experience the winner effect, with one player taking (almost) all. Superstars expand over an increasing share of the market, leaving less and less room for local competition.

The concept of the so-called knowledge-based economy also has a group of detractors who find it unlikely that such as economy can be achieved or that the knowledge workers it requires can be supplied. Doubts emerge concerning the various statistical measures international organisations use to describe this entity, mixing beliefs (the enthusiasm generated by the idea of such an economy) with empirical research based on the assumption that this type of economy simply exists (Dzierzgowski 2012: 27–30). One might also question whether this type of economy uses knowledge to a greater extent than does the traditional labour of experts, farmers, or officials. Freeman and Louçã (2001: 132) observe that all forms of human economy deserve to be deemed knowledge-based – not just the latest iteration that has arrogantly claimed the privilege. Learning has accompanied humanity since time immemorial. What has changed are the methods of knowledge accumulation and dissemination. Sceptics believe that 'knowledge worker' is merely a new name for the well-established expert (Dzierzgowski 2012: 11–23). After all, there is ample proof that employees in the so-called knowledge-based and creative sectors mostly engage in repetitive and algorithmic labour, even if their workplace is an office rather than a factory. This brings to mind the example of Fordism, forcing the question whether technological progress actually increases the demand for advanced competencies, or rather for specific abilities and knowledge. Critics contend that the knowledge-based economy has a clear ideological component related to the promise (usually unfulfilled) of freedom, meritocracy, and elasticity (Dzierzgowski 2012: 37–50).

In reality, however, that ideology may be mobilised to legitimise and naturalise hierarchies without naming them outright. In spite of the fluidity of the context, the competitiveness that innovations in the knowledge-based economy are supposed to foster effectively decides who is better and who is worse, who is a winner and who is a loser (Zarycki 2014: 28).

Subsequent technological changes in capitalist states propel institutional change and the exchange of the elites; these alterations serve as the foundation for new fortunes and powerful enterprises, another face of Schumpeter's 'creative destruction' (Freeman and Perez 1988; Perez and Soete 1988). Regulatory regimes and institutions also need to undergo a reconfiguration (Perez 1983, 1985, 2002). Explosions of labour productivity typically result in conflict and are accompanied by crisis and the need for adaptation. As a result, thousands of people lose their livelihoods, and their professions become a remnant of history (Braudel 1984: 592). Some societies adjust successfully, while others experience a lasting decline.

As the examples of Germany and the USA illustrate, changes in economic and technological paradigms can provide an opportunity for advancement for states that do not number among the world powers (Samuelson 2004: 142). This, in turn, constitutes one of the factors affecting the emergence of new powers and shifts in the international configuration. The desire to exploit the change necessitates the introduction of technological, organisational, and social innovations. However, these processes cause even greater strain for poorer states, granting additional privileges to the current leaders, better accustomed to the vectors of change and possessive of more resources for the necessary adjustment. In spite of the often quite utopian faith in innovation as a driver of the improvement of the human condition, economic history proves that, thus far, innovations have, in fact, contributed to the rise of inequality in the wealth of nations. Technological change may have increased the overall wealth, but the benefits were not distributed equitably. This is due, for instance, to the persistent gap between innovators, those who adapt early, and those who prepare for the change at a later time (Rogers 2003: 460).

Education, knowledge, and the global value chains

The concept of global value chains has emerged from at least two separate currents of debate about world economy. On the one hand, the more liberally minded experts, such as the aforementioned Michael Porter, approach it as an indelible part of capitalism in an era of globalisation; on the other, the proponents of world-system theory inspired by Fernand Braudel and Immanuel Wallerstein perceive the same phenomenon as a mechanism for the formation of an economic dependency described as the relationship between the centre and the periphery (Gereffi and Korzeniewicz 1994). In the era of globalisation, capitalism brings about a far-reaching disaggregation of the various stages of production extended beyond state borders and reflected by the strong ties between global corporations. Terence Hopkins and Immanuel Wallerstein (1986: 159) define the commodity chain as a network of labour and production processes culminating in the finished good. Every single process is a link in the chain; the boundaries of a process are not rigidly defined, and they can split (specialise further) or combine (e.g. with the advent of a technology that simplifies production). Like other liberally minded scholars of the value chains, Porter focuses on the micro level, that is, particular enterprises involved in the value chain, while Wallerstein and his proponents are drawn towards a macro perspective, analysing specific links in value chains through the categories of centre and periphery of the world system.

Value chains contain multiple functions, from the exploitation of natural resources, through various stages of commodity production, up to R&D and marketing. Within a given chain, not all links are equally profitable either for the companies involved or for the states in which they operate. The hierarchy of links can be illustrated by the classification of economic activities by the order of their quality (Reinert 2007). High-quality economic activity is typified by new knowledge of high market value, a steep learning curve, a high increase in productivity, rapid technological advancement, a high share of R&D, obligatory learning through practice, imperfect information, imperfect (but dynamic) competition, high earnings, high industry concentration, high entry and exit barriers, trademarked products, and connection and synergy effects, with no adherence to standard neoclassical assumptions. Meanwhile, low-quality economic activity is characterised by the deployment of well-known knowledge of little market value, flat learning curves, low increases in productivity, low technological advancement, low share of R&D, low education requirements for both individuals and institutions, perfect information and competition, low earnings, industry fragmentation, low entry and exit barriers, and few connections and synergies. Here, the standard assumptions of neoclassical economics are fulfilled: in low-quality economic activity on the global market, the competition is perfect; the higher the quality, the more imperfect the competition and the more profitable the state's position in the global economy, provided the right links of the chain are located within its territory.

It is believed that companies which control the most profitable links of the chains, including R&D and marketing (e.g. by operating a strong trademark) earn disproportionately more than those involved in the other links of the chains. Control of R&D and marketing often translates into control over the entire value chain (Lundvall 2015: 16). According to Porter (1987: 29), the study of competitive advantages should refer to specific branches, the battlefield on which these advantages are won or lost. Success on a global scale requires integrated and systemic management of connections within global value chains.

The effect of globally unequal technological progress and high differentiation in human capital development was additionally reinforced by advances in international trade, which contributed to specialisation, strengthening the states which had already achieved a high level of advancement. Commodities whose production requires more complex abilities also provide greater added value. Increasing demand for qualified labour results in the gradual increase of investment in 'quality' in states which can afford to cover such expenses (Galor 2011: 199). In a feedback effect, this contributes to technological progress and reinforces competitive advantages of the relevant economies. The process also creates incentives for those less developed to specialise in the production of labour-intensive – rather than knowledge-intensive – commodities. It is typical for specific chains to assign a comparatively larger share of the profits from production to links that are located in states of the centre, rather than those competing mostly in the peripheries. Consequently, the pressure of competition is greater in the peripheries than at the centre, which gains an advantage thanks to innovations. Reliance on cheap labour provides a competitive advantage of the lower order, inevitably blighted by instability.

Competition and innovation are the key elements of the historical shifts in the global value chains. To move up in a chain or switch to another, one needs the right kind of human and social capital, as well as knowledge and research support and a superior market position. Hopkins and Wallerstein's (1986) concept of global commodity chains updates the world-system theory, providing a more nuanced identification of the types of production present in various areas and moving away from the previous hierarchies based on resource economy, industry, and services. As a result, it can more consistently avoid becoming tangled in the myth of post-industrial economy. In many developing countries, labour-intensive services such as programming or data processing can have a greater impact on growth than the industry. Within the commodity chain, profitability moves across the links according to the relative intensity of competitions on the level of particular links (Gereffi and Korzeniewicz 1994: 4).

The spatial transition of parts of the chains into states in the periphery entails an increase in the labour intensiveness of work, while the links that consume the most capital and knowledge are to be found in states of the centre. This means that the amount of added value decreases in proportion to the distance from the centre. In comparison to the era of industrialisation, the global centre does not require high-density industry. Labour-intensive industries that have no use for advanced human capital or technological knowledge can be located in semi-peripheries. As illustration, one might consider a wealthy player such as Apple, the company that symbolises modern economy, whose devices bear the legend: 'designed in California, assembled in China'.

Apple is a well-respected owner of one of the most perfect and best developed value chains that is also typified by an exceptional elasticity. The company acquires parts and materials from dozens of suppliers, and then dispatches them to the factory in China which assembles the devices; once complete, these go to the users. Suppliers compete for the privilege of participating in the value chains for particular products offered by the global giant. The diagram below illustrates the share of companies from different states in iPhone's value chains (data from 2010).

What typifies capitalism is consumer resistance to monopoly in the most profitable links of the value chains, which often motivates a technological 'escape forward', or an attempt to transform the commodity qualitatively.

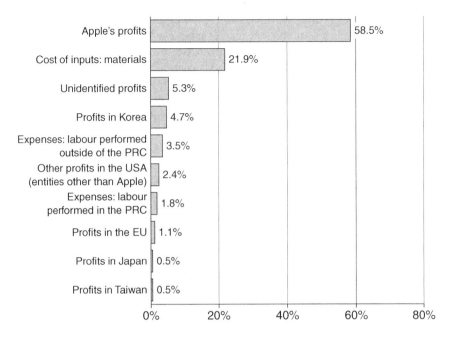

Figure 3.3 Costs and gains in iPhone's value chain.
Source: own elaboration based on Kraemer, Linden, and Dedrick 2011: 5.

Central links can be located in a limited number of states which meet the necessary conditions, including human capital and technological know-how, while links of low added value are easily divided among peripheral states, which engage in fierce competition. In this respect, proponents of the centre-periphery theory find it highly unlikely that multinational corporations should ever invest in developing states to a degree sufficient to raise the local competencies to a level enabling those states to reap comparatively larger rewards from participation in global value chains. In light of this, the transition to a knowledge-based economy would only deepen the chasm between the poor and the rich (Grieco and Ikenberry 2003: 271, 335).

As the previous fragment shows, liberally minded and Marxist-leaning experts share a significant proportion of the diagnosis of the contemporary world economy. Where they differ is, first, in the axiological layer – liberals gaze in awe at the efficiency with which capitalism produces wealth, while proponents of Marxist approaches concentrate on the unequal distribution thereof. Second, while liberals believe that the system ensures generally fair rules of the game that allow various entities to win provided they choose the right strategy and apply themselves sufficiently (as in the economic advance of China since its inclusion among the global economic institutions under Deng Xiaoping), leftist thinkers stress the dependency of the weak, which, in fact, prevents them from advancing within the system. In their view, the liberal order in the world economy favours those who already are privileged, thus consistently reproducing the centre and the periphery at ever-new levels.

The impact of education and science on economic development in market economies

The development of education systems was concurrent with the political processes that created the modern state. In its latter stages, in particular, it coincided with the Second Industrial Revolution. Education systems in different countries reflect the economic model assumed by each of them in the course of history. The different forms of capitalism and the consequent variety of school systems, particularly with regard to the abilities being taught (skills regimes in primary, secondary, tertiary, and professional education), became the object of comparative studies of institutions in the 1990s. This interest derives from the observation that the analysis of quantitative data describing social policies leads to incomplete and distorted conclusions (Esping-Andersen 1990). Michał Federowicz (2004: 171–172) stresses that institutions are not easily transposed from one country to another, and the understanding of the architecture of an entire economic system demands reflection on the specific, local context of the emergence of particular configurations of coordinating mechanisms. John W. Meyer and Michael T. Hannan (1979) attempted to show that, while paradigms for the modern state, including school systems, gained prominence, with each state establishing institutions according to models successfully implemented in Western states, local adaptations were made, as well. Thus, what took place cannot be simply identified as institutional convergence, since the reactions of the governments and companies depended on the context (Federowicz 2004: 175). Furthermore, even in the West, no single, identical model prevailed, as discussed in Chapter 2.

Peter Hall and David Soskice (2001) proposed one famous typology of models of capitalism that focused in particular on differences in education systems. The part of their study devoted to education systems was subsequently expanded by Kathleen Thelen (2004), who concentrated on the evolution of institutions, analysing the influence political coalitions and conflicts had on their development. Pepper Culpepper and David Finegold (2000) conducted an in-depth analysis of the German system, which was credited with the greatest efficiency in providing the necessary skills for the industry. Their analysis stems from the observation that, since industrialisation, the delivery of relevant competencies is troubled by coordination problems due to the fact that enterprises need to ensure access to employees endowed with the right skills, while the employees need to decide how much to invest and in which skills. Coordinated market economies deal with this challenge in a different manner than liberal market economies do. The degree to which enterprises are willing to invest in training depends on the degree of security that the employee that had been invested in will keep faith with his employer, while the employees are mostly interested in using the competencies they invested in.

In coordinated market economies of the German and Japanese mould, specific institutions oversee state-subsidised public training systems. In Germany, there are employer associations and labour unions, while Japan has *keiretsu*, or networks of companies from different sectors within a single 'family of enterprises'. Labour associations and families of enterprises ensure that companies do not buy off employees trained by the competition and that the abilities taught are standardised to yield comparable results even as training is provided by different companies (Hall and Soskice 2001: 24–25). Here, employment is based on long-term contracts, with entities prevented from exploiting the mobility of scientists and engineers, including technological transfers. Such is the cause of the strong ties between enterprises involved in a coordinated, government-supported transfer of knowledge, in spite of mutual competition. Companies finance research jointly, often in coordination with public research institutions. In coordinated market economies, it is easier to achieve variety in products and exploration of niches, that is, complementarity rather than competition with other entities inside the same industry, a typical feature of liberal market economies.

On the other hand, the latter, which include the USA, Great Britain, New Zealand, Canada, and Australia, possess a far more elastic labour market, which impacts the strategies employed by companies and labourers alike. It is more profitable for companies to exploit the emerging possibilities of enlisting the services of useful workers than to invest heavily in training with a view to the long-term exploitation of their skills. Thus, while coordinated capitalism exhibits advanced specialisation, this model is primarily dominated by general competencies that employees invest in on the assumption that these will prove useful in various lines of employment. School systems in those states, too, respond to the demands of the highly fluid labour market. Professional qualifications are mostly gained in institutions of formal learning that offer training in skills of general use in a given branch of the industry. Companies are unwilling to organise high-level training for fear of losing the employees they had invested in. In liberal market economies, a high level of general competency means that employees adapt easily to new responsibilities. As a result, though the labour force is less specialised, it is also more adaptable, more suited to the service sector than advanced production. However, this model is characterised by a consistent shortage of specific abilities. Given the absence of cooperation between enterprises, technological transfer occurs thanks to the mobility of the employees – particularly scientists and engineers.

An ideal institutional order is impossible to achieve, since every particular model has inherently mutually related virtues and vices. From a historical perspective, coordinated economies fared better in some periods, while liberal ones did so in others (Moore 2010: 19). Some virtues are particularly useful in specific periods, but not in others; similarly, some vices are more detrimental in certain circumstances, but not in others. A closer look at the origins of school systems and the organisation of education in the formative period of capitalist models explains why both main paradigms of exploiting opportunity established by the Second Industrial Revolution are as efficient as they are.

Germany invested in a highly qualified labour force, offering guaranteed, stable employment. America's success drew more from innovative use of new technologies to simplify work, which enabled the maintenance of high mobility and provided a solution for cases of labour shortage and qualitative inadequacy of competencies. While Germany had to build up the competencies of their citizen, the USA offered attractive opportunities to immigrants and used technologies to simplify the processes of production (Thelen 2004: 177). These two states, representing the two main modes of capitalism, became the major winners of the Second Industrial Revolution in spite of applying two divergent strategies.

In this part, I will analyse two cases of states showing the mechanisms through which the education and science were historically included in the process of economic development. Studies of the role of education and science in economic development of two exemplary coordinated market economies: Germany and Japan will allow me to identify common pathways among those types of mechanisms. Among those two success stories, the first one built its education and science elaborating its own model, while the other achieved comparable results willing to learn about efficient solutions already implemented elsewhere. Interestingly, both countries achieving formidable economic results, at some point of their history experienced aggressive nationalism, which led to the war and, afterwards, internationally supervised reconstruction of the countries and redesigning the states and nations.

Germany – efficiency that astounded and frightened

Prussian absolutism differed significantly from the French one (described in Chapter 2). The former relied to a far greater extent on repressing the peasantry, with the entire political system infused more deeply with violence (Anderson 1974: 195, 223). Pressure from more advanced societies in Europe forced the Hohenzollern and – to a lesser extent – Habsburg monarchies to seek their own route to a stronger state (Kennedy 1987: 211). The political conditions in the countries differed from those in France – the dominance of the aristocracy was greater, the political power of the poorest infinitely weaker, and the pre-absolutist regime posed less of a challenge to the citizen, particularly in border areas. In effect, Prussian absolute monarchy was much more repressive than its French counterpart, which had provided the blueprint for the trend towards centralisation.

The contours of the respective education systems reflected these general outline of the state. In France, the state intervened early to promote the establishment of vocational and technical schools, but did not extend compulsory education to the peasantry the way Friedrich II in Prussia and Marie Therese in Austria did. During the eighteenth century, development of public systems of compulsory education became the specialty of Central Europe rather than France or Great Britain. Trying to overcome various delays in relation to the centre located in the West, European absolutist latecomers made use of education as a significant instrument of the state. During the Enlightenment, these monarchies were also more linguistically diverse and demographically diffuse, struggling against the challenge of local particularisms. The network of pre-absolutist, decentralised relations of power continued to exhibit greater density and efficiency than in Western Europe, necessitating the imposition of new institutions enforcing vertical solidarity and social control as the foundation for absolute monarchies. Furthermore, the geopolitical challenges faced by these states were also greater, requiring efficient management of borders, which, in turn, required the maintenance of cohesion and centralisation – both on the inside, safeguarding against centrifugal forces, and on the outside, protecting from potential aggressors.

The rulers of Prussia borrowed a page from the playbook of fully trained planners, choosing the shortest and most efficient path to advancement. Using the status of latecomers to their advantage, they boasted a more advanced education system in the nineteenth century than states that had outpaced Prussia in technological advancement and modernisation of political life. As a result, Germany became the model to follow for other powers, including Great Britain (Fischer and Lundgreen 1975: 56).

In the absence of diffuse, pre-absolutist institutions of social control, the emerging structure was already centralised and universal in nature. Later, during the nineteenth century, the existing institutions were infused with a strong nationalist component, with the education system increasingly used as a tool for furthering various social reforms, often demanded by the process of industrialisation. The Prussian education system served as a key component of the wholesale, centrally driven state-building effort that transformed a society built on serfdom and royal absolutism into a reformed Junker state fully prepared to take its place in the capitalist world.

The direct impulse for the development of this most advanced education system of the nineteenth century came from the defeat suffered at the hand of Napoleon. It was then that Friedrich Wilhelm III proffered:

> we have indeed lost in territory, and fallen in external power and splendor, but we must see to it that we gain in internal power and splendor; and hence it is my earnest desire that the greatest attention be given to the instruction of the people.
>
> (Quoted in Painter 1896: 292)

Schools would bring on a national renaissance, fulfilling the peculiar Prussian ideal of individual submission to a common, corporate spirit. Karl Altenstein, one of the foremost reformers of education in the first half of the nineteenth century, claimed that:

> [i]n order to transform the people, to inspire them with confidence and to make them endure any sacrifice for independence and national honour, we must educate the youth of the country. All the forces of the spirit must be

developed and no ability on which the dignity of man rests must be neglected. We shall see a generation growing up which is physically and morally of such vigour that a better future will open before us.

(Quoted in Green 2013: 126)

In subsequent decades, Prussian and then German reformers focused their efforts on industry. The fact that Prussia lacked the strong and energetic bourgeoisie of Great Britain meant that industrialisation followed a completely different path. This revolution from above, to use Barrington Moore's term (1966: 433), was conducted by a group of Junker aristocratic farmers, under efficient support from the state and bureaucracy. Educated bureaucrats played a key role in providing technical knowledge to the emerging industry. After 1830, as a result of the most significant batch of Altenstein's reforms, education – already compulsory – became universal in fact. The established tradition of extending access to education ensured the near absence of obstacles to enforcing compulsory education in the nineteenth century.

Even before then, Prussian theoreticians had devised the method of teaching to an entire class, which was more effective than individual work with every student, as applied in other countries, since the latter meant one child could only receive a few minutes of the teacher's time. By then, teacher training had already advanced, so that even primary school teachers boasted several years of training. Already in the nineteenth century, Prussian teachers used the most innovative methods of instruction and exhibited professionalism superior to their counterparts in other countries. The education programme itself was quite ambitious and substantially instrumentalised by the state. Primary education consisted in transmitting a specific range of knowledge considered vital to socio-economic life and in inculcating submission and patriotism. Middle school, on the other hand, was aimed at forming the cadres for the state bureaucracy, and in time also for the rising industry. Already in the nineteenth century, observers from other countries were fascinated by Prussian, and then German, schooling, and visited the country to learn about the methods involved. These drew mixed responses: both admiration and doubts concerning the impact of such a technocratic approach.

The Prussian education system reflected the numerous contradictions in the society revealed and, at times, reinforced by change. Though state institutions and the education system were created by aristocrats and Junkers, their purpose was a transformation of the society. For this reason, the strict control imposed by the schools was paradoxically accompanied by a greater potential for social mobility than in Great Britain, where decentralised and class-specific education contributed to the reproduction of class distinctions, or France, where a thoroughly centralised and unified state education system likewise hampered mobility. The leadership role of the aristocracy in industrialisation necessitated the opening of paths to social advancement for a certain section of the bourgeoisie. The education system provided a means for this social transformation (Green 2013: 132). In this case, a strongly autocratic regime proved quite amenable to modernisation through education, while the clearly liberal system found in Great Britain delivered stagnation and exclusion of mobility at the point of democratisation (Landes 1969: 348).

According to Paul Kennedy (1987: 241), German industry, technology, education, and science, along with modern administration and the military, became the foundation for a world power. The historian also ascribes the unprecedented aptitude of the German soldiers to the dynamic development of education and science. Prior to World War I, 330 out of every 1,000 Italian recruits were illiterate; in Austro-Hungary, the ratio was 220 to 1,000, in France – 68 to 1,000, while in Germany – just 1 to 1,000. As a result, Kennedy contends, the German army could mobilise and equip millions of reserves and sent them to the front without risking any loss in efficiency. Meanwhile, French reserves were at best fit for second-line service due to their inability to learn the rules of war sufficiently quickly and comprehensively. The educationally backward Russia, in turn, did not possess enough competent officers capable of leading hundreds of thousands of newly mobilised, illiterate peasants (Kennedy 1987: 270, 273).

During the nineteenth century, Germany also came to treat science as a profession, which led the German higher education system to eventually become an inspiration for many other countries. The model of scholarly career was strongly network-based and more open than in France. It was here that the typically modern idea of the 'virtuoso of science' gave way to the expert. Already by the mid-nineteenth century, German science was completely free of self-taught scholars and eccentric experimenters and inventors. The University of Berlin, designed by Wilhelm von Humboldt, set the paradigm for other German universities. The role of the professor was to make scientific discoveries and reproduce experiments with his students. The German system not only transmitted current scientific knowledge, but also provided training in research. Knowledge itself was not enough – one also had to know how to expand it. The focus shifted from the lecture hall to the laboratory (Gilpin 1968: 99–100).

Already Francis Bacon predicted that individual genius in science would one day bow to the achievements of groups of less distinguished, but properly trained and organised common men. This prediction was fulfilled in Germany in the second half of the nineteenth century. German universities trained hundreds of 'common' men, providing them with advanced analytical and technical skills. They housed research laboratories equipped with modern instruments and offering an atmosphere that fostered activity and desire for new challenges. Meanwhile, French science basked in its elitism, high qualification requirements, and deep isolation between its institutions. The French followed the path staked out by Descartes' solitary genius rather than Bacon's intuition, which Germans took as their guiding principle.

The German model of organisation of educational and scientific institutions within their broader surroundings provided a vital reference point for other states, both in Europe and elsewhere. Most importantly, it inspired reforms in Japan, and in several of the areas mentioned above, in spite of the divergence of the modes of capitalism involved, also in the USA. Germany managed to achieve unprecedented economic leaps twice – first in the second half of the nineteenth century, and then in the troubled conditions after World War II.

This model underwent a major transformation after World War II, when the country resigned from the use of nationalism for state-building and economic advancement. However, the peculiar education system, enabling workers to gain advanced competencies at the workplace, remained. The system is unique on a global scale and provides a major reason why Germany's industry is yet to relocate abroad, to countries that offer cheaper labour. Such delocalisation is impossible for those sectors of the industry that Germany plays a major part in precisely due to the competencies and organisation of labour that cannot be transported outside of the country. Compared to the Anglo-Saxon counterparts, German technical universities continue to command respect and enjoy popularity among gifted and ambitious students, unaffected by negative selection. The system is decentralised, managed at the regional level, which facilitates close relations with the industry. The schools provide an even and solid scientific and technical education; in comparison with other economically advanced states, they are distinguished by the large number of doctorates and the prestige attached to academic careers in these fields in Germany. Management programmes, in turn, are a weak spot, leading some German companies to employ foreigners as directors. German academic institutions, however, find it increasingly difficult to maintain their superior international standing, struggling to resist the competition of American universities with their wealth and mass exploitation of the potential of gifted immigrants.

The world-famous German apprenticeship system, jointly organised by regional authorities and private enterprises, operates on a massive scale, involving hundreds of thousands of students in many branches of the industry every year. Traditionally, apprentices spend a half of every week at work, perfecting their practical skills, and the rest at school, receiving professional training as well as in-depth theoretical instruction. Apprenticeships also enable access to qualifications in very rare disciplines. As a result, workers possess not only superior technological skills, but also theoretical insight than their foreign counterparts. In Germany, qualified workers enjoy higher social status than in other developed states. The country leads the way in well-established branches of the industry, such as chemistry, metallurgy, and medicine; however, it is not as innovative as the USA. It is harder to begin production in new, advanced fields, such as electronics, biotechnology, or material engineering, in Germany.

Japan – from avoiding colonisation to challenging the greatest superpower

Changes in education and science constituted a significant aspect of the Meiji Revolution – a series of reforms that led Japan through the process of modernisation on the European model. The 1871 visit to Europe by Prince Iwakura Tomomi and Okubo Toshimichi exhibited to the Far Eastern travellers the extent of Japan's developmental delay in relation to Great Britain and other European states. It also suggested a sense of kinship with the recently unified Germany.

Japan's case is a classic example of an educational reform designed for the purposes of state-building, to secure the country from European domination and colonisation, which then brought spectacular economic success. Applying a common programme and disseminating the national language, schools promoted a sense of national unity. The process of replacing regional identities with national loyalty faced serious challenges, given that the state comprised 300 separate feudal entities (Passim 1965; Burks 1985: 257; Cummings 1980). As in states of continental Europe, education helped establish new bureaucratic elites. However, Japan's transformation was distinguished by the fact that the adoption of Western science, technology, and education was accompanied by the highlighting of the exceptional character and historical continuity of national culture and tradition. The resulting state was highly efficient and modern, but with an identity rooted in its peculiar, pre-modern values.

Already in 1871, the newly established Ministry of Education began to extend the network of schools, adopting the French, centralised model and introducing a modern programme of education based on American examples. Over the following years, this far-reaching Occidentalism was overturned, with focus turned towards Japanese values and traditions. Portraits of the Emperor hung in every school, and on national holidays, each hosted ceremonies according to the same ritual. During the 1880s, a compromise was achieved between the modern and the traditional. Mori Arinori, the Minister of Education at the time, defined his goals thus:

> In the administration of all schools ... what is to be done is not for the sake of the pupils, but for the sake of the country.... Our country must move from its third class position to second class, and from second class to first, and ultimately to the leading position amongst countries in the world.
> (Quoted in Green 2013: 348)

One of the Meiji reforms consisted in the creation of a public education system, initially on a four-year and, since 1907, seven-year programme. At the outset, compulsory education was extended only to boys, but, in time, girls were also admitted. The radical ramifications of the universal educational reform are all the more astounding given the patriarchal character of Japanese culture. As a result, since the Meiji Revolution, the proscription on women's participation in social life only applied to the highest classes. In 1890, only 30 per cent of girls of adequate age attended schools; within thirty years, that number rose to 97.4 per cent (Nolte and Hastings 1991: 157). The state enforced universal education for girls in spite of parents' resistance spurred by anxieties over the resulting loss of income. The reform caused a massive social change, in fact doubling the workforce.

The nationalist character of the Japanese educational reforms increased markedly with the advent of the twentieth century. On the one hand, compulsory military training became a part of the middle school curriculum; on the other, the Ministry of Education took and consistently exploited its monopoly in textbook publishing (Cave 2003: 35). The nationalist-militarist tendencies peaked in the 1930s; textbooks idealised soldiers as an example for the entire society, asserted the divine origin of the Emperor as fact rather than myth, glorified self-sacrifice while castigating individualism, and depicted Japan as an exceptional nation, undefeated in battle and endowed with a special mission and responsibility in Asia (Akiyoshi 2008: 56).

Even at its outset in 1868, the Meiji Revolution saw the state put significant effort into absorbing knowledge from the West. At the time, employment of foreign experts as consultants and specialised technical personnel in various industrial undertakings was the key aspect of the process of making up for delays in development. Students were dispatched abroad to learn and train at companies, schools, and educational institutions. On the other hand, though, the Japanese government also established various educational institutions of its own, staffed to a large degree by foreigners, but these concentrated on training cadres rather than independent scientific research. The year 1873 saw the establishment of the Imperial Polytechnic, with a programme modelled on that of ETH in Zurich and a British staff. Later on, the institution merged with the engineering department of Tokyo University. The government's efforts focused on the formation of a strong Imperial University in Tokyo. The pioneers of Japan's late-nineteenth-century industrialisation received training at the local universities, expanded with one or two years of foreign apprenticeship.

Once the war was lost and Americans occupied the country, nationalist elements were struck out from the programmes, moral education was proscribed, and instruction in history and geography was suspended until new textbooks were prepared. When the occupation ended, some of the nationalist tropes returned to the programmes, providing a lasting cause of controversy and tensions between Tokyo and the governments of other Asian states that had suffered from Japanese aggression (Akiyoshi 2008: 58). The most vocal critiques of one-sided and tendentious readings of history in Japanese textbooks emerge from Beijing.

The state operates a coordinated market economy, but with different institutional solutions than those applied in Germany. Traditionally, education is endowed with significant prestige, and educated people command public respect. Comparative studies from the 1990s indicated that the Japanese exhibit high competency in mathematics and natural sciences, as proven in international tests. In addition, they are adept at group work and diligent. As a coordinated market economy, Japan – much like Germany – functions in conditions that favour the expansion of advanced competence among its workers. At its disposal is a vast array of well-educated engineers, some of whom received education at the finest foreign universities, primarily in the USA. At its economic apex during the early 1980s, Japan trained 50 per cent more engineers than the United States and employed 700,000 people in the R&D sector – more than Great Britain, France and West Germany combined (Kennedy 1987: 599). However, Japan's higher education institutions do not compare favourably to American counterparts. Japanese universities provide good technical instruction, but are not particularly renowned for training in hard sciences, and even more so in social sciences. The relative feebleness of higher education in comparison to the economic and industrial potential of the country has driven public debate for years. Yet, within Japan's economic model, enterprises matter more than scientific and research facilities. Much of the knowledge is produced by private enterprises. On-the-job training is executed with exceptional rigour, continues throughout the period of employment, and is often of high quality. Some companies even train their employees beyond the doctoral level. Scientific research, too, is often the domain of enterprises rather than universities. The most gifted graduates in hard-scientific or technical disciplines tend to prefer a career in business to the academia. This is reflected in expenses on R&D: 80 per cent come from private enterprises, while only 20 per cent is provided by the state. Characteristically, Japan also has a framework for cooperative research by different companies, coordinated by the Ministry of International Trade and Industry (MITI) (Johnson 1982).

Japan's strength is also in the ease with which it adapts foreign technology, the willingness to learn from others, and the ability to independently develop the imported solutions. Due to its cultural conditions, Japan also does not benefit from immigration, relying instead on the foundations provided by the education of its own citizen. For this reason, Japan's universities provide instruction geared towards knowledge transfers rather than independent advances, while the state operates an extensive scholarship system for its own citizen, providing funding for studies at the best foreign institutions on the condition that the student returns home after graduation.

After World War I, the government began to create research laboratories and initiated public support programmes for private research and development undertakings (Mazzoleni and Nelson 2009: 390–393). Japan, like the Republic of Korea which adopts the similar approach, constitutes an example of a developmental bureaucratic state. The most significant means of implementing this strategy was MITI, Japan's Ministry of Trade and Industry, which offered centralised aid to local companies in their efforts to make up for delays in development, and then also to challenge foreign rivals on the markets for specific products (Johnson 1982). Government planners designed sets of economic incentives and subsidies for existing companies to enable them to compete in areas that would have carried excessive risk without such assistance. While supporting advancing branches of the industry, the government discreetly bypassed those that were deemed insufficiently competitive. In the 1980s, the share of R&D expenses in the GDP increased from 2 per cent to 3.5 per cent, thus expanding beyond the levels found in the USA (in relative terms), where this indicator stood at 2.7 per cent.

In its coordination of Japan's policies, MITI concentrated not on identifying the winners, but rather on creating cross-sector connections, ties between companies and between the private and the public (Johnson 1982). In the 1950s and

1960s, it was believed that Japan's only strength – and major limitation – was its reliance on copying, imitating, and importing foreign technologies. During the 1970s, the state devoted 2.5 per cent of its GDP to R&D, but, in contrast to the USA and the Soviet Union, it invested more heavily in civilian technologies, advancing in multiple directions and fostering the integration of R&D, production, and technological transfers on the company level (Freeman 1995: 12). In time, the projects became more ambitious, and Japan managed to improve some of the copied technologies well beyond the quality levels achieved by the original producers (Freeman 1995: 11).

The system, which favoured competition against the extant leaders, became such a success at the turn of the 1970s – fuelling Japan's irrepressible rise – that some of the American elites began to believe that Tokyo, rather than Moscow, would become the first rival economy to overtake Washington. During the 1990s, however, the Japanese approach betrayed its limitations. At the time, it was thought that the developmental bureaucratic state did not leave room for the radical innovation that is vital for states and economies seeking to become world leaders (Block 2008: 171). The recommendation for Japan was to revert to a more network-based model, with the state conceding some of its influence on the directions of technological advance and embracing the role of the centrepiece of the network, as a facilitator for new connections and disseminator of knowledge. The challenge is still in front of the Japanese education system, whose high efficiency in the inculcation of basic abilities does not translate into an easy transformation to a model oriented on high-level competencies, especially those rooted in a critical and creative attitude to knowledge. Even today, Japanese schools relay the same values that fed the state's economic miracle: precision, efficiency, discipline, and deference. Parents perceive schools as the surest means to a successful career, as their children are burdened with heavy requirements and forced to apply themselves to learning. A child's future professional standing is very strictly determined by the schools it graduates from. Selection begins at pre-school level, with social divisions reproduced on all stages of education. The pattern is hard to overcome. Next to public education stands a parallel and nearly universal system of cram schools, accessible by way of costly exams. These schools themselves are deeply varied in terms of quality. The pressure of exams that define the educational and professional future of a person is massive, with virtually no alternative routes. Since the 1990s, this standardised system, which leaves so little room for individuality and gives ultimate preference to repetition and reproduction over critical thinking, has been the subject of increasing criticism. Its opponents argue that, while the Japanese 'educational miracle' was erected on a solid and algorithmic foundation that gave birth to the 'economic miracle', it is not clear whether this approach would succeed in the twenty-first century. Among the youth, too, signs of fatigue caused by the heavy toil and high expectations of the generation of their parents are becoming increasingly visible.

Questions such as the excessive burdens shouldered by children and teenagers or the stress induced by the exams, leading to overwork, attract attention. The assumption of a key role by the parallel cram schools is also perceived as problematic. Criticism is levelled against the overburdening of teaching programmes with repetition- and memory-based material. From the social perspective, critics sought to limit the oppressive nature of the system, which had a negative impact on the pupils; in relation to economics, on the other hand, suggestions were made concerning new abilities required for technological change (Central Council for Education 1996: 13).

These recommendations aimed to radically differentiate and liberate the traditionally centralised and standardised Japanese schools. The government set about implementing some of the changes: time spent at school was decreased, with the scope of compulsory instruction somewhat limited, and schools were encouraged to diversify their programmes and teaching methods. However, there is much to suggest that Japan has still not achieved a radical reform of its education system or established world-class research universities. Japanese schools still derive their power from deep-set social control, both on the part of the institutions themselves and the parents, and the content they disseminate is of an obviously algorithmic and memory-based nature (Green 2013: 376–379; Akiyoshi 2008).

Critiques of the commodification of knowledge and abilities

Aside from charges against the theoretical clarity of the notion of human capital and the methodology of measuring it, liberal research programme has sparked serious axiological controversies resulting primarily from the philosophical leanings of particular critics in the areas of politics and the economy. This fragment provides a brief discussion of these controversies.

One important current of critique focuses on the instrumentalisation of both knowledge and humanity, treated in this approach as merely the means to economic growth. The focus here is on the reductionism and limited purview of the approach, concentrated on a narrow range out of the wealth of social processes, only to the extent that they contribute economically. The proponents of human capital theory point out that their approach does not decide the value of other aspects of life, simply leaving them be. However, critics reply that this line of thinking – the commodification and commercialisation of knowledge and subjection of everything to the market – leads to real negative change both in state education policy and in the goals and rules of the game that educational institutions define for themselves. In a longer view, this contributes to the rise of forms of social behaviour identified with the *homo oeconomicus*, tying individuals ever more strongly to economic gain and rational calculation, engagement only in those pursuits that are the most profitable. Marxists, on the other hand, criticise human capital theory on the assumption that the conventional education system performs more duties than just the dissemination of abilities. More importantly, it achieves the segmentation of the labour force and prevents the formation of class-consciousness among the workers, legitimising economic inequalities with an open, objective, and ostentatiously meritocratic mechanism assigning individuals to workplaces of divergent worth (Bowles and Gintis 1975: 77–78). School should serve as a means to emancipation and social change and teach democracy instead of inculcating abilities of use to business (McLaren 2007). Finally, it is vital that attention be devoted to care of a broader community and cooperation for the common good rather than being turned primarily towards individual welfare. The dominant mode of socialisation today reinforces social Darwinism, which Marxists perceive, in fact, as an indelible part of capitalism as a socio-economic system.

Critiques are also levelled against the notion of competitive advantages. Philip Cerny (1999) points out that providing favourable conditions for business often becomes the most important, if not the only, goal of the state, at the expense of most of the society. The goals of business are not always – and not completely – aligned with those of the entire society; a part of the concept of the competition state entails the acceptance of a drastically narrow definition of public good, understood solely through the prism of economic efficiency and optimised allocation, and not justice. As a result, public welfare provided for by the state now arbitrarily includes everything that business requires and fosters favourable conditions for investment – human capital, infrastructure, support for new technologies, and basic services related to 'quality of life', as requested by the elites. Meanwhile, redistributive goods historically provided by welfare states are excluded. Common welfare, of course, is beside the point. The transition from static comparative advantages to competitive advantages which the state can affect deepened its marketisation as an entity, diverting an increasing part of attention and resources in that direction. It also subjected the state to ever more pressure from the perspective of transnational relations and mutual dependency. As a result, Cerny observes (1999: 18), states find it harder to operate strategically in the way that the so-called developmental states used to.

Fierce opposition is also expressed against the category of employability and lifelong learning (LLL). Though the mainstream accepts the value of schools and universities as institutions teaching individuals to be elastic in the face of unpredictable shifts on the labour market, critics note that this only serves to accustom the employees to a reality that denies them the security of stable employment (Moore 2010: 3). By the same token, the necessity to constantly improve in response to technological advances reflects the decline in quality of life within the society as well as the dissolution of social bonds due to frequent changes between workplaces, which increase competition between workers and destroy solidarity. Criticism is also levelled against the marketisation of not merely the goals of education and science, but also their infrastructure and management, shaped exclusively by the efficiency of cognitive aspects of instruction at the expense of other values (Ball 2003).

Humanist approaches alternative to human capital theory indicate that education is a value even when it cannot be translated into income or economic growth. In fact, in their view, it is income increases that are instrumental to general welfare and high quality of life. Proponents of this line of thinking question the implications of teaching to the young that they are harnessed to the common effort by the state to produce and sell as many goods as possible at maximum productivity and profit. What this message implies is that labour and consumption are the most significant features of the model of citizenship taught at school, most importantly at the universities.

It is not by accident that the opposition and resistance to this type of change found most vivid expression in states of the global centre, where market reforms in science and academic education went the farthest – Great Britain and Australia. The various dangerous and negative effects of these shifts have been identified – the most significant include the divestment of the academic world from social responsibility, which had traditionally been a feature of these milieus. Critics of the cooperation between science and business argue that rigorous attachment to this model may also lead to the collapse of those academic disciplines whose presence would not be easily represented in terms of economic gains and global competitiveness. The reduction of the goals of knowledge to the production of wealth can only be achieved through divestment from other values, such as the creation of critical scenarios and a critical image of the world or the formation of independent experts, versatile practitioners, and inner-directed citizen. Thus, the negative effect in this context consists in the weakening of those disciplines, which, in spite of their value for the state and society, do not generate economic productivity or innovation and are unlikely to yield cooperative networks with the industry.

Conclusion

Chapter 3 analyses economical mechanisms through which the level of education and science is translated into state power. Engaging writings in economics and economic policies concerning such subjects as human capital, growth theory, competitive advantages, and national innovation systems, I show how skills contribute to wealth and prosperity. I also discuss the challenges that the Third Industrial Revolution brings to education and science and argue that development in those issue-areas is necessary for any state that seeks to occupy a favourable position in the global value chains. From this perspective, education and science serve as additional means of gaining superiority over competitors and of establishing the boundary between economies of the centre and of the periphery. Finally, I show that there are different ways to succeed in education and science, but what works in terms of policies is always embedded in the model of capitalism a given country represents.

Modern education systems formed throughout the nineteenth century in European states, as part of broader state-building processes. Meanwhile, industrialisation gained pace, introducing such a qualitative change to contemporary societies that the period is often referred to as the Second Industrial Revolution. States in which education was made universal and science reached an advanced stage, as well as those that gained access to the knowledge and abilities of people educated in other countries thanks to immigration, proved to have adapted better to economic changes. The scientific discourse that attempts to systematically explain the causal mechanisms within this relationship only emerged in the 1960s, on the foundation of economic models describing growth theory and the implications of the increase of human capital for productivity. Over subsequent decades, debates continued within economic sciences in the attempt to answer the question of the relationship between human abilities and knowledge and its applications. Though these relationships are conceptualised in various ways even today – for example, due to difficulties with isolating and measuring particular variables – it is commonly accepted that education, science, and the uses of knowledge for technological and extra-technological innovation constitute a necessary, though insufficient condition of the economic development of states and of the welfare of societies. The globalisation of international trade, and the development of international value chains in the production of goods and provision of certain services that it entails, alter the conditions of economic competition, with states coming to specialise not so much in any specific commodities, such as agricultural or industrial products or services, but rather partake in various links of production chains. Some of those links yield far greater economic benefits than others. The most profitable phases of the productive processes usually require advanced knowledge, technology, and significant human abilities – resources possessed by the economies of states that reap the greatest rewards from globalisation. They are aided not solely by a greater added value resulting from the kinds of labour they provide, but also by favourable conditions of global competition. The attraction of low costs of labour is highly unstable, since events in other regions may easily exert a negative effect on them: delocalisation of labour-intensive links of the production chains is relatively easy to achieve. Meanwhile, though states which control the knowledge-intensive phases of production also engage in fierce competition, the advantages that they enjoy are more reliable, leading to greater security and stability. The cases of Germany and Japan provide convincing illustrations of the manner in which unique competencies and the system of organisation of labour insulate states against competition, which could cause profitable branches of production to relocate.

The institutional organisation of systems of knowledge and abilities takes a different guise in states that profited the most from the Second Industrial Revolution. Clear differences appear between the political economy of coordinated and liberal market economies, determining, in turn, the kinds of abilities available in specific states. Liberal market economies exploit greater mobility and adaptability resulting from the general skills and conditioning to lifelong learning among the citizen, ranging as far as gaining qualifications in completely new professions. However, they suffer from a lack of specific skills, which are found in abundance in coordinated market economies, whose stable, cooperative relations between the state, the employers, and the employees enable greater stability of employment and long-term investment in professional training of employees within specific trades. The two models, which function as ideal types for the discussion of the mode of organisation of training systems, were elaborated during a lengthy evolution of the local state structures and capitalism as an economic system – and not produced to a pre-determined design.

The observation of various models of capitalism provides a good reference point for the discussion of the degree to which the state should engage in the production of human capital and science and in stimulating innovativeness. It is commonly agreed that the state should provide its citizen with good education and finance basic research, since market mechanisms cannot guarantee the supply of these goods, which, in turn, yield positive externalities, that is, increased gains. Far more divergences emerge in the recommendations for higher education, which some believe to benefit from competition and the differences in quality that it entails, while others put faith in a more even, though still solid offer provided to a broader section of the society instead of the maintenance of a narrow group of institutions of global pedigree. Even more contrast is exhibited in attitudes towards state involvement in stimulating business activity based on knowledge. More liberally inclined experts claim that being able to provide education at a good level and operating scientific institutions capable of applying the findings of scientists from across the world constitute sufficient conditions for entrepreneurs to be able to devise innovative applications. It is the latter, after all, that know better what is worth investing in, and should also bear the cost of the trials they engage in.

Proponents of state involvement, in turn, point out that private enterprises are risk averse, making them unlikely to engage in the truly daring undertakings that decisively affect the international standing of a state. The ability to apply the knowledge produced in another context does not suffice; the government should stimulate, at least selectively, the pursuit of the kinds of knowledge that can generate ground-breaking implementations, while securing the relevant institutional arrangements that will establish the entire infrastructure of relations between science, business, and public institutions.

The debate over which model of public policy is most worth choosing is reasonable, since the league of states which own both advanced knowledge and ground-breaking innovations remains narrow and exclusive. Few states managed to stake a claim to membership in that league since the Second Industrial Revolution. A further perspective in this discussion concerns the issue of the broader conditions of success within these strategies: to what extent does it depend on a more extensive context. Thus returns the question of state-specific economic policies, the quality of institutions, social confidence, and, finally, of culture. Another important aspect is the question of the phase a given state is in, since the few states that have achieved a relative economic progress on a global scale are known to have relied on knowledge transfers rather than taking their own risks at specific stages, while accepting a broader state intervention to secure better conditions for local business enterprises at others.

The commodification of education and knowledge is, finally, an issue that raises major axiological controversies. They find expression in the critique of the reduction of some of the most important institutions of every society to the role of infrastructure for economic growth. In this context, questions are raised over other values endorsed by these institutions. Resistance emerges against attempts to subjugate applied solutions to the demands of the economy, whose global form necessitates a degree of uniformity in teaching and research, leading to the globalisation of education and science. Doubts abound whether humans who truly achieve the highest productivity and operate with ease under international competition also possess the traits most valued in a citizen and member of a national, local, or family community. Questions are raised over the branches of knowledge that focus on identity rooted in a given culture while not generating any economic gains. Among those whose confidence in capitalism as an economic system is limited or non-existent, its transformations cause particular anxiety, since the education of the younger generations and the existence of independently minded academic elites capable of critical reflection on the normative foundations of institutions is traditionally perceived as the foremost means to social change and emancipation of various groups. States which cannot escape the conditions of global competition now find themselves under enormous strain of expectations whose fulfilment does not always translate into harmonious growth. At times, instead, the choice of an alternative entails a loss on the side of other values.

Notes

1 Before that, the idea of human capital was invoked by William Petty, who in 1676 compared the arms, machines, and other wartime losses to the loss of human life.
2 The contemporary discourse attaches major significance to innovation while completely overlooking the role of imitation in the development of civilisation. One interesting context here is the evolutionary approach, which indicates that for most individuals in a majority of cases the optimal strategy is imitation, which minimises the risk of failure (and accounts for the so-called incremental innovation), while radical innovation requires massive investment. In his analysis of cumulative culture, Michael Tomasello (1999) shows how the advantage humans enjoy over other species derives from his ability to accumulate knowledge and reproduce it accurately.
3 Due to the unclear meaning of the term 'neoliberalism', as well as its very broad and ambiguous frame of reference and ideological deployment, I refrain from using it in this work. Vivien Schmidt and Mark Thatcher (2013) propose an interesting analysis of neoliberalism, claiming that the term has recently expanded to include some of the ideas advanced by opponents of the doctrine, effectively deflecting the social resistance to the solutions it proposes. Traditionally, neoliberalism entailed a belief in the free market reinforced by global trade and the mobility of capital, with a market-friendly, limited state – a 'night watchman' promoting an elastic labour market, reducing dependency on welfare, and implementing reforms aimed at floating public services on the open market. Neoliberalism highlights individual responsibility, the value of competition, and the significance of allocation by the market, with the state posited as a problem, and the market as a solution. In Schmidt and Thatcher's opinion, neoliberalism is resilient because, in response to social-democratic assaults, it incorporated some of the values of the welfare state, even as it pursues them by its own peculiar means. The two authors ascribe the expansiveness of the category, first, to the elasticity of the fundamental precepts of neoliberalism, and second, to gaps between neoliberal rhetoric and reality, the strength of neoliberal discourse in public debate, the power of interests behind the strategic deployment of specific ideas, and the tenacity of the institutions that carry those ideas forward

(see also Plant 2009). Moderate liberals criticise neoliberalism for putting too much faith in the market and the excessive deregulation that removes the state from the purposes it is designed to fulfil to maintain the operation of the market, including certain necessary regulations devised to prevent the imperfections of the market from manifesting themselves.

References

Acemoglu, D. (1998). Why do New Technologies Complement Skills?: Directed Technical Change and Wage Inequality. *The Quarterly Journal of Economics* 113(4): 1155–1089.

Acemoglu, D. and D. Autor (2012). What does Human Capital Do?: A Review of Goldin and Katz's the Race Between Education and Technology. *Journal of Economic Literature* 50(2,) http://economics.mit.edu/files/7490 (accessed 8 October 2015).

Akiyoshi, Y. (2008). Facing Crisis. Soft Power and Japanese Education in a Global Context. In W. Yasushi and D.L. McConnell (eds), *Soft Power Superpowers: Cultural and National Assets of Japan and the United States.* New York: M.E. Sharpe, 54–74.

Anderson, P. (1974). *Lineages of the Absolutist State*. London: Verso.

Arrow, K. (1962). Economic Welfare and the Allocation of Resources for Invention. In *The Rate and Direction of Inventive Activity: Economic and Social Factors*. Princeton, NJ: Princeton University Press.

Ashton, D., F. Green, D. James, and J. Sung (1999). *Education, Training and the Global Economy*. Cheltenham: Edward Elgar.

Ball, S. (2003). *Politics and Policymaking in Education: Explorations of Policy Sociology*. London: Routledge.

Barnett, C. (1988). *The Audit of War: The Illusion and Reality of Britain as a Great Nation*. Cambridge: Cambridge University Press.

Barro, R.J. and J.-W. Lee (2001). International Data on Educational Attainment: Updates and Implications. *Oxford Economic Papers* 53(3).

Becker, G.S. (1962). Investment in Human Capital: A Theoretical Analysis. *Journal of Political Economy* 70/5(2): 9–49.

Becker, G.S. (1964). *Human Capital: A Theoretical and Empirical Analysis with Special Reference to Education*. New York: National Bureau of Economic Research.

Block, F. (2008). Swimming Against the Current: The Rise of a Hidden Developmental State in the US. *Politics & Society* 36(2): 169–206.

Bowles, S. and H. Gintis (1975). The Problem with Human Capital Theory: A Marxian Critique. *The American Economic Review* 65(2): 74–82.

Braudel, F. (1984). *Civilization & Capitalism 15th–18th Century: The Perspective of World*. Collins: London.

Brown, P., A. Green, and H. Lauder (2001). *High Skills: Globalisation, Competitiveness and Skill Formation*. Oxford: Oxford University Press.

Brynjolfsson, E. and A. McAfee (2011). *Race Against The Machine: How the Digital Revolution is Accelerating Innovation, Driving Productivity, and Irreversibly Transforming Employment and the Economy*. Lexington, KY: Digital Frontier Press.

Bukowski, M. (ed.) (2015). *Zatrudnienie w Polsce 2014: Praca czasu innowacji*. Warsaw: Centrum Rozwoju Zasobów Ludzkich.

Burks, A.W. (ed.) (1985). *The Modernizers: Overseas Students, Foreign Employees, and Meiji Japan*. Boulder, CO: Westview Press.

Cave, P. (2003). The Inescapability of Politics: Nationalism, Democratisation and Social Order in Japanese Education. In M. Lall and E. Vickers (eds), *Education as a Political Tool on Asia*. London: Routledge.

Central Council on Education (1996). *The Model for Japanese Education in the Perspective of 21st Century: First Report*. Monbusho.

Cerny, P.G. (1995). Globalization and the Changing Logic of Collective Action. *International Organization* 49(4): 595–625.

Cerny, P.G. (1997). The Dynamics of Political Globalization. *Government and Opposition* 32(2): 251–274.

Cerny, P.G. (1999). Reconstructing the Political in a Globalizing World: States, Institutions, Actors and Governance. In F. Buelens (ed.), *Globalization and the Nation-State*. Cheltenham: Edward Elgar.

Chattopadhyay, S. (2012). *Education and Economics: Disciplinary Evolution and Policy Discourse*. Oxford: Oxford University Press.

Cimoli, M., G. Dosi, and J. Stiglitz (2009). *Industrial Policy and Development: The Political Economy of Capabilities Accumulation*. Oxford: Oxford University Press.

Cooper, R. (1961). American Competition in World Markets 1953–1960 (PhD dissertation). Harvard University.

Culpepper, P. and D. Finegold (eds) (2000). *The German Skills Machine: Sustaining Comparative Advantage in a Global Economy*. New York: Berghahn Books.

Cummings, W.K. (1980). *Education and Equality in Japan*. Princeton, NJ: Princeton University Press.

Dee, T. (2004). Are There Civic Returns to Education? *Journal of Public Economics* 88(9–10): 1697–1720.

Denison, E.F. (1962). *The Sources of Economic Growth in the United States and the Alternatives Before Us*. New York: Committee for Economic Development.

Dzierzgowski, J. (2012). Gospodarka oparta na wiedzy: niespełnione obietnice i problem umiejętności (PhD dissertation). Warsaw: Instytut Socjologii UW.

Esping-Andersen, G. (1990). *The Three Worlds of Welfare Capitalism*. Princeton, NJ: Princeton University Press.

Etzkowitz, H. and L. Leydesdorff (1998). The Triple Helix as a Model for Innovation Studies. *Science and Public Policy* 25(3): 195–203.

Etzkowitz, H. and L. Leydesdorff (2000). The Dynamics of Innovation: From National Systems and 'Mode 2' to a Triple Helix of University-Industry-Government Relations. *Research Policy* 29: 109–123.

Farkas, G. (1996). *Human Capital or Cultural Capital? Ethnicity and Poverty Groups in an Urban School District*. New York: De Gruyter.

Federowicz, M. (2004). *Różnorodność kapitalizmu. Instytucjonalizm i doświadczenie zmiany ustrojowej po komunizmie*. Warsaw: Wydawnictwo IFiS PAN.

Fischer, W. and P. Lundgreen (1975). The Recruitment and Training of Administrative and Technical Personnel. In Ch. Tilly (ed.), *The Formation of National States in Western Europe*. Princeton, NJ: Princeton University Press.

Freeman, Ch. (1995). The 'National System of Innovation' in Historical Perspective. *Cambridge Journal of Economics*, 19: 5–24.

Freeman, Ch. and F. Louçã (2001). *As Time Goes By: From the Industrial Revolutions to the Information Revolution*. Oxford: Oxford University Press.

Freeman, Ch. and C. Perez (1988). *Structural Crises of Adjustment, Business Cycles and Investment Behaviour*. London: Pinter.

Freeman, Ch. and A. Young (1965). *The R and D Effort in Western Europe, North America, and the Soviet Union*. Paris: OECD.

Galor, O. (2011). *Unified Growth Theory*. Princeton, NJ: Princeton University Press.

Galor, O. and D. Weil (2000). Population, Technology, and Growth: From the Malthusian Regime to the DEMOGRAPHIC TRANSITION. *American Economic Review* 90: 806–828.

Gereffi, G. and M. Korzeniewicz (eds) (1994). *Commodity Chains and Global Capitalism*. London: Greenwood Press.

Gerschenkron, A. (1962). *Economic Backwardness in Historical Perspective: A Book of Essays*. Cambridge, MA: Belknap Press of Harvard University Press.

Gibbons, M., C. Limoges, H. Nowotny, S. Schwartzmann, P. Scott, and M. Trow (1994). *The New Production of Science and Research in Contemporary Societies*. London: Sage.

Gilpin, R. (1968). *France in the Age of the Scientific State*. Princeton, NJ: Princeton University Press.

Goldin, C. (2014). Human Capital. In C. Diebold and M. Haupert (eds), *Handbook of Cliometrics*. Heidelberg: Springer.

Goldin, C. and L. Katz (2010). *The Race between Education and Technology*. Cambridge, MA: Harvard University Press.

Green, A. (2013). *Education and State Formation: Europe, East Asia and the USA*. Basingstoke: Palgrave Macmillan.

Grieco, J. and J. Ikenberry (2003). *State Power and World Market: The International Political Economy*. New York: W.W. Norton & Co.

Ha, J. and P. Howitt (2006). Accounting for Trends in Productivity and R&D: A Schumpeterian Critique of Semi-Endogenous Growth Theory. *Working Paper*, http://citeseerx.ist.psu.edu/viewdoc/download?doi=10.1.1.182.7331&rep=rep1&type=pdf (accessed 27 August 2015).

Hall, P. and D. Soskice (eds) (2001). *Varieties of Capitalism: The Institutional Foundations of Comparative Advantage*. Oxford: Oxford University Press.

Hamilton, A. (1791). *Report on manufactures*, www.constitution.org/ah/rpt_manufactures.pdf (accessed 22 August 2015).

Hanushek, E.A. and D.D. Kimko (2000). Schooling, Labour-Force Quality, and the Growth of Nations. *The American Economic Review* 90(5): 1184–1208.

Hanushek, E.A. and L. Wössmann (2007). The Role of Education Quality in Economic Growth. *World Bank Policy Research Working Paper, 4122*, https://openknowledge.worldbank.org/bitstream/handle/10986/7154/wps4122.pdf (accessed 7 June 2015).

Hanushek, E.A. and L. Wössmann (2010). Education and Economic Growth. In D.J. Brewer and P.J. McEwan (eds), *Economic of Education*. Amsterdam: Elsevier.

Heckman, J., J. Stixrud, and S. Urzula (2006). The Effects of Cognitive and Noncognitive Abilities on Labor Market Outcomes and Social Behavior. *Journal of Labor Economics* 24(3): 411–481.

Herbst, M. (2012). *Edukacja jako czynnik i wynik rozwoju regionalnego*. Warsaw: Wydawnictwo Naukowe Scholar.

Hobsbawm, E.J. (1969). *Industry and Empire*. Harmondsworth: Penguin.

Hopkins, T. and I. Wallerstein (1986). Commodity Chains in the World-Economy Prior to 1800. *Review (Fernand Braudel Center)* 10(1): 157–170.

Johnson, Ch. (1982). *MITI and the Japanese Miracle: The Growth of Industrial Policy 1925–1975*. Stanford, CA: Stanford University Press.

Kennedy, P. (1987). *The Rise and Fall of Great Powers*. New York: Vintage Books.

Kohli, A. (2004). *State-Directed Development: Political Power and Industrialization in the Global Periphery*. Cambridge: Cambridge University Press.

Kraemer, K., G. Linden, and J. Dedrick (2011). Capturing Value in Global Networks: Apple's iPad and iPhone. *Working Paper*, http://pcic.merage.uci.edu/papers/2011/value_ipad_iphone.pdf (accessed 12 July 2015).

Landes, D.S. (1969). *The Unbound Prometheus: Technological Change and Industrial Development in Western Europe from 1750 to the Present*. New York: Cambridge University Press.

List, F. (1841). *The National System of Political Economy*. English Edition (1909). Longman: London, http://oll.libertyfund.org/titles/315 (accessed 4 June 2015).

Lucas, R. (1988). On the Mechanics of Economic Development. *Journal of Monetary Economics* 22: 3–42.

Lundvall, B.-Å. (1985). *Product Innovation and User-Producer Interaction: Research Report*. Aalborg: Aalborg University Press.

Lundvall, B.-Å. (2015). The Origins of the National Innovation System Concept and its Usefulness in the Era of the Globalizing Economy (paper presented at the 13th Globelics Conference 2015 in Havana, 23–26 September).

McLaren, P. (2007). *Life in Schools: An Introduction to Critical Pedagogy in the Foundations of Education*. Boston, MA: Allyn & Bacon.

Mankiw, G.N., E. Phelps, and P.M. Romer (1995). The Growth of Nations. *Brookings Papers on Economic Activity* 1: 275–326.

Mazzoleni, R. and R.R. Nelson (2009). The Roles of Research at Universities and Public Labs in Economic Catch-Up. In M. Cimoli, G. Dosi, and J. Stiglitz (eds), *Industrial Policy and Development: The Political Economy of Capabilities Accumulation*. Oxford: Oxford University Press.

Mazzucato, M. (2011). *The Entrepreneurial State*. London: Demos.

Meyer, J.W. and M.T. Hannan (eds) (1979). *National Development and the World System*. Chicago, IL: University of Chicago.

Milligan, K.M., E. Moretti, and P.E. Oreopoulos (2004). Does Education Improve Citizenship?: Evidence from the United States and United Kingdom. *Journal of Public Economics* 88(9–10): 1667–1695.

Mincer, J. (1958). Investment in Human Capital and Personal Income Distribution. *Journal of Political Economy* 66(4): 281–302.

Moore, B. Jr. (1966). *Social Origins of Dictatorship and Democracy: Lord and Peasant in the Making of the Modern World*. Boston, MA: Beacon Press.

Moore, P. (2010). *The International Political Economy of Work and Employability*. Basingstoke: Palgrave.

Moretti, E. (2004a). Estimating the Social Return to Higher Education: Evidence from Longitudinal and Repeated Cross-Section Data. *Journal of Econometrics* 121(1–2): 175–212.

Moretti, E. (2004b). Human Capital Externalities in Cities. *Handbook of Regional and Urban Economics* 4: 2243–2291.

Moretti, E. (2004c). Workers' Education, Spillovers, and Productivity: Evidence from Plant-Level Production Functions. *The American Economic Review* 94(3): 656–690.

Nelson, R. (1959). The Simple Economics of Basic Scientific Research. *Journal of Political Economy* 67(3): 297–306.

Nolte, S.N. and S.A. Hastings (1991). The Meiji State's Policy Towards Women, 1890–1910. In G.L. Bernstein (ed.), *Recreating Japanese Women, 1600–1945*. Berkeley, CA: University of California Press.

North, D. (1990). *Institutions, Institutional Change and Economic Performance*. Cambridge: Cambridge University Press.

North, D. and R. Thomas (1973). *The Rise of the Western World: A New Economic History*. Cambridge: Cambridge University Press.

OECD (2002). *Frascati Manual: Proposed Standard Practice for Surveys on Research and Experimental Development*. 6th edn. Paris: OECD.

Painter, F.V.N. (1896). *A History of Education*. New York: D. Appleton & Co. (facsimile: Elibron Classic series 2006).

Passim, H. (1965). *Society and Education in Japan*. New York: Teachers College Press.

Perez, C. (1983). Structural Change and Assimilation of New Technologies in the Economic and Social Systems. *Futures* 15(4): 357–375.

Perez, C. (1985). Microelectronics, Long Waves and Structural Change: New Perspectives for Developing Countries. *World Development* 13(3): 441–463.

Perez, C. (2002). *Technological Revolutions and Financial Capital: The Dynamics of Bubbles and Golden Ages*. London: Edward Elgar.

Perez, C. and L. Soete (1988). Catching Up in Technology: Entry Barriers and Windows of Opportunity. In G. Dosi et al. (eds), *Technical Change and Economic Theory*. London: Francis Pinter.

Plant, R. (2009). *The Neo-Liberal State*. Oxford: Oxford University Press.

Porter, M. (1987). Changing Patterns of International Competition. In David Teece (ed.), *The Competitive Challenge: Strategies for Industrial Innovation and Renewal*. Cambridge: Balliner.

Porter, M. (1990). The Competitive Advantage of Nations. *Harvard Business Review* March–April.

Porter, M. (1998). *The Competitive Advantage of Nations*. New York: Free Press.

Prettner, K. (2012). Public Education, Technological Change and Economic Prosperity: Semi-Endogenous Growth Revisited. *Working Paper No. 90*, Harvard Program on the Global Democracy of Aging, www.hsph.harvard.edu/program-on-the-global-demography-of-aging/WorkingPapers/2012/PGDA_WP_90.pdf (accessed 27 August 2015).

Pritchett, L. (2001). Where has all the Education Gone? *World Bank Economic Review* 15(3): 367–391.

Reich, R.B. (1992). *The Work of Nations: Preparing Ourselves for 21st Century Capitalism*. New York: Vintage.

Reinert, E. (2007). *How Rich Countries Got Rich and Why Poor Countries Stay Poor*. London: Constable & Robinson.

Reinganum, J. (1984). Practical Implications of Game Theoretic Models of R&D. *American Economic Review* 74(2): 61–66.

Rifkin, J. (1996). *The End of Work: The Decline of the Global Labor Force and the Dawn of the Post-Market Era*. New York: Penguin.

Rodrik, D. (2014). The Past, Present, and Future of Economic Growth. *Challenge* 57(3): 5–39.

Rogers, E.M. (2003). *Diffusion of Innovations*. New York: Free Press.

Romer, P.M. (1990). Endogenous Technological Change. *Journal of Political Economy* 98(5): 71–101.

Romer, P.M. (2007). Economic Growth. In *The Concise Encyclopedia of Economics*, www.econlib.org/library/Enc/EconomicGrowth.html (accessed 24 May 2015).

Samuelson, P.A. (2004). Where Ricardo and Mill Rebut and Confirm Arguments of Mainstream Economists Supporting Globalization. *Journal of Economic Perspectives* 18(3): 135–146.

Schmidt, V. and M. Thatcher (2013). *Resilient Liberalism in Europe's Political Economy*. Cambridge: Cambridge University Press.
Schultz, T.W. (1960). Capital Formation by Education. *The Journal of Political Economy* 68(6): 571–583.
Schultz, T.W. (1961). Investment in Human Capital. *American Economic Review* 51: 1–17.
Schumpeter, J.A. (1943). *Capitalism, Socialism, and Democracy*. London: Routledge.
Schwab, K. (ed.) (2012). *The Global Competitiveness Report 2012–2013*. World Economic Forum, www3.weforum.org/docs/WEF_GlobalCompetitiveness-Report_2012-13.pdf (accessed 14 May 2015).
Sedláček, T. (2011). *Economics of Good and Evil: The Quest for Economic Meaning from Gilgamesh to Wall Street*. Oxford: Oxford University Press.
Sharif, N. (2006). Emergence and Development of the National Innovation Systems Concept. *Research Policy* 35(5): 745–766.
Smil, V. (2006). *Transforming the Twentieth Century*, vol. 2: *Technical Innovations and Their Consequences*. Oxford: Oxford University Press.
Smith, A. (1977). *Inquiry into the Nature and Causes of the Wealth of Nations*. Chicago, IL: University of Chicago Press.
Solow, R. (1957). Technical Change and the Aggregate Production Function. *Review of Economics and Statistics* 39: 312–320.
Thelen, K. (2004). *How Institutions Evolve: The Political Economy of Skills in Germany, Britain, the United States, and Japan*. Cambridge: Cambridge University Press.
Tilak, J.B.G. (2002). *Building Human Capital in East Asia: What Others Can Learn*. New Delhi: National Institute of Educational Planning and Administration.
Tomasello, M. (1999). *The Cultural Origins of Human Cognition*. Cambridge, MA: Harvard University Press.
World Economic Forum (2015). *The Human Capital Report. Employment, Skills, and Human Capital: Global Challenge Insight Report*. Davos: World Economic Forum.
Zarycki, T. (2014). Innowacjonizm jako legitymizacja. Dyskursy innowacji, gospodarki opartej na wiedzy, społeczeństwa informacyjnego i pokrewne w perspektywie krytycznej. *Zarządzanie Publiczne* 1(27): 20–34.
Zysman, J. and L. d'Andrea Tyson (eds) (1983). *American Industry in International Competition*. Ithaca, NY: Cornell University Press.

4 International distribution of power and state strategies

This chapter is devoted to a comparison of the power of states in the areas of education and science, and a survey of the scale of global inequalities, which divide the world into the centre and the periphery in this context, as well. Like before, I will focus on the agential aspect of power as defined by Stefano Guzzini in the model applied herein. While discussing state-building processes and the role of education and science in economic welfare, I already devoted some space to the various leaders in these areas across modern history, whose ascendancy often coincided with their status as major powers. Here, aside from presenting the international distribution of power, I will also analyse the strategies that allowed various players to achieve success in the past. The paths they followed were diverse, but always tied to the particular model of capitalism developed in specific instances. The strategies they applied corresponded to the institutional architecture and other conditions peculiar to each case, including access to the supply of talented individuals, in particular. In the absence of such a supply, attempts were made to achieve progress by the means available within the state itself and its own population.

In contrast to the previous chapters, my interests will extend beyond education and science, focusing – though narrowly – on the research and development sector (R&D). The part devoted to the analysis of state strategies discusses the United States, select European countries, Japan, Republic of Korea, Singapore, and China. Unique within this group, the USA owes its position, in part, to the cumulative effect of immigration of thousands of gifted individuals from around the world throughout the twentieth century, which continues today. Europe is closer to representing the strategy of self-reliance, that is, educating its own citizen in local high-quality institutions. Japan and the Asian Tigers thrive on knowledge transfers. Meanwhile, China provides a somewhat distinct case – in spite of enormous advances in the aforementioned areas, it does not warrant naming among global leaders. The PRC owes its presence in this chapter to its status as the most prominent emerging power and a major rival to the USA in international policy.

The previous chapters provided a more general outline of the nineteenth-century patterns of modern state-building and the emergence of twentieth-century theories binding education and science to economic welfare. This part uses empirical data to expand the breadth of those considerations. The description of the distribution of power in education and science and of the specific strategies is based on the theoretical assumptions discussed in Chapters 2 and 3, and present contemporary phenomena against the backdrop of a certain vision of the world. Though this vision might sit comfortably within the mainstream of international debate, this should not be taken to mean that it evokes no controversy or criticism.

International distribution of power in education and science

The international distribution of power in education and science expresses a high degree of variety in the potential of states at all levels of education. With respect to the quality of primary, secondary, and tertiary education, as well as the status of scientific research, one can identify a group of states which occupy dominant positions and achieve remarkable results. Here, the more advanced the level of instruction, the greater the advantage enjoyed by those at the centre. Even as the abilities of pupils in high schools in developed and developing states from the middle of the range do not diverge significantly from those possessed by their counterparts in the most developed states, the dominance the latter exert in higher education and science is undisputable. This difference correlates strongly with expenses, particularly once cumulative investments across many decades are factored in.

Primary and secondary education

There is significant variety in levels of education in different societies across the world, as even the most basic indicators – such as the rate of literacy or the average duration of schooling – show. Though they reflect the quality of instruction only in the most basic skills of reading and writing, these variables capture the extent of the distance between the most advanced states of the world and the global peripheries (Herbst 2012: 10–16). Millennium Development Goals data indicate that, in 2015, 743 million people aged fifteen or over were illiterate, two-thirds of them women. In spite of not being listed among the worst offenders in that regard, India is the state with the largest illiterate population – 273 million.

The number of years spent at school strongly correlates with literacy, though some states, such as Honduras, El Salvador, Kirgizstan, Turkmenistan, and Myanmar, boast low illiteracy rates in spite of comparatively short schooling. On the other hand, there are states which experience consistent levels of illiteracy in spite of longer schooling; such is the case with Botswana, Guyana, Jamaica, Saudi Arabia, and Syria.

All states in the world exhibit a tendency to increase the amount of time young people spend in schools. In addition, record-breaking numbers of people move on to study at universities. This ongoing process began in the nineteenth century, when a handful of the most developed countries introduced compulsory

142 *Power distribution and state strategies*

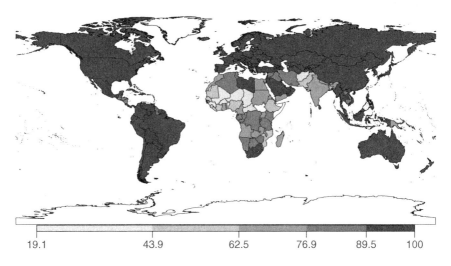

Figure 4.1 Percentage of literate persons in the population of people aged fifteen or more.

Source: own elaboration of UNDP 2012.

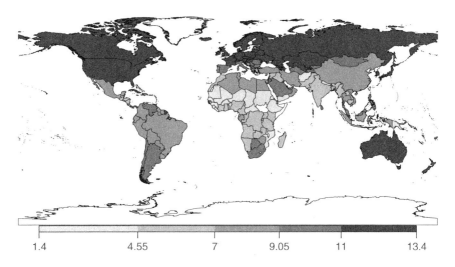

Figure 4.2 Average number of years of schooling for people aged twenty-five or more.

Source: own elaboration of UNDP 2012 (data refer to 2015 or the most recent year available).

education, initially limited to the primary level. Since the 1960s, common access to schooling in developed states was extended to the secondary level, while universities expanded. The distance between the West and the rest of the world in terms of education, though quite substantial in the nineteenth century, motivated developing countries to engage in efforts to mitigate the deficiency during

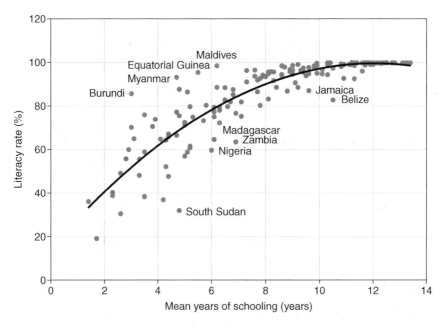

Figure 4.3 Correlation between average duration of schooling and literacy.
Source: own elaboration of data provided by the UNDP.

the second half of the twentieth century. On the one hand, governments were encouraged by the rising educational aspirations of an increasing number of social groups; on the other, the political elites themselves believed that education was a driver of economic development and a means to state-building (Bashir 2007). Public investment in education enabled a larger degree of involvement than private funding would allow. In consequence, educational expenses consumed an increasing share of state expenses; however, outlay in absolute terms remains highly varied between developed and developing states (Attewell and Newman 2010: 5). In the latter, including the Sub-Saharan Africa, substantial progress has been achieved, with education becoming increasingly common and illiteracy on the wane. However, given the fact that these competencies are among the most basic and have become common in developed states of Europe already by the turn of the nineteenth century, and keeping in mind the disparity of resources and investment in education in these states, it is clear that the developing states have not caught up with those in the lead to any degree.

Even comparisons to other underdeveloped states indicate the challenges African populations face in securing access to education. While enrolment at the primary level has increased, the secondary and tertiary levels suffer from massive dropout rates. UNESCO data show that as many as 30 million children in Sub-Saharan Africa do not attend school regularly – over half of all children in the world outside of the school system. Quality is no less of an issue: many pupils finish education without basic abilities, such as reading, writing, or counting. It is estimated that in states with the lowest education levels, as much as 50 per cent of formally literate persons remain functionally illiterate. Without these competencies, the development of more complex abilities is impossible. Shortages of properly trained teachers and quality materials and textbooks remain a challenge (UNESCO 2011). The situation is exacerbated by the fact that the population of Sub-Saharan Africa is the youngest and fastest-growing on all continents, with roughly a third – that is, 300 million people – in the ten to twenty-four age bracket. By 2050, this group is expected to expand to 550 million.

The shortage of basic skills that typifies substantial percentages of the populations of states in the region puts to question their future development. Furthermore, it hampers industrialisation and the implementation of new technologies, both for the expansion of knowledge and abilities, and in labour itself. While the digital revolution has not passed by the least developed states in Africa, with many people using cell phones as well as smartphones, its impact is relatively negative, contributing to the technological gap. These states still face the challenge of expanding secondary education, which has become a standard feature – and a bare minimum – in developed states often as far as fifty years back. Meanwhile, the poorest states in the world still concentrate on ensuring universal access to primary schools with instruction at the lowest quality level. It is still common practice for children of the local elites to be sent to foreign high schools. Educational infrastructure in this region requires substantial qualitative and quantitative improvement if this sizeable group of young people is to fulfil its aspirations, find employment, and contribute to the development of their native states.

The quality of post-primary education may be assessed based on Programme for International Student Assessment (PISA) tests, conducted by OECD on children aged fifteen since 1999 (in three-year intervals). The tests are organised in all member states (thirty-four most-developed states of the world in 2012), as well as partner states (thirty-three in 2012). Thanks to PISA data, Finland's education system achieved worldwide fame due to its ability to ensure both equality of opportunity and formidable effects; at the same time, local public opinion in such states as the USA or Germany was disturbed by surprisingly low results, with expectations far exceeding the outcomes (Wojciuk, Michałek, and Stormowska 2015). PISA tests proved that even among the most developed states of the West, the youth exhibit a diverse range of competencies in mathematical thinking, natural sciences, and reading comprehension. The tests also uncovered the high competencies of the youth in East Asia, while proving the substantial advantage of developed states in the West and Asia – including select cities in China – over the developing states.

Varied educational levels among societies are largely the reflection of the extent of public outlay on education. Twenty per cent of states with the lowest public outlay assign no more than US$16 per year per student; in 20 per cent of the states with the largest expenses in this area, the amount is over US$674. The latter group is very diverse – it includes the borderline case of Norway, investing US$4,500 a year in every student.

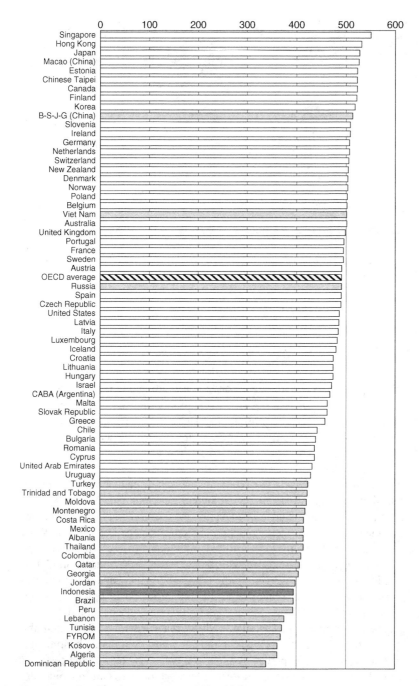

Figure 4.4 Combined average score, PISA 2015.
Source: own elaboration of OECD data.

146 *Power distribution and state strategies*

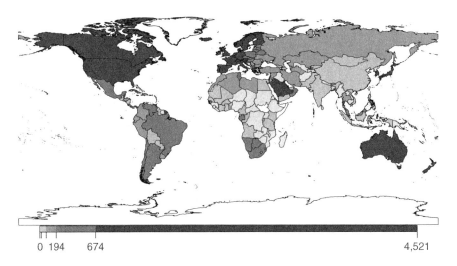

Figure 4.5 Average educational expenses, 1990–2014, represented in constant US$ (2005).

Source: own elaboration of data from the World Bank.

Higher education

Complete expenses on higher education exhibit an even greater variety. Owing to limited participation on the one hand, and underfunding on the other, developing states can offer only low-quality instruction at their universities. Meanwhile, highly developed states carry a substantially larger share of this burden, especially when both public and private expenses are taken into account, allowing for the level of investment in this regard to be compared more effectively between states that deploy different institutional models.

Approaches which underline the economic aspects of education, particularly those that bind it to questions of technological development, ascribe special significance not merely to the general education level of a society, but even more so to hard sciences and engineering (S&E). National Science Foundation (NSF) data indicate that in 2010, over 5.5 million individuals in the world received their first diplomas in these fields, of which 24 per cent were granted in China, 17 per cent in the EU and 10 per cent in the USA. The first decade of the twenty-first century saw a very sharp increase in the number of S&E diplomas, which doubled within just ten years in China, Turkey, Germany, Poland, and Taiwan. In such developed states as Australia, Italy, Great Britain, Canada and the Republic of Korea, the increase fell within the 25–56 per cent range. In spite of a marginal decrease in the percentage of diplomas in hard sciences and engineering, Japan remained on world-record levels at 60 per cent. In China, the recorded increase translated into a 50 per cent share of all diplomas, and in the USA – one-third. The focus on technology that typifies Asian states finds

Power distribution and state strategies   147

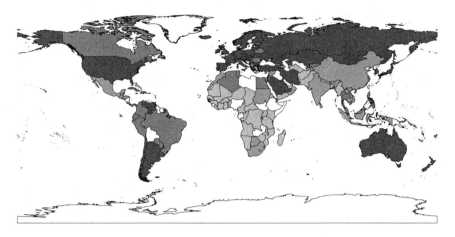

Figure 4.6 Gross schooling rate at ISCED 5 and 6 level.

Source: own elaboration of data from the World Bank. For Canada and Brazil, net schooling levels are represented, based on OECD data.

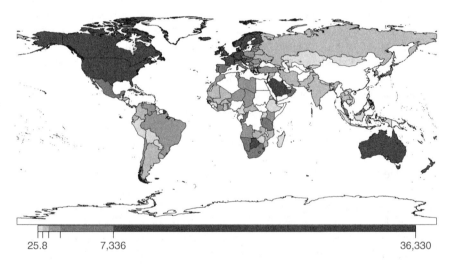

Figure 4.7 Average yearly expenses (public and private) on higher education, 1998–2014, per student in constant US$ (2005).

Source: own elaboration of data from the World Bank (for Germany, owing to gaps in the information available from the World Bank, the data used come from the OECD 2013).

reflection in the ratios of engineers trained there; in the USA, engineers represented 5 per cent of all graduates in 2010, while in Asia the rate was roughly 18–31 per cent in China alone.

However, the United States remain unmatched in terms of the number of doctorates in S&E, arguably an even more representative indicator of the advancement of technological progress.[1] In 2011, 38,000 of such doctorates were granted in the USA, with China, Russia, Germany, and Great Britain being the other major contributors in this category. The number of S&E doctorates has increased at the greatest pace in China and the USA, with the Republic of Korea and many states of the EU achieving more modest results. American research universities clearly switched their focus primarily onto research, with a far lesser interest in instruction, as indicated by statistics on the number of diplomas at specific levels of education. Within the USA, research universities granted as many as 74 per cent of all S&E doctorates, but only 42 per cent of master-level diplomas and 38 per cent of those on the bachelor level, the most common type of S&E diploma in the country.

The processes of establishing major science centres bind together the aspirations of individuals, academic institutions, and states. The most prestigious institutes located in wealthy states of the West find it particularly easy to attract students, doctoral candidates, and scholarly personnel. The best universities and the most advanced states strive to retain the most talented foreigners, who moved there to study or gain academic experience. Due to the personal aspirations of individuals seeking to secure better working conditions, and the actions of institutions and states designing sufficient incentives in the context of global competition and maintaining their talent pool, less developed states lose at least a section of their most intellectually endowed citizenry. There is also a group of states that are in the process of making up for the delay in development, which engage in an active policy of knowledge importation – first, by attracting their own citizen, as well as foreigners, who had acquired it at top institutions, and second, by sending out their citizen to study or engage in post-doctoral work under the condition that they would return to the home country. Universities in developed states grant access to foreign students seeking education – whether to fulfil their own ambitions or as part of government programmes – on a commercial basis. Some states, such as Great Britain and Australia, derive a significant profit from this practice.

The United States and Western Europe educate over two-thirds of all foreign students; the USA remains the most common destination for a majority of internationally mobile students (on the BA and MA levels), though the American share of this market decreased from 25 per cent in 2000 to 19 per cent in 2010. Within the OECD, the USA experienced a relative loss in popularity as the destination for candidates in natural sciences and engineering, while gaining ground in social sciences. Of the 38,000 doctorates in natural and social sciences and engineering granted in the USA in 2011, 56 per cent of candidates in engineering, 51 per cent in computer science, 44 per cent in physics and 60 per cent in economics were foreign nationals.

This illustrates the level of internationalisation of American science and points to one of the sources of the state's unmatched global standing. While education is what the global centre sells to the periphery, the most prestigious institutions in the world actively compete for gifted students. Exploiting the enormous advantage in resources, they can provide their employees with financially and socially unparalleled working conditions and offer possibilities of self-improvement and career development beyond the reach of their poorer competitors. American universities process a disproportionately large number of the most gifted young scholars from around the world in relation to the size and wealth of the USA.

In the early twenty-first century, 67 per cent of foreign-born persons who received doctoral diplomas in S&E from American universities remained in the country for at least five years. Though the ratio decreased in the wake of the 2008 crisis, by 2011, it bounced back at 66 per cent. While some of the most gifted young scholars return to their home countries – either as part of a strategy of developing their potential, or for personal reasons, not having considered permanently relocating to the USA – a significant percentage remains at American universities. A proportion decide to seek employment in other states of the OECD, where competition is not as intense as in the USA, and conditions remain highly favourable. Thus emerges a system in which the USA operates as a global magnet for students, reaping the benefits of immigration by retaining some of the most gifted foreigners trained in America. Owing to their prestige and financial resources unmatched by any other institution of higher learning, American universities also have the most drawing power for scholars from outside of the USA. In 2010, of $c.360,000$ doctoral candidates in the country, $c.295,000$ have previously received education in the USA, while the rest did not. The percentage of US-trained doctors employed at American universities dropped from 55 per cent in 1973 to 44 per cent in 2010, while the share of immigrants among them increased from 12 per cent to 26 per cent in the same period. In 2010, as well, roughly 50 per cent of graduates of doctoral studies in the USA who went on to enrol in post-doctoral programmes inside the country were foreign-born, with nearly 75 per cent of all employees in these programmes being immigrants. A substantial percentage of foreign-born scholars – over 40 per cent in 2011 – is recorded in Switzerland, too. The strategy is also broadly applied by institutions in France, the Netherlands, and New Zealand.

The number of students seeking further education outside of their home countries has clearly grown, currently reaching almost three million people. A major part of this international migration of students has a commercial character at least for one side of the exchange. Foreign students become a source of increasing income for universities in host countries, most of which are in the English-language sphere. On the other side, the motives for migration vary, with data providing only ambiguous accounts of the types of migration taking place. A significant proportion of student migrations are an expression of individual aspirations for improving one's education, but conscious actions by states, which implement scholarship programmes promoting such migrations, have an increasing impact on the situation.

Foreign enrolment generates the most profit for the USA (US$22 billion in 2012), Great Britain (US$15 billion), Australia, Canada, New Zealand, Denmark, the Netherlands, and Switzerland (OECD 2008; Global Demand for English Higher Education 2014). States which export education actively promote their services; candidates receive the necessary information and support in dealing with formalities from such programmes as Study in Germany, Study in Australia, or Education UK. In the USA, campaigns of this kind are organised on the federal level by Education USA (a programme operated by the Department of State) and Study USA (controlled by the Department of Commerce), as well as certain specific states (e.g. Study New York, Study Oregon, or Study Maine).

Though the USA enjoys global superiority in terms of the number of foreign students at its universities – 764,000 in 2012 (rising from 200,000 in 2006) – in Great Britain, foreigners make up the highest proportion of the student body (nearly 50 per cent). In the academic year 2012–2013, 300,000 foreign students (including EU nationals) were enrolled in British institutions on all levels of higher education – a sixfold increase in comparison to 1980. At the same time, the proportion of students from outside of the EU – primarily East Asia and Brazil – also grew (Global Demand for English Higher Education 2014). Meanwhile, the number of students from India and Pakistan is in relative decline owing to the fact that they increasingly choose to enrol in Australia and the USA. Great Britain, Australia, and the USA are especially popular among BA students; however, the percentage of foreigners in the student body is higher in doctoral and post-doctoral programmes.

Among the Chinese, who provide the most foreign students, the five most popular destinations are the USA (110,000), Japan (78,000), Australia (58,000), Great Britain (45,000), and the Republic of Korea (31,000). Indian students enrol in the USA (95,000), Australia (27,000), and Great Britain (24,000). Of Brazilians pursuing studies abroad, a third choose the United States.

American and British universities also draw a sizeable profit from their foreign-based campuses and programmes, which allow students to obtain a diploma from an Anglo-Saxon school without setting a foot in its home country, usually by way of a partner institution. Foreign campuses are higher education

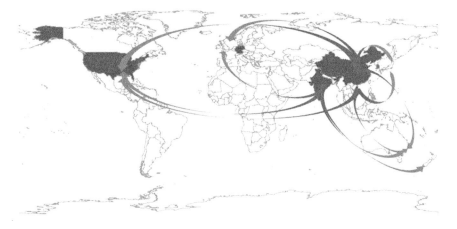

Figure 4.8 States exporting the most students abroad and main directions of migration.
Source: own elaboration of data from the UNESCO.

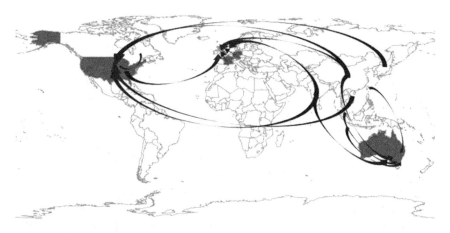

Figure 4.9 States hosting the most foreign students and major sources of migration.
Source: own elaboration of data from the UNESCO.

institutions owned partly by a foreign university, which use its name and offer an at least partially stationary programme (i.e. not solely online), providing the opportunity to obtain a diploma of the institution the given campus represents (Wojciuk 2018). The campuses established in this manner differ widely in size and offer, ranging from just one to dozens of programmes. The number of students enrolled at foreign campuses also varies, from a few dozen to several thousand. While these campuses essentially focus on teaching, they show an increasing tendency to engage in scientific research.

In 2014, over 220 of such institutions existed, the greatest proportion of them (roughly 30 per cent) belonging to American universities, with Australia and Great Britain also enjoying a considerable share of the market. Foreign campuses were also operated by scientific institutions from Russia, China, Malaysia, the Netherlands, and Venezuela. Some states both admit foreign scholarly institutions and fund them, as is the case with Canada, Malaysia, Belgium, France, Italy, Mexico, the Netherlands, Russia, the Republic of Korea, and Switzerland. Though such institutions typically add to the existing local higher education offer, in such states as Qatar and the United Arab Emirates, they constitute the most important centres for higher education. In the Gulf States, foreign campuses also serve as a tool for technological transfer, especially with regard to the oil industry. In many cases, they also act as culture centres for the exporting states. Foreign campuses should not be confused with the chapters that scholarly institutions establish abroad for research purposes. The practice has a long history, and the posts of this kind serve to further the development of various disciplines, from formal sciences, through natural sciences, to the humanities. Foreign research chapters increasingly serve as a means to providing practical experience abroad for students from leading universities.

Internationalisation is also achieved by way of joint-diploma and dual-diploma programmes. Here, too, the USA and Great Britain dominate. Dual diplomas are the more common solution, since they allow both universities to retain control over the programme, while joint-diploma programmes only demand common didactic requirements. In the academic year 2012–2013, these programmes provided access to higher education for nearly 550,000 people, mostly in Asia, in such states as Malaysia, China, and Hong Kong. Outside of East Asia, a mass presence of such joint operations is observed in Nigeria.

Though the internationalisation of higher education can be traced back to the hegemony of Western science and culture during the colonial era, its current mass form is mostly defined by commercial considerations. In English-speaking countries, universities charge higher fees from foreign students, unless they come from states within the EU, which has banned such practices. These means provide a significant source of income for universities, especially during a period marked by decreasing public investment in higher education, particularly pronounced in recent years in Great Britain. Profit is also a motive for those universities which establish campuses abroad. On the one hand, the international mobility of students can be seen as an opportunity to combat educational inequality and pursue an equalisation of the potential of states, but on the other, the end result is often a 'brain drain' that leads talented individuals from less developed countries to emigrate permanently to richer states, increasing the gap between the scholarly centre and the peripheries.

Due to the increasing importance of education and science for economic progress and social development broadly conceived, it has become more common for peripheral and semi-peripheral states to pursue knowledge and skill transfers by advocating specific forms and directions of migration, and to attract educational institutions from the centre. On the other hand, states of the centre typically treat knowledge transfers as business ventures, rarely seeing them as instruments of development aid. As a result, the exchange of knowledge, abilities, and the people who bear them begins to subscribe to the rules of commodity trading. Increasingly, terms such as export and import are used in reference to knowledge. Such an approach to education does generate controversy and resistance from its detractors. Proponents of Marxist approaches identify this phenomenon as a part of the broader process of commodification, which transforms goods heretofore immune to the exigencies of the market into saleable products. According to critics, commodification leads to the erosion of social values, displaced by a market-dominated ethic, while various means of social coordination and the axiological layer of education dissolve.

The structure of international trade in higher education clearly reflects the centre-periphery distinction, with the centre cast as the exporter and the peripheries and semi-peripheries as the importers. Semi-peripheral states, in particular, seek to expand human capital to improve their global economic standing and move to a better position in the value chains. Within the same interaction, states of the centre use their higher education systems to export knowledge and extract a rising profit from the transaction. As a result of the global increase of demand, the higher education sector comes to play an ever-more significant role in the economy. Aside from such benefits as the extension of access to higher education for increasing numbers of people from various countries, the phenomenon also creates threats, as the ideal of the university as the location of an independent pursuit of the truth becomes untenable in these conditions outside of elite institutions. In addition, the tension between instruction geared towards general development and an entirely utilitarian approach based on the dissemination of purely practical knowledge with debatable long-term use value is on the rise.

Subjected to the pressures of competition, British and Australian universities, as well as their American counterparts which operate under conditions of massive demand, have increasingly shifted to a business model to maximise productivity. An analogous process is taking place in scientific research, with incentives designed to foster the publication of partial, and even incomplete results, while undervaluing scientific programmes which require a long-term investment and tend to yield new ideas and solutions. This tendency towards the commodification of higher education is increasingly expressed in the practice of replacing scholars at the highest levels of leadership with professional management, oftentimes transferred directly from the corporate world.

Aside from using higher education and science to establish their scientific and research potential or produce immediate economic gains, states sometimes use the transnational mobility of scholars and students for purely political purposes. By inviting representatives of other states into their universities, they attempt to improve their prestige, and in some cases affect their future influence abroad, even though this mechanism is far from direct and not easily controlled. In special circumstances, when the policy goal is to promote democracy and human rights in other states, strengthening the local oppositional elites might serve as an intermediate tool. Such exchanges also often serve to establish a common understanding between the foreign guests from national elites and the host state. This strategy is distinguished by the absence of commercial interest, with no immediate gain for either the state or the host institution. Furthermore, such programmes usually do not foresee the possibility of allowing participants to extend their stay beyond the stated length. To limit the risk of brain drain, those invited are sometimes forced to sign a pledge to return to the home country after completing training or studies (Wojciuk 2014: 221–222).

These programmes tend to be administered by ministries (usually of foreign affairs, education, higher education, science, or development), state agencies, private foundations, and sometimes by academic institutions themselves, using government funding. The practice dates back to colonial times, when the elites of conquered societies pursued studies in the capitals and other major academic centres of the metropoles. During the nineteenth and twentieth centuries, such activities were not subjected to any institutional or bureaucratic control – they progressed spontaneously, inadvertently establishing paradigms for conscious policies (Wojciuk 2014: 222–223).

The mechanics of such interventions are based on the assumption that foreigners will serve as a sort of conveyor belt for the ideas and norms inculcated at the metropolis, becoming informal ambassadors of the host states. The efficiency of these programmes depends on the successful selection of candidates – thus, governments usually extend their invitations to actual or potential civic leaders, as well as scientists, intellectuals, and journalists considered important for shaping public opinion. In contrast to commercial mobility, recruitment for such programmes can sometimes occur by way of deliberate selection, by inviting specific persons. Though these invitations may be accompanied with certain public pronouncements, applications often involve informal contact between the parties, practically limiting the extent of free competition for a given scholarship. One exemplary case of such activities is the Fulbright Programme, in operation since the Cold War, which became a means to influencing the process of elite formation in real socialist states. The initiative dates back to 1946 and was designed to involve students, scholars, teachers, and artists in the pursuit of peaceful understanding through an international educational exchange. Established by a special act of the US Congress, it came under the administration of the Department of State. The programme allows US citizens selected on a competitive basis to travel abroad for study and research, and foreign nationals to organise and finance analogous stays in the USA. In operation for seven decades, the programme involved over 325,000 persons from 155 states, almost two-thirds of them non-US citizen. The success of the recruitment policy is attested to by the fact that the list of participants includes fifty-three Nobel Prize winners and seventy-eight Pulitzer Prize recipients, as well as eighteen future heads of state and prime ministers.[2]

Broader participation and less elitism are exhibited by EU's Erasmus-Socrates programme, whose goals include fostering a sense of European identity, citizenship, and common understanding between Europeans from various member states. The assumption that participation in a foreign-based programme permanently moulds a political leader, however, can prove erroneous. One infamous case is Hungarian Prime Minister Viktor Orbán, once a recipient of a scholarship funded by George Soros, who has since chosen to lend voice to convictions quite distinct from those promoted by Soros. Limited evidence about the perception of host countries among international students suggests, in fact, that exchanges do not necessarily produce positive attitudes towards another culture (Wojciuk 2018).

Some states also use knowledge export as a tool of development policy. An analysis by UNESCO (2005: 192) indicates that countries such as Canada, Finland, and Norway attach relatively large significance to education as an element of development aid. In absolute terms, though, the greatest spenders in that regard are France, Japan, and Germany. In contrast to the training of the elites, the use of education as a part of development aid generally involves only primary and secondary education.

Scientific research

International comparisons are particularly affected by the intensity of scientific activity, which constitutes a key aspect of a state's ability to attract foreign talent, both among scholars and doctoral candidates. Indicators that both measure the intensity of scientific activity and take the size of the population into account include the number of scholars, the number of Journal Citations Index (JCR) publications, and the amount of JCR citations per 1,000 inhabitants. The absolute number of scholars employed in a given state again highlights the advantage enjoyed by the USA, which employs over one-third of all scholars in the OECD, even though the rate per 1,000 favours other states, such as Switzerland, Germany, and Sweden. Meanwhile, the publication indicator underlines the unparalleled advances of scholars from Sweden.

An analysis of S&E publications proves that the impact of the USA, the EU, and Japan – the traditional global centre in terms of science – has been waning over the past few decades, while that of China increased dramatically. In 2011, 26 per cent of all S&E articles originated in the USA (a drop from 30 per cent in 2001). The EU's share declined from 35 per cent in 2001 to 31 per cent in 2011, while Japan accounted for 9 per cent and 6 per cent, respectively. China, on the other hand, experienced the highest rise, from 3 per cent to 11 per cent, becoming the third biggest producer of basic research articles after the EU and the USA. Other states with a heretofore insignificant presence – Brazil (2 per cent), India (3 per cent), and Iran (1 per cent) – have also markedly increased their impact.

Articles written in the USA tend to gain the most citations, but the numbers have lessened in the last decade. In 2012, articles by individuals from the USA made the top 1 per cent in the amount of citations at a likelihood exceeding the expectation based on the actual number of works originating in the USA by 75 per cent (a relative decline in comparison to 2002, when the rate was assessed at as much as 85 per cent). The impact of articles from the EU has increased: in 2002, they exerted an impact 21 per cent lower than expected given their number in terms of the likelihood of breaking into the 1 per cent of the most cited items, while by 2012, the index recorded a rise to just 6 per cent below expectations. As far as articles produced in China are concerned, the likelihood of making the top 1 per cent of most cited articles was lower by 37 per cent than the number of articles published would suggest.

The degree of internationalisation of science and research also exerts a significant influence. Since the resources – both intellectual and financial – of states and institutions are limited, a large proportion of the necessary knowledge must come from abroad. International networking allows universities to increase their development potential by reinforcing the general level of competency and adding to the resource pool. International mobility provides the opportunity for cooperation with leading experts and formation of scientific relations, exchange of scholarly views and didactic experiences, and the use of infrastructure unavailable at one's home institution.

Aside from such obvious benefits, engagement in an international network provides an opportunity of access to so-called tacit knowledge, which can decide the fate of scholarly undertakings to nearly the same degree as openly expressed knowledge. The most common indicators in this context are the number/percentage of foreign students and doctoral candidates and the mobility

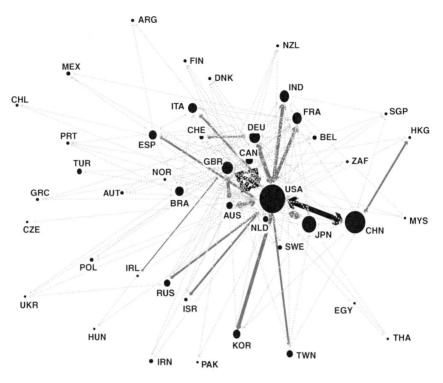

Figure 4.10 Analysis of network of international mobility of scientists.
Source: own elaboration of OECD 2013.

of students, academic teachers, and experts at universities and polytechnics. The directions of mobility and the vectors of international cooperation in science and research again exhibit significant divergence, betraying a major contrast between states of the global centre – English-speaking countries, Western Europe, Japan, and certain East Asian states, as well as countries rich in potential and involved in the process of catching up with their more developed counterparts, most prominently China – and the rest of the world, often completely absent from these maps. Network analysis also clearly shows that the internationalisation of science, as indicated by cooperative publications of scientists from countries all across the world, is on the rise. Over the last twenty years, the number of such publications has doubled. More than two-thirds of S&E publications from 2012 were authored by representatives of more than one institution. The weak are already at a disadvantage for being unable to strategically exploit the new conditions.

The aforementioned inequalities in educational and scientific potential largely explain the dominance of American universities in international rankings. In spite of many methodological reservations that such comparisons attract, they

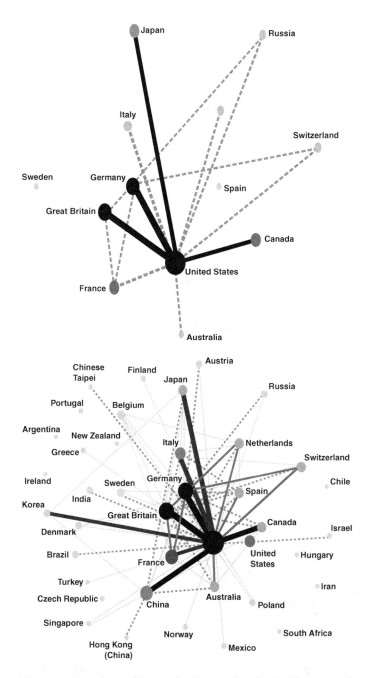

Figure 4.11 Analysis of international networks of scientific cooperation as measured by cooperative publications in 1998 and 2011.

Source: own elaboration of OECD 2013.

remain a relevant reference point. As far as they are concerned, the Anglo-Saxon hegemony is uncontested. Once the range of analysis is limited to the top 100, or even the top 400, as in ARWU (the so-called Shanghai Ranking), a sharp boundary emerges between the global centre of science and states in the peripheries. In this regard, the position of the USA seems unthreatened – there are merely a handful of other significant players: Great Britain, Germany, the Netherlands, Japan, Canada, France, Australia, Switzerland, Sweden, and Israel. Meanwhile, Italy, Belgium, China, and Denmark constitute a 'contact group' behind the world leaders. At least one 'top 200' university can also be found in Brazil, the Russian Federation, Austria, Argentina, Finland, Singapore, Hong Kong, Mexico, the Republic of Korea, and Norway.

The other countries have no university among the best 200, which illustrates the distance between these states in spite of the critiques levelled at the methodology of the ranking. The use of the number of universities in a state as a measure of advancement in higher education is misleading in the sense that it privileges large states. These conditions serve to highlight even more vividly the achievements of smaller states in Scandinavia and East Asia, which, though wealthy in per capita terms, do not possess populations comparable to those of the global powers; yet, they do figure prominently on the world map of science. At the same time, not all states with sizeable per capita income are a presence on the global scientific scene. In particular, the Gulf States, whose economies depend on the exploitation of natural resources, perform far below the expectations based on their GDP.

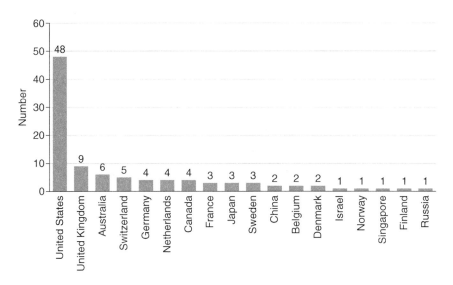

Figure 4.12 The number of universities in the top 100 of the Shanghai Ranking (ARWU) of higher education institutions, by state.

Source: own elaboration of data from ARWU (www.shanghairanking.com; accessed 29 October 2017).

Power distribution and state strategies 159

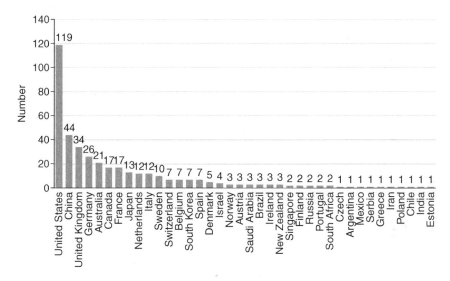

Figure 4.13 The number of universities in the top 400 of the Shanghai Ranking (ARWU) of higher education institutions, by state.

Source: own elaboration of data from ARWU (www.shanghairanking.com; accessed 29 October 2017).

A simple regression of the results from the Shanghai Ranking of research institutions and the Global Competiveness Index of the World Economic Forum for 2012–2013 indicates a clear positive correlation between the number of ARWU 'top 400' research institutions per 10,000,000 inhabitants and competitiveness. Comparisons of the listings of recipients of the Nobel Prize and the Fields medal – an equivalent of the former in mathematics – in states at low, average, and high degrees of development show that activity in the field of hard sciences and mathematics is almost completely dominated by the most developed states, while achievements in culture and social activity provide a more balanced relationship, as reflected in Nobel Prizes for literature and peace.

Today, universities are increasingly perceived as a key means to internationalisation of the economy and society, attracting a highly skilled labour force and foreign investment, and contributing to a positive environment for business. According to now-fashionable precepts, internationalised higher education and science should facilitate a state's adjustment to economic change. Though not all contemporary universities have an international profile, the processes of globalisation apply to any and all of them as its objects or victims, but also, in part, as its subjects and key actors (Scott 1998: 122). Merely a generation ago, international relations had negligible impact on the life of universities outside of a narrow range of research. The contemporary shift is accompanied by the emergence of new players, particularly China and India, and the increased significance of market forces. The pressure of rankings, comparisons, and benchmarks

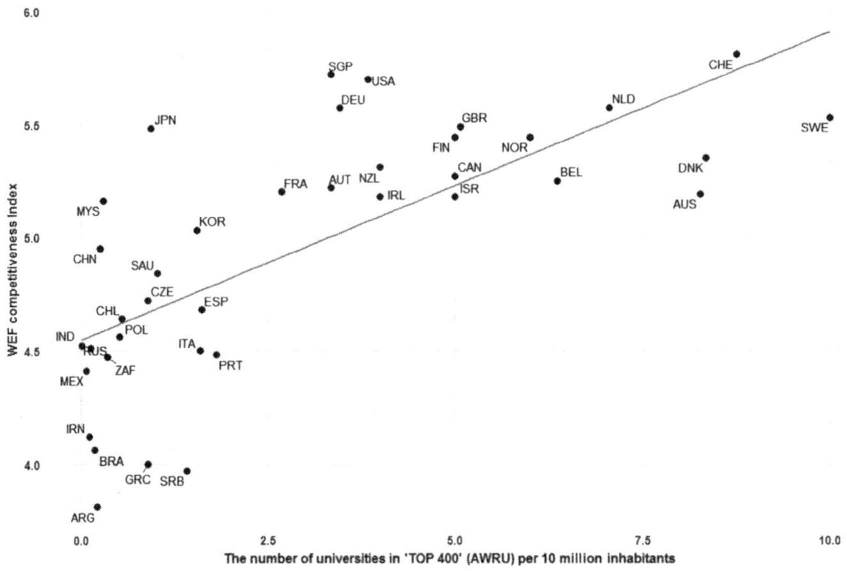

Figure 4.14 Correlation of the number of universities in the 'top 400' (AWRU) per ten million inhabitants and WEF competitiveness index.

Source: own elaboration of data from ARWU (www.shanghairanking.com; accessed 29 October 2017).

is on the rise, as is the demand for financial efficiency. To a degree, this leads to the convergence of academic and research institutions, as the measurable effects of their labours increasingly transform into informal requirements and measures of the fulfilment of global standards. The commercial activity of the university also encourages both the recipients and the providers of its services to comparisons. The interest in rankings of educational and scientific effects and lists of top universities are gaining in popularity. However, this is rarely paired with an in-depth analysis of the components of these indicators.

Given that a rising number of states seek to establish world-class universities, and international rankings are mostly based on research-related indicators, the rivalry for scientific talent heats up. The competition is even more tense due to the fact that access to research funding is regulated externally rather than according to rules established by professional academic unions, as had been the case thus far. Reforms are usually justified with the need for accountability in research activity.[4] While the impact of higher education and science on the labour market is appreciated, comparatively less attention is devoted to expenses that had attracted the most attention up to now. In spite of the rising significance of demand-driven methods of assigning research funds, most OECD states still largely subscribe to the traditional mode of funding, based on supply mechanisms. Yet, reforms bring forth a gradual expansion of the Anglo-Saxon model

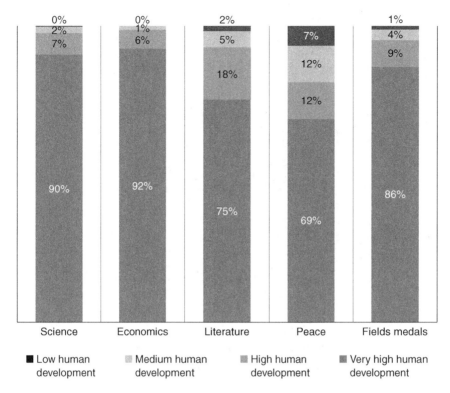

Figure 4.15 The share of states on all levels of development (according to HDI) in the overall amount of Nobel Prizes and Fields medals.

Source: own elaboration of information from nobelprize.org (accessed 29 October 2017).

of organisation of the university, fostering competition in disregard of the distinct local traditions. In many states, the implementation of the foreign model results in protest from the academic circles. Even in Anglo-Saxon states, changes spark resistance against the incorporation of ever-broader market solutions in higher education and funding allocation for basic research. The promotion of the image of a proper scholar as, among other things, an enterprising person invested in the commercial application of their achievements, evokes similar distaste (Jemielniak and Greenwood 2015).

The strong position of universities in English-speaking states and the most advanced regions of Asia and Europe is also reflected in the flow of students and scientific workers. The global distribution of power correlates with this map of migrations both in terms of directions and extent. The benefits of globalisation in higher education are distributed unevenly. Strong states and top universities act like magnets, drawing in gifted scholars, doctoral candidates, students, as well as research sponsors and profits from enrolment fees. For some institutions, international activity has become the most important driver of development and a

162 *Power distribution and state strategies*

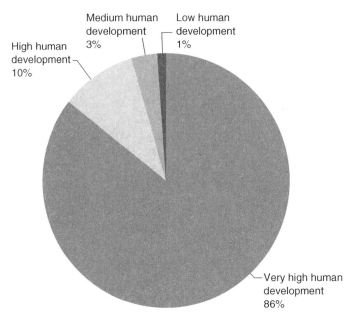

Figure 4.16 The share of states on specific levels of development (according to HDI) in the overall amount of Nobel Prizes and Fields medals.

Source: own elaboration of information from nobelprize.org and mathunion.org (accessed 29 October 2017).

major source of income. In weaker states, on the other hand, these phenomena result in brain drain and loss of talent – often fostered at a relatively higher cost than in states of the centre.

The globalisation of higher education and science is, in part, a result of strategies applied by states which, on the one hand, attempt to gain capabilities in these areas, and on the other, seek to reap the rewards of the potential they have by exploiting the high demand for specialised knowledge. Knowledge importation plays a significant part here, usually taking the guise of individual mobility on the part of students and scientific workers equipped with experience from the global centre, whether gained through own activity or as a result of the policies of a government. They are encouraged to seek employment in states that are only establishing their capabilities. Governments are equally involved in the regulation of student flows, both on the side of the countries of origin and the hosts. Through intervention, or lack thereof, authorities maintain a decisive role in regulating policies for higher education and science in their international aspect. Though academic and scientific institutions often enjoy a significant autonomy and take part independently in transnational interactions, states that carry the most weight in these areas engage in an active pursuit of involving these institutions in activities aligned with the state interest (Wojciuk 2014: 220).

Research, development, and applications

The effort put into forming and attracting foreign talent is supposed to achieve the expansion of a state's economic potential, which, in turn, depends on the efficiency of the transfer of knowledge and human capital to enterprises. This efficiency depends on a distinct logic quite removed from simple automatism. For it to occur, it is necessary that, first, the right enterprises exist which can exploit the available potential. Even before the internationalisation of science and higher education had intensified, the very high incidence of highly qualified persons among immigrants in developed states was recognised as a fact. It was estimated that towards the end of the twentieth century, up to a third of scientists and engineers born in developing states were employed in states of the global North (Carrington and Detragiache 1998). Their productivity, as measured by publications and patents, is significantly higher in their current places of residence than it would have been in their home countries, where the necessary infrastructure is lacking in institutional, physical and basic human terms, scientific cooperation within teams of specialists being far harder to achieve (Meyer and Brown 1999). While knowledge is mobile, its dissemination on the international level is not entirely spontaneous, but rather largely the result of conscious state policies.

In the USA, 70 per cent of holders of S&E diplomas find employment in private enterprises, while 19 per cent work in education, and 11 per cent – in the government; however, in terms of doctorate distribution, the distribution among the particular sectors is much more even-handed, with roughly 45 per cent apiece going into business and academia. Interestingly, companies with 100 or fewer employees provide employment to as much as 37 per cent of S&E doctorate recipients. However, since the 1990s, the highest dynamic of increase in the number of these workplaces has been observed in China and the Republic of Korea, while the USA and the EU experienced consistent, but less dramatic growth than these East Asian states. In Japan, the number remained constant, while in Russia, it declined.

The extent of the brain drain in the poorer countries is best described by statistics provided by the World Intellectual Property Agency. The poorer the state, the more inventors leave it for developed countries. Between 2007 and 2012, 86 per cent of patents submitted by the Vietnamese were filed outside of Vietnam, while only 8 per cent of Norwegian patents were not filed in Norway. Large states endowed with rich research infrastructure, such as the USA or China, lose few inventors, while small ones – even relatively wealthy – struggle to retain them; Estonia is one of the exceptions to this rule (*The Economist* 2015).

R&D occurs at the highest intensity in the USA, China, and Japan, which account for over half of the US$1,430 billion in expenses within this sector, combined. In 2011, the USA, the leader in this aspect, covered 30 per cent of the global expenses on R&D. This marked a decrease in relation to 2001, when the state's share amounted to 37 per cent. Meanwhile, states in East and South-East Asia made a mark – their combined share reached 25 per cent of the global R&D

expenses in 2001, and increased to 34 per cent within a decade.[5] The biggest players within that group were China, responsible for 15 per cent of activity, and Japan, with a 10 per cent share. China's rise occurred at an unprecedented pace, averaging 18 per cent year-on-year (adjusted for inflation). In 2011, the European Union accounted for 22 per cent of R&D activity, registering a 4 per cent drop since 2001.

During the period in question, the USA maintained a stable GDP outlay on R&D, in the 2.6–2.9 per cent range. Higher intensity of involvement was exhibited by Israel, the Republic of Korea, Finland, Japan, Sweden, Denmark, Taiwan, Germany, and Switzerland; however, in terms of absolute expenses, no state matched the USA. Within the EU, Germany held the lead in 2011, with GDP involvement in R&D amounting to 2.9 per cent, followed by France with 2.2 per cent, and Great Britain with 1.8 per cent. In Eastern Asia, the extent of involvement was higher, reaching 4 per cent in Korea, 3.4 per cent in Japan, and 1.8 per cent in China (it should also be noted that it had doubled since 2001).

In 2008, a record year, American enterprises spent US$267 billion on R&D. In spite of the delocalisation of production, American international corporations still continue to conduct up to 85 per cent of their R&D activity within the United States, with the rest taking place mostly in the EU, though even in this respect, Asian states are seeing a positive change. Public expenses on R&D (GERD) grew in all Western states (in constant cost). In the USA, prior to the 10 per cent reduction instituted in 2010, they amounted to almost US$150 billion. More than half of the federal expenses on R&D were made toward military technologies, followed by research into health, whose share in the overall cost had been rising in the past two decades. The expenses were administered by fifteen American ministries and twelve agencies.

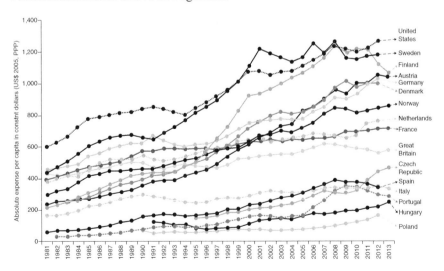

Figure 4.17 Government expenses on research and development (GERD) per capita.
Source: own elaboration of data from OECD.

The role of the conveyor belt between basic and applied research and economic effects is played primarily by the industry, characterised by large knowledge and technology intensity (KTI). The USA exhibits the highest involvement of KTI in the GDP among all major states, posting at 40 per cent, while the EU and Japan record a 30 per cent share. In Brazil, China, and India, the share amounts to roughly 20 per cent, and among middle development states, KTI plays a relatively large role in Turkey (23 per cent). The United States provides 32 per cent of knowledge-intensive services, the EU coming in second with a 23 per cent share in the market. China saw a dramatic increase, reaching an 8 per cent share, on par with Japan. In advanced technologies, the USA is responsible for 27 per cent of production, while China for 8 per cent (doubled between 2002 and 2012).

In 2012, more investment into renewable energy technologies was recorded in developing states than in their developed counterparts. China took the lead, with complete cost of investment in the field reaching US$60 billion in 2012, rising exponentially (the share of the USA and the entire EU amounting to

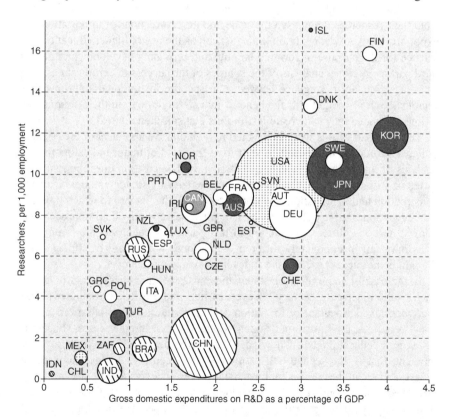

Figure 4.18 Correlation between the number of scientists per 1,000 employees and R&D expenses in relation to GDP.

Source: own elaboration based on OECD 2013.

between US$27 and US$29 billion each). The United States and Japan found themselves in the lead in terms of public investment in this area, with the USA spending US$1.5 billion in 2004 even without the stimulus package provided for under the American Recovery and Reinvestment Act implemented five years later, which increased expenses to a record level of US$7 billion before another decrease two years later brought the amount back to US$3 billion. These data illustrate that, in spite of popular opinion, developed states are indeed conscious of the significance of, and potential future profits from, the development of renewable energy sources. It is also clear that the USA is treating the development of these technologies as a strategic goal.

Examples: strategies of select states in education, science, and innovation

The discussion of the international distribution of power in education and science uncovered the strategies deployed by the states for the purpose of building up their potential in this field or reaping the financial or political benefits from their resources. I analysed the scale and main directions of importation and exportation of knowledge, brain drain, as well as the use of higher education and science for the purpose of forming an elite and providing developmental aid for third parties. A closer analysis of the sources of the success of certain states indicated a significant divergence between the specific institutional solutions they established. It also highlights the benefits that states draw from their unique conditions, provided they can create institutions that suit their context.

The next part of this work is devoted to a qualitative appraisal of the peculiar policies introduced in this area, a shift from the level of major indicators into an analysis of institutional solutions and strategies. The cases in question represent different instances both of market economies and of strategies applied to the construction and exploitation of a state's potential; the manner in which it organises education and science represents in all cases an individual approach that allows these institutions to function in this particular country – the same solutions may fail in completely different conditions. What these examples share, though, is the success each of the states in question has achieved.

In the case of some of those states, the causes of their success can be traced back to the nineteenth century, or even earlier, and are strictly bound with the aforementioned processes of formation of nation-states, industrialisation, and, in many instances, their position as international powers. In other cases, success in developing education and knowledge can only be dated to a rather recent moment, that is, the second half of the twentieth century. A closer look at the progress made in these areas by East Asian states uncovers an important, though often overlooked context of their developmental achievements. Case studies are of necessity synthetic; their purpose is to capture the peculiarities, highlight both the characteristic conditions and the implemented solutions. Therefore, the accent here is on the most important aspect of each of the states in question, rather than a systematic comparison of the same aspects in all states.

The United States: a global magnet

The American state did not follow the same line of development as its European counterparts, exhibiting a far greater decentralisation and dispersion of power, which also reflected upon the rise of education systems. Schools were mostly established by private entities. In territories inhabited by immigrants representing various cultures and speaking different tongues, in the absence of any time-honoured state institutions, education came to serve as a crucial means of nation-making. Prior to the American Revolution, schooling was typically considered a private matter, but for the thinkers who contributed the most to American independence – such as George Washington, Noah Webster, Thomas Jefferson, and Benjamin Rush – it became political due to its usefulness in transmitting specific values and convictions. In the case of a newly established state, it was particularly important to disseminate the republican idea. For Enlightenment thinkers, it also provided a crucial safeguard against tyranny.

The Constitution of the United States authorised Congress to impose and collect taxes and ensure national security and common welfare. Some of the proponents of universal education interpreted that last item as an injunction to establish public schooling. In his 1790 report to Congress, aside from recommending the creation of a national army, currency, and system of measurements, Washington argued:

> Nor am I less persuaded that you will agree with me in opinion, that there is nothing which can better deserve your patronage than the promotion of science and literature. Knowledge is in every country the surest basis of public happiness. In one, in which the measures of government receive their impression so immediately from the sense of community, as in ours, it is essential.
>
> (Quoted in Painter 1896: 315)

Jefferson, on the other hand, drew inspiration from humanist ideals – natural law, equality, and freedom. He advocated for a state-sponsored system of free universal education for all children. Issuing a directive for schools in Virginia, he prefaced it by stating that the goal of these institutions was to instruct the pupils in civic abilities that would allow them to function as citizen (A Bill for the More General Diffusion of Knowledge 1779). Education in America continued to be dispersed in the first few decades of the nineteenth century – consolidation would only begin in 1830, with efforts towards establishing a public system. The process was initiated in the north-eastern states, branching out to the west and south at an uneven pace.

The fact that the United States formed in clear distinction from European traditions posed a challenge to the leaders of the independence movement, demanding the formation of a separate identity and identification of values that would differentiate between the American society and the former colonisers. Though the newly established state claimed no control over schools, leaving education in the hands of the particular states, ideas about education put forward by Jefferson and Rush had a significant effect on the operation of a system marked by great divergence – in fact, a divergent set of education systems. Paradoxically, though not directly tied to the federal government, American schools played a major part in the state-building process, fulfilling the desires of the Founding Fathers in their own decentred ways (Green 2013: 179).

In the USA, the role education played in state-building did not conform to the Prussian or French model. There was no feudal, aristocratic heritage to dismantle. Furthermore, nineteenth-century schools did not yet serve as a major source of cadres for bureaucracy, army, and major public investments. However, they contributed greatly to erecting an identity rooted in the American version of republicanism, which necessitated the dissolution of immigrant identities.

American education proved highly successful in assimilating various cultures. During the nineteenth century, one significant task national schools performed in relation to the children of immigrants was to redirect their loyalties from the communities their parents belonged to towards the national community (Tyack 1974). Teachers would even consciously target the remnants of immigrant cultures for destruction (McDonough and Feinberg 2003: 8). Today, few would dare profess such radical views on the purpose of schooling. Noah Webster, who authored English schoolbooks, believed that he was redefining the purpose of schooling from the purely technical transmission of skills, towards a far broader perspective, involving the inculcation of moral norms and rules. Socialisation of immigrant children into the Protestant ethic became a major effect of American schooling. In effect, it contributed to standardisation by devoting particular attention to teaching the language and forming values (Katz 1976: 384).

Though religious schools initially exerted a significant influence in America, the dominant Protestant majority accepted the creation of public schools according to a model that limited instruction in religion to readings from the Bible and common prayer, with no discussion of doctrinal controversies. This compromise paradigm enabled the socialisation of children from other denominations to the Protestant values on which the United States were founded, thus curbing the risk of tensions between different denominations (Green 2013: 198). Schooling served to teach morality, rather than instruct in doctrine. The ideal of good citizenship it disseminated concentrated on the culture of labour and respect for private property.

Another purpose of schooling was to teach young people to be active citizen, directly involved in democratic processes. The creators of the public school system believed that the government of a free state needed civic virtue and intelligence, and that lasting freedom and equal rights and duties could only be achieved through proper instruction across generations. According to Webster, knowledge enables the citizen to appreciate the virtues of democracy; without it, people cannot judge whether their government is working well or recognise the privileges they enjoy and the positives of a given regime. This makes them prone to various manipulations that counteract democracy (Taylor 1835).

Towards the end of the nineteenth century, a debate began in the USA over the practicality of compulsory education. The opponents of this solution believed it contradicted the entire philosophy of the state – after all, compulsion impinges directly upon the prerogatives of the parents and its absence does not endanger other national institutions, suggesting – its opponents believed – that it was not necessary. Proponents of compulsory education, in turn, argued that ignorance constituted an ill that the state had to counteract, and that the parents do not have the right to raise their children in the dark. According to this line of argument, it was the duty of the state to implement laws that ensured internal security and cohesion. The positive effects of compulsory education in Europe were used as an example. With time, the number of proponents of universal education in the USA increased, with more and more states adopting it (Painter 1896: 323).

While the correlation between industrialisation and the establishment of education systems was far from strong in Europe, the United States serves as an example of a state where schooling took shape to a far greater extent in response to the requirements of the rising industry. The consolidation of education in the northern states coincided precisely with a period of intense industrialisation in 1830–1860. Interestingly, the USA hosted at least two highly divergent models of education. The southern states followed the example set by Virginia, where education was perceived as a private affair resolved by parents and private associations. The north adopted the model put forth in Massachusetts, the state that boasted the first universal public education system (Painter 1896: 313).

The leaders in the drive towards institutionalisation of education in the USA openly declared that its purpose was to achieve an increase in productivity and provide newly established factories with a workforce equipped in useful skills, and thus to contribute to the wealth of the country (Green 2013: 53). European theoreticians of education would rarely reflect so unambiguously and openly on the economic benefits of increasing the education level. One reason might be that, in distinction from Europe, the USA experienced workforce shortages throughout the nineteenth century, highlighting the need for productivity and quality, which were of lesser concern on the overpopulated Old Continent.

Even in the USA, however, it is easy to overestimate the actual usefulness of knowledge and skills transmitted by nineteenth-century schools – particularly on the primary level. Samuel Bowles and Herbert Gintis (1975: 169) believe it unlikely that an owner of a nineteenth-century textile factory or any other industrial institution would agree that the school programme had in any way contributed to the productivity of the workers in his employ.

The United States has already been characterised as, first, the state that most convincingly represents the liberal model of market economy, and second, one that owes its advantages in education and knowledge largely to immigration, which, in turn, is due partly to the attraction the state has as a destination for educated migrants, and partly to the implementation of an efficient policy of acquiring talent. Being the only state whose status as a world power has not been challenged for 100 years and also an economic hegemon of the first order, the USA is able to assign the most funding in these fields and possesses vast amounts of human and infrastructural resources. The primacy of the USA, which takes the guise of hegemonic domination of a number of disciplines of science, is, at the same time, the result of cumulative advantages across many decades. It is also the fruit of the ambition for leadership in scientific and technological progress that typifies the major powers. The standing of the USA in education and knowledge should therefore be viewed in the context of the state's position as a global power, the wealth it possesses, and the aspiration to maintain superiority in both areas. In view of the constant competition between ever-newer actors, it is only possible for a state to remain at the top if it escapes forward rather than contenting itself with the advantages it possesses at any given moment.

The potential of the USA in human capital and science is the result of the immigration of the most gifted people from around the world, a process that had typified the state from the very outset and intensified in the inter-war and postwar periods. This population transfer usually occurred spontaneously, but a few government programmes had also had an impact, attracting outstanding scholars. Such was the goal of Operation Paperclip, initiated in 1944, which allowed German scientists to relocate to the USA, with special consideration given to aviation engineers and scholars in hard sciences. Similar policies have been applied continuously ever since, throughout the Cold War and after its conclusion, even if not to as spectacular effects. Many of the well-educated scientists who contributed to the success of the USA came from Europe. For instance, between 1956 and 1963, about 1,500 European scholars and engineers (6 per cent of all graduates of Western Europe's universities) migrated to the USA every year; according to the OECD, the immigrants brought with them extraordinary qualifications (L'Émigration des scientifiques et des ingénieurs vers les États-Unis 1966: 38–53). During the nineteenth century, it was Europe that made unparalleled advances in education and science; the USA gained its potential from the exploitation of the relative decline in international significance experienced by the European powers, and particularly the destabilisation of the Old Continent brought on by fascism, repression, war, and then the East–West confrontation, which forced many gifted persons to abandon their home countries. Even without direct repression, many simply chose the workplace that guaranteed peaceful conditions for scientific activity, and sometimes even unmatched material resources.

Up until World War II, education in the USA – still outside the purview of the federal authorities – maintained a level below that of the European counterparts. The average quality of education in the USA did not improve until after World War II, when the state invested in the generation whose formative years were spent on the frontlines. The GI Bill was devised to allow veterans to gain education, and it affected several million people. Only in the 1960s would the USA assign significant funding to the education system, visibly improving the quality of instruction.

These changes did not eradicate the significant divergence of schools and universities, which typifies the American system to this day. Aside from hosting institutions renowned for their unattainably high academic level, the USA is also the locus of inequalities unknown to other developed states. While certain universities, such as Harvard, Stanford, and Princeton, have very high name-recognition, an enormous number of higher education institutions in the USA offer a level of instruction low enough to be unthinkable in similarly wealthy European states. The average American university is inferior to the average German university. The same can be said about the education system itself, which leads to frequent critiques and accusations of reproduction of social inequalities in economic and cultural capital. Enormous educational inequalities leave children from families of low socio-economic status with very limited chances for a quality education. The many poorer schools set a very low bar for the students and face major problems with student conduct. On average, the skills in mathematics, hard sciences, and reading comprehension exhibited by American high school graduates are lower than the scientific advantage enjoyed by the United States in comparison to other developed states would lead one to expect. In some instances, American unqualified labourers remain functionally illiterate (Goldin and Katz 2010).

World War II also left a lasting mark on the relationship between the American state and science. It was during the conflict that the government gave scientists a very distinct role in the war effort (Price 1954). Its first decision was to endow laboratories, whether at universities or in the industry, with massive contracts for R&D in the area of military technology. For the first time in history, a lasting, firm connection was instituted between basic research conducted at the universities and applied research in the industry and military programmes. This mode of organisation allowed scientists and engineers involved in work for the army to combine affiliations at universities and in the industry with service for the country. World War II became a turning point for American science and technological development also because technological transfers, previously conducted from civilian science to military applications, now followed a reverse polarity thanks to the efforts of such institutions as the Office of Scientific Research and Development and the Manhattan Project.

The Manhattan Project provided the first major instance of this cooperation between science, industry, and the state, leading to the production of the atomic bomb. Later on, the Pentagon cooperated with security agencies, the Atomic Energy Commission, and NASA, eventually ensuring the development of 'civilian' applications, including in computers, aviation, nuclear power, lasers, and biotechnology (Block 2008: 175). The experiences of the early 1940s convinced American political decision-makers of the significance of technological advantage, both in terms of security and the economy.

Leading scientists of various backgrounds who participated in the Manhattan Project went on to make spectacular discoveries and applications in civilian industry, revolutionising the social life of the 1950s and 1960s. The efficacy of this project provided the rationale for continued state involvement in scientific policy and implementation against established economic tradition. Foreign to the USA, this approach typified nineteenth-century Germany; in America, it drew widespread opposition due to the rather common investment in the tradition of the limited state. For this reason, maintaining the degree of public investment in these areas in peacetime required mobilisation and special efforts on the part of advocates. It should be stressed that, while research expenses in the USA come mostly from state treasury, the country's universities – especially the most prestigious ones – remain under private control to a degree not seen in any other developed state. This is due, first, to the aforementioned limitation of the role of the state, and second, to the unique tradition of the richest Americans and major private companies providing funding for non-commercial ventures.

Immediately after World War II, the significance of science and technology for maintaining the international status of the state was well recognised in the USA. Contemporary attitudes on the state-science relationship are reflected in Vannevar Bush's famous report *Science, the Endless Frontier* (1945), compiled at the behest of President Roosevelt by then-director of the Office of Scientific Research and Development. It was decided that the most important questions for the future concerned technological transfer and industry applications capable of creating high-quality workplaces that would lead to increased wealth and welfare for the entire American society, as well as the challenge of ensuring access to the most gifted youth for work in science. The development of antibiotics, radar, radio, air conditioning, synthetic fabrics, and plastic is merely an example of the rising tide of inventions associated with the development of contemporaneous military technologies. World War II, particularly the struggle against U-boats, the invention of radar, and the creation of defences against V-2 rockets, proved – the authors of the report surmised – that the advance of science in the twentieth century is also a vital aspect of national security. Civilian and military technologies not only increase welfare and security in a state, but also directly affect quality of life by providing new methods of farming which ensure vital provisions, expanding medical and pharmaceutical knowledge that improve public health, and allowing workers to earn more while working fewer hours thanks to increased productivity – which, in turn, gives the workers more free time to spend on recreation and entertainment. The report stipulated that the progress of science is a condition of possibility of the welfare of the state, but not a guarantee thereof – technologies can, after all, be turned against humans.

Bush stressed that, among other factors, the power of the state is defined by what he called scientific capital. He contended that the United States continued to remain dependent on Europe, the leader in this field, and that its welfare and security as a major power also hinged on the sturdiness of this pillar. From this perspective, state support for basic research and the implementation of an effective policy of attracting talent, and in large numbers, are of particular significance. The shortage of properly trained persons becomes a 'ceiling' for technological progress.

Answering the question of the best way to transition from war to peace in science without losing in quality and dynamism of research, Bush recommended the creation of an agency guaranteeing the stability of funding for long-term projects, whose employees would be recruited based solely on merit, and which would promote studies conducted by non-governmental entities with grants and contracts. Thus emerged prototypes of two institutions that would be established a decade later – the National Science Foundation and Defense Advanced Research Projects Agency (DARPA).

Though Bush's propositions were not immediately endorsed, the race between the United States and the Soviet Union, and especially the technological aspect of that rivalry, contributed significantly to the consistency and institutionalisation of state support for science. The nearly absolute freedom which used to dominate in academic research succumbed to increasing coordination by the government, which sought to enforce useful directions of research and effect an increase of its pace. At the start of the 1950s, up to 75 per cent of the R&D conducted in the USA, both at universities and in private enterprises, was financed from the federal budget (Lesher and Howick 1966: 20). As a result, a scientific-technological system emerged typified by a dense network of connections between universities, the industry, and the government, with the power of distributing research funds vested in the numerous and highly specialised government agencies.

Marked by immense efficiency, the American system owed its success to the highly competitive structure and contracts which provided diverse possibilities of funding. At the same time, it enabled consistent long-term support for all institutions as well as dedicated funding for those whose value was not defined by their current activities, for projects deemed vital by the government or the scientists themselves, or certain specific disciplines, etc. These various forms of funding worked so well not only because the incentive-creating mechanism itself was so well designed, but also, no less significantly, due to enormous investment on the part of the federal government.

The 1960s were the period when the international advantage of elite American universities became apparent, and they continued to increase the distance over the competitors while still benefitting from the influx of foreigners.

One should not underestimate the role played in this process by parents, whose educational aspirations for their children drastically increased during the 1960s, leading to a rise in private expenses on education. The United States was the first country to achieve mass higher education, with 40 per cent of the age cohort attending post-secondary education in 1960. The expansion of higher education propelled American qualified workers (managers, engineers) to the status of the best-educated specialists in the world. Regardless of the broad divergence in quality of instruction among higher education institutions, one should stress that the USA is home to a very large group of universities ranked at the global top, and not merely the handful of famous names – the group includes at least several dozen institutions. Already at the time, the massive scientific base included not merely the renowned research universities, but also the federal outlay on R&D and numerous scientific laboratories owned by private companies. Federal expenses on basic research reached far higher levels than in any other state in the world.

Another injection of funds and effort came with the so-called Sputnik effect caused by the launching of the eponymous satellite in 1957 by the Soviet Union, which became a symbol of the technological challenge involved in the Cold War rivalry. The launch evoked incredulity and anxiety among the American political elites. The response of the USA consisted partly in the decision not only to train more scientists and engineers, but also to engage in the conquest of space. This development allowed America to gain a dominant position in the space industry as well as in semiconductors and medical and computer equipment for years to come.

It was at that time that DARPA – a famous institution (though minor in terms of employment and its share of expenses on science and R&D). Its stated purpose was to oversee projects whose implementation horizon extended beyond twenty years. The agency provided employment for researchers and visionary engineers, giving them significant autonomy in dispensing with the funds; only at a later phase would it define directions of research more proactively (Block 2008: 175–176). Today, the institution has a budget of more than US$3 billion and employs over 250 people, responding flexibly to the needs of the government while maintaining operational independence. Its function extends well beyond financing basic research. It specialises in, among others, goal-specific expenses in particular areas and directions of research, creation of new opportunities for innovation, negotiation of transactions between public and private partners – including venture capital – and support for commercialisation. The structure of the agency is relatively informal, which distinguishes it from traditional bureaucracy and enables effective combinations between the abstract thinking of academics, the long-term goals of the government, and the military demand for improvement in existing technologies.

The agency not only provided funding for, but also actively shaped a network that enabled the sharing of some of the knowledge and information on negative results of studies, or blind alleys, between mutually competitive entities, thus lessening the risk of repeated funding of unproductive ideas. In this manner, using managers as architects of a social network between science and the industry, DARPA came up with a third way, balancing the free market against the central control characteristic of the developmental state (Fuchs 2010: 1134). The agency concentrated on supporting small, efficient companies which competed in the area of innovative technological solutions (Mazzucato 2011: 75–79). The projects which received early funding from DARPA contributed significantly to the development of personal computers (PCs) during the 1960s and 1970s.

Though DARPA is unique on the global scale as well as within the USA itself – contributing to interest from both the media and technology enthusiasts – it does not operate in a vacuum, and its success is strictly tied to the context it operates in. That context consists in a dense network of exceptional universities equipped in copious amounts of financial resources for basic and applied research, accompanied by American venturesomeness and an unprecedented accumulation of capital. Finally, the agency serves the most powerful military machine in the history of humanity.

During the 1960s, in a famous report for the House of Representatives, Carl Kaysen (1965: 149–150), then-director of the Institute for Advanced Study, advocated further increase of expenses on basic research on the basis of its significance for applied research and new technologies. He also addressed the strict relationship between high-end research and the quality of instruction, primarily in natural sciences and engineering. Adhering to Bush's school of thought, he contended that applied R&D efforts should be aimed at solving specific practical issues to yield better results. In Kaysen's view, scientists involved in basic research played a vital role in national security as well.

At the time, divergences in outlay on R&D between the United States and Western Europe had become readily apparent. For instance, in 1962, the USA devoted US$93 per capita on R&D with GERD at 3.1 per cent GDP, while states of the EEC spent US$25 per capita on average with GERD at 1.5 per cent in France, 1.3 per cent in the Federal Republic of Germany and 2.2 per cent in Great Britain, in spite of an inferior base compared to the USA. America's expense on R&D in 1962 was four times higher than that of the most industrialised part of Western Europe, even as the populations of the two were comparable (Freeman and Young 1965: 32). Though specific states and their statistical bodies used their own definitions of a scientist and an engineer, necessitating a cautious approach to comparisons, data for 1962 indicate that 436,000 scientists and engineers worked in the USA, 415,000 in the Soviet Union, and 148,000 in the entire Western Europe.[6] Thus, already in the 1960s, the comparable populations of the USA and Western Europe yielded numbers of scientists and engineers disparate by a factor of three (Freeman and Young 1965: 72). Even at that early stage, the USA benefitted from the brain drain, mostly of Europe, and not merely in terms of quantity, but rather quality.

In 1962, while roughly 5 per cent of all American scientists had received education abroad, as many as 21 per cent of the members of the elite National Academy of Sciences were born outside of the USA, and 18 per cent had completed studies abroad. Their migration occurred mostly at the expense of Great Britain, Germany, and certain minor states, such as Ireland, Greece, Norway, Switzerland, and Austria, whose losses in relation to their population were the most palpable. In the latter 1950s, the USA received over 6,500 scientists and engineers in all from Western Europe. By the early 1960s, a major increase in migration of scientists from Asia was recorded (Freeman and Young 1965: 58).

In 2012, American academic institutions spent over US$65 billion on basic research in all areas, with as much as US$62 billion going to S&E; 60 per cent of the outlay was covered by the federal government (as had been the case since the 1980s). Six agencies distributed 90 per cent of the funds – National Science Foundation and entities operated by the Department of Health, Department of Defense, NASA, Department of Energy and Department of Agriculture. Over the past two decades, investment in life sciences increased – mostly at the expense of physics – to cover over 60 per cent of all funds for basic research in S&E. Public funding for R&D remains significantly skewed towards the defence sector, resulting in far fewer discoveries of use for the broadly conceived economy while the military-industrial complex benefits. It is also not uncommon for these funds to serve very specific military purposes. Today, American expenses on R&D, though unmatched in absolute terms, are lower than those of Germany and Japan in relation to GDP, even with defence spending factored in. Aside from a few elite universities, technical education in the USA is also inferior to that found in competing states; the dearth of good technical and vocational schools is particularly palpable on the secondary level. Apprenticeship and on-the-job training systems are also insufficient.

Due to the high stage of advancement of entrepreneurship, the United States is a country where establishing a company – or a few – is seen as a natural professional activity. Meanwhile, one rarely hears of the extent of American government's investment in developing general-purpose technologies by way of active intervention and major public contracts. The federal government's engagement is relatively less apparent from mainstream debate. Fred Block (2008: 183) goes so far as to call the United States a 'hidden developmental state' (see also Motoyama, Appelbaum, and Parker 2011: 109) whose public embrace of the liberal mode of capitalism does not prevent it from engaging in goal-oriented, area-specific deployment of the kind of coordinated capitalism that led Germany and Japan on the path of economic progress in the nineteenth and twentieth centuries. The surreptitious character of these practices is necessitated by the public distrust of an active state. In absolute terms, the breadth of public intervention in R&D in the USA is due to the extent of the base; in comparison to other states, however, the disproportionate relationship to the cost borne by private enterprises in this area becomes apparent. Tracing the sources of America's potential in this regard, therefore, one should also take into account the massive public expenses in absolute terms and even greater private investment, incomparably higher than those in any other state. Roughly 70 per cent of all expenses on R&D, which amounted to US$450 billion in 2012, come from the business sector.

The tradition of federal support for R&D continues today, with different initiatives put forward by Democratic and Republican administrations. Under Ronald Reagan, the Small Business Innovation Development Act (SBIR) was introduced, obliging government agencies endowed with large research budgets to contribute a minor proportion of their budget (initially 1.25 per cent) to a research fund supporting ideas put forward by small and independent, but highly innovative enterprises. SBIR currently controls over US$2 billion, providing funding for minor hi-tech firms to support the development of many new undertakings and the commercialisation of results. The same administration oversaw the passage of the Orphan Drug Act (ODA), geared towards the formation of a comparable innovation system in biotechnology, and the pharmaceutical industry in particular. Research on orphan drugs played a significant part in the development of biotechnology, with the United States a major player – investing in the production of knowledge, subsidising new drugs, protecting the drug market, and financing drug acquisition (Mazzucato 2011: 84).

The latest initiative of the American government is aimed at fostering an innovation system around nanotechnology. It was initiated as early as the 1990s, when few expected nanotechnologies to become another key general-purpose technology. It was then that the National Nanotechnology Initiative (NNI) was introduced (Motoyama *et al.* 2011). The idea grew out of the conviction that nanotechnology would revolutionise the market in the same way that the Internet did. Funding was approved by the administration of Bill Clinton and maintained by that of George W. Bush. The American government played a major part by defining directions for research, mobilising potential stakeholders to formulate a programme for development, and providing extensive public funding distributed in a manner that would ensure a future return in case of success. Institutionally, development in this area was supported primarily by the NSF, SFIR, and the Department of Defense, and the yearly budget amounted to US$1.8 billion in 2010 (Motoyama *et al.* 2011: 109). Barack Obama's administration, on the other hand, is responsible for investing billions of dollars in new energy technologies, as reflected by budget allocations for the American Recovery and Reinvestment Act. Aside from providing the money, the government also established ARPA-E – an institution modelled on DARPA and tasked with decentralised support for high-risk innovative initiatives in energy.

The American innovation system transformed the functioning of many branches of business and successfully convinced scholars to engage in the search for applications of technological inventions in production and services. The United States itself, however, provides proof that companies which profited from public funding are loathe to pay back even a part to the state or invest in new undertakings of the same kind on their own. Thus, to be able to provide support for innovations while maintaining broad acceptance for public expenses in this area requires a careful weighing of the pros and cons and balancing of risk and gain, so that the state – being the primary risk-taker – reaps the rewards of the commercial success of an innovative process. However, it is of primary importance that the involvement of the American government in R&D is perceived as merely a part of, and complement to, the broader context, in which R&D costs and the risk involved in technological and extra-technological innovation are mostly borne by private entities. For this reason, the American 'covert developmental state' is only apparent at certain points – most of the burden rests on the liberal market economy with a peculiar, highly competitive mode of capitalism supported by massive private capital.

Europe: multiple models between internal competition and cooperation

Europe is a region of great diversity in terms of potential in education and science, as well as in applications. Several states provide important examples of effective policies in this area, while the European Union as a whole pursues greater competitiveness. On primary and secondary level, young Europeans rank among the best; there is less inequality between students as far as the abilities measured in PISA studies are concerned than there is, for instance, in the USA. In terms of the advancement of science, the Old Continent still trails the United States. Two countries are renowned for their strength in the areas of higher education and science – Great Britain and Germany. Yet, both have lost in significance in comparison to the nineteenth and early twentieth centuries, when they enjoyed the status of global leaders. Great Britain is additionally benefitting from the ability to reap the rewards of commercialisation thanks to the widespread knowledge of the English language across the world. Germans, in turn, dominate on various levels of technical education (analysed more broadly in Chapter 3). In recruitment policies for scientific cadres, Great Britain follows a similar course to America, taking advantage of immigration, even though its capabilities in that regard are much more limited. Germans, in turn, are far more self-reliant, maintaining stable cadres and structures, as well as investing in their development.

Even before World War II, Great Britain began to lose its competitive advantages, in part due to the dearth of qualified workers – a challenge that Germany did not face due to its reliance on advanced competencies (Freeman and Louçã 2001: 251). At least since the turn of the twentieth century, the British education system has been proving itself inferior to those of other leading states in terms of adjustment to the demands of subsequent stages of capitalism (discussed in Chapter 2). After World War II, Great Britain failed to retain many of the most gifted scholars in its research institutions – instead, they emigrated in search of better working conditions, primarily to the United States.

In spite of its status as an unquestionable world power, many areas of British education and science exhibit a peculiar weakness due mostly to divergences in the quality of instruction (Green 2013: 204–297). While British elite high schools and universities are famous the world over, the average Briton receives education of a lower quality than in other highly developed states, with lower access to higher education. Up until the Margaret Thatcher era, the British education system put a particular stress on equality in teaching, with little attention devoted to competitiveness; it was under Thatcher that the focus turned towards increasing the role of parents and diversifying the educational offer. Education reforms implemented by the conservative government continue to attract much controversy, highlighting the conflict between social cohesion and equality of opportunity on the one hand, and global competitiveness on the other.

A similar degree of variety is found in higher education, represented by several formidable universities of illustrious history, such as Oxford University, Cambridge University, London School of Economics, and Imperial College. On the one hand, they form an elite endowed with advanced competencies which achieves success on an international scale in services, consulting, and information technologies, as well as world-class scholars in hard sciences and social studies; on the other, the British system is blighted by the absence of ties between universities and business. Elite education focuses either on the humanities, or on theoretical hard sciences, while the practical engineering sciences do not enjoy particular renown or popularity with the young. The apprenticeship system works poorly, and existing traineeships often fail to meet the demands of entrepreneurs. Teacher-training also leaves much to be desired. As a result,

British labourers are often inferior to foreign competitors in terms of knowledge and abilities. The industry likewise fails to effect a change in this area, investing comparatively little in the professional development of employees. In effect, graduates of local schools and universities, already hampered by lower education, fall ever farther behind to their competitors. The case of Great Britain reveals the shortcomings of the liberal market economies institutional models.

Yet, Great Britain invests heavily in basic research, primarily for the purposes of the defence sector (a major part of the public expense). Private outlay on R&D is lower than in states at a comparable level of development and concentrates in a few specific sectors – mostly pharmaceutical and chemical – where ties between the industry and universities are uncommonly strong. In spite of isolated successes, ever more branches of industry fail to match foreign competitors.

Europe is made up of numerous small states, which maintain global economic competitiveness by flexibly adapting to economic change while compensating domestically in order to counter some of the harmful effects of international liberalisation. Just as in other fields, they play to the strengths of the weak in education and science, as well (Katzenstein 1985). The mix of policies they apply differs from those pursued by large states. They are more likely to support employment directly, up to the implementation of various policies for increasing labour power, including vocational training and skills importation policies. Since R&D requires significant expenses while carrying uncertainties and risk, small European states eagerly pursue common research projects that would not have been feasible for any one of them in isolation (Katzenstein 1985: 45).

In terms of competitive advantages, the minute Switzerland is uncontested. It leans more towards the coordinated market economy model when it comes to the organisation of training, but the state refrains from direct investment in R&D (with the exception of nuclear energy). Aside from other favourable conditions it enjoys, the country has access to a vast reserve of well-educated workers with advanced abilities, characterised by high work culture. Switzerland boasts a public, common, and high-quality education system which is invested with significant social confidence. Swiss teachers are much more highly qualified than their American or British counterparts. Roughly 80 per cent of students who finish primary school continue education in high schools, with as many as 70 per cent going into vocational schools, while the other 30 per cent attend the more conventional baccalaureate schools. The bias towards vocational training is even more pronounces in German-speaking cantons. Baccalaureate schools only admit candidates with academic ability. A high school graduate gains admittance to a university within the same canton or one of two federal institutions immediately after graduation. Swiss universities conduct high-quality research in select areas, particularly in natural sciences, such as physics or chemistry, and are rated highly in international rankings. As a result, as much as a half of all students in Switzerland graduate from institutions from the global top 200. Though the USA has more universities in that group, only 20 per cent of American students graduate from them. Swiss vocational schools provide training for over 200 professions (SKBF 2010). Like its German cousin, the Swiss education system offers expertly devised apprenticeships for all students. Most students enrolled in vocational programmes follow a dual track, which requires students to serve as apprentices at a firm several days a week. Industry associations were heavily engaged in the formation of the curricula, and the companies which admit apprentices are expected to provide them with training. The low earnings of the apprentices compensate for the expenses incurred in this context by Swiss companies.

The selectivity of the Swiss system, and particularly the limitation of access to university education, invites controversy and pressure to enlarge admittance to the institutions. These ideas are opposed both by a part of the academic elites, which fear a decline in the quality of instruction, and by entrepreneurs, who argue that this would limit their ability to obtain gifted pupils for vocational training (Tauxe 2004). Companies invest heavily in worker training, playing an active part in improving the welfare of their employees not only by offering them appropriate wages, but also through generous social funding. The cooperation between private enterprise and the universities operates smoothly, contributing to the success of Swiss pharmaceutical companies, among others (Katzenstein 1985: 109–110). The local companies exhibit a remarkable facility in establishing contacts with foreign scientific centres when a given technology is unavailable in Switzerland and a technological transfer is needed. The Swiss do not assume that all the technologies they need should be devised within their country; to facilitate technological transfers, the country's pharmaceutical industry established research centres in the United States and Great Britain. As in the USA, the state has been reaping the rewards of an influx of gifted immigrants for decades, with particularly beneficial shifts after World War II.

Another minor European state which also boasts an education system that favours economic prosperity under conditions of global competition is Sweden, a country typified by a long tradition of public access to education and the deployment of a unified programme of instruction. Sweden provides high-quality technical education tied to an apprenticeship system reminiscent of its German counterpart. Many Swedish managers and engineers have received education or worked abroad – formerly mostly in Germany and Great Britain, today primarily in the United States. In an attempt to meet the global challenge, Sweden reformed its education system to allow more competition between schools and thus partly abandoned its egalitarian principles. As a result, schools pursued different paths of development while reproducing and increasing social inequalities. These reforms polarise public opinion, with some stressing the necessity to adapt to international arrangements, while others criticise the dismantling of another element of social policy distinguishing the welfare state from economies shaped by a more liberal vision of capitalism. In relative terms, basic research receives less attention than applied research designed for implementation, conducted by major companies – or rather clusters – in cooperation with universities. Unlike other small European countries, Sweden maintains a technologically independent program of national defence. That is why R&D has received much more government support there than, for example, in Switzerland. The Swedish government has also committed to the national innovation system. In addition, Sweden proved very efficient in borrowing foreign technological innovations, which already in 1970s earned it the label of 'the Japan of Europe' (Katzenstein 1985: 110). High costs of labour (workers with low qualifications receive relatively high wages) necessitates innovation in production processes, primarily through automation, a major source of Sweden's high productivity.

In its official statements, the European Union attaches particular significance to competitiveness and innovation as foundations for its advancement. Such pronouncements can be found in the 2000 Lisbon Strategy, a programme for transforming Europe into the most competitive economy in the world within a decade. The transformation was to be effected primarily through the deployment of knowledge-based economic thinking and innovativeness, as well as increased spending on basic research. The Strategy drew intellectual inspiration from Joseph Schumpeter, who perceived growth as the result of innovation, and was authored by scholars associated with the concept of national innovation systems. The guidelines found in the document were not binding and many governments did not fulfil their obligations, leaving most of the goals of Lisbon Strategy unachieved, including higher employment rates among women, extension of the productive period, and increased outlay on research.

The Lisbon Strategy was replaced by Europe 2020. Aside from other goals, the document foresees a limitation of the dropout rate from 15 per cent at the time of signing to 10 per cent and increased enrolment on the tertiary level, from 31 per cent to 40 per cent for people aged thirty to thirty-four. Goals also include increases in R&D spending to at least 3 per cent GDP, including both private and public expenses. Among major initiatives, the strategy names improvements in the quality of education systems, drawing power of higher education, and mobility in the labour market – including the acquisition of new qualifications – as well as the creation of an infrastructure for financing research and innovation. These stipulations are implemented through the Horizon 2020 programme which will see the EU distribute roughly US$90 billion during the years 2014–2020. The main pillar of Horizon 2020 is the high level of science directed towards basic research. These resources are assigned to research projects, scientific mobility, research infrastructure, and the pursuit of new technologies, on a competitive basis.

The current priorities of the EU in the areas in question include mobility and competence transfer, the achievement of a modern higher education, high level of science, reliable scientific infrastructure, scholar and student mobility, mutual qualification recognition, an open and competitive labour market for scientists, and accessible knowledge. The EU has also established several institutions tasked with achieving the aforementioned goals, including the European Institute of Innovation and Technology, a network of universities, research institutes, and enterprises; European Research Council, responsible for improving the quality of basic research; and Joint Technology Initiatives, public-private partnerships focused on enterprises. Competitiveness and innovativeness are also the watchwords of the EU's initiatives in education and science, accomplished by way of soft governance through open coordination, with highly limited oversight from the European Commission. Here, the European Union implemented two initiatives strictly tied to education and instruction – first, the Bologna Process, and second, the European Qualification Framework.

EU's strategy for science and innovation is not free from internal tension. One particularly contentious issue is the definition of the desired extent of competition within national systems and the Union, relative to the benefits of inter-institutional cooperation on the national and European levels. On the one hand, a simple competitive model would reinforce vertical disparity, strengthening some institutions in specific research areas while weakening others, and consequently leading to the restraining of variety. On the other hand, limiting competitiveness among universities to achieve uniform levels, for all the good it does to social cohesion within the Union, reduces the likelihood of the emergence of even a narrow group of institutions capable of competing with the global leaders. In this field, the application of the European strategy is hard to achieve in part because it requires an effective distribution of labour as well as a balance between global competition, the quality of European institutions, and national priorities, including questions of culture and linguistic variety. Member states find it difficult to define the right proportions of incentives for competition and cooperation.

An analysis of the Bologna Process, designed to promote both a globally competitive European system and internal cooperation within the Union, has indicated similar internal conflicts (van der Wende 2004). To achieve the latter goal, the unification of education levels, academic titles, common qualification frameworks, and quality safeguards was to be implemented.

Inside the EU, there is also the peculiar microcosm of student exchange. Citizen of member states have the right to free education in universities of other states within the Union. Here again, the asymmetry of flows rears its head, as persons from states which offer instruction of inferior quality tend to seek access to countries with superior higher education. State governments that oversee net positive student migration are not completely satisfied with the practice, which creates a financial burden on an investment that does not yield sufficient profits. Since EU laws prohibit the discrimination of citizens of the Union, governments of hosting states attempt to improve their gain–loss ratio by encouraging young, well-educated people to remain where they received their education. For instance, the government of Denmark estimates that retaining a young person with high competence and placing them on the local labour market allows the state to recoup the losses (through taxes) from educating the young foreigner in about five years.[7]

The European Innovation Scoreboard, based on twenty-five indicators describing eight dimensions and three areas – enablers, company activity, and outputs – highlights significant divergence among European states. In 2013, it identified Denmark, Finland, Germany, and Sweden as leaders of innovation.

A second group of states, which scored above the EU average included Austria, Belgium, Cyprus, Estonia, France, Ireland, Luxembourg, the Netherlands, Slovenia, and Great Britain. Among those scoring somewhat below the average were Czech Republic, Greece, Hungary, Italy, Lithuania, Malta, Portugal, Slovakia, and Spain. The poorest performers, the so-called modest innovators, included Bulgaria, Latvia, Poland, and Romania (Innovation Union Scoreboard 2014: 5). Between 2008 and 2012, the most dynamic improvement in innovation was recorded in Estonia (7.1 per cent), with significant advances in Lithuania (5 per cent) and Latvia (4.4 per cent); the least dynamic increases, on the other hand, typified Poland (0.4 per cent), Bulgaria (0.6 per cent), and Sweden (0.6 per cent). The latter, however, is too far ahead of the pack to be capable of making significant advances. In the same period, Greece and Cyprus saw their innovativeness decrease by 1.7 per cent and 0.7 per cent, respectively.

The divergence in innovation within the EU is due to the disparity between the pace with which those at the bottom of the list catch up and that with which the leaders advance further. For all its variety and strong international standing, Europe remains the victim of the paradox that its leadership in basic research does not translate effectively into profitable innovations. The source of this incapacity is found in the weakness of the system of applied research and a relative lack of innovative enterprises (Dosi, Llerena, and Sylos Labini 2006).

The Republic of Korea and Singapore: educational miracle in conditions of high coordination

Japan provided a model of development for many Asian states (Johnson 1995; Cummings 1980, 1995; Kohli 2004). In spite of the enmity shared among East Asian states towards Japan – a result of brutal occupation during World War II – it was the occupier state that served as a principal source of inspiration for local modernisers. In Korea, Park Chung-hee revered the Meiji Revolution and Japan's transition to modernity, and cooperated closely with the powerful neighbour when implementing his own reforms in the 1960s and 1970s. The top officials of Singapore, Prime Minister Lee Kuan Yew and the architect of economic reforms Goh Keng Swee, also drew intellectual inspiration from Japan

In 1949, following the abolition of Japanese dominance, South Korea established a uniform, compulsory, and publicly financed education system. Donn Adams and Esther E. Gottlieb (1993: 26) believe that here, too, the idea of using education to mould the state was a major inspiration for the development of primary schooling. The modernisation in the 1960s led to an increase of nationalism; it was then that the history of Korea as a unified state with a continuous history going back 5,000 years was 'discovered anew'. Even today, the Korean education system is not unaffected by nationalist tendencies, be it of a slightly more palatable ideological tone. Aside from building up the national identity, much attention was devoted to developing cadres and infrastructure. Park established thousands of schools, eradicated illiteracy, and provided access to higher education to a significant proportion of the youth.

In Singapore, as well, the development of education was clearly intended to aid the establishment of an independent state following the country's withdrawal from the Federation of Malaya in 1965. The adopted model differed markedly from the ones found in Japan and Korea. Those other states relied on historical particularity and time-honoured traditions, stressing the relative ethnic homogeneity of their populations and developing an ethnocultural sense of nationhood. Meanwhile, due to its ethnic, religious, and linguistic diversity, Singapore was forced to devise an idea of nationhood from scratch, using a civic model centred on the concept of multiculturalism. The country's Minister of Education claimed in 1968 that:

> young state struggles with many challenges, one of the most important is the survival as an independent nation. In order to overcome this challenge the Republic needs people loyal to the state and ready to receive education which strengthens our country. Our individual capacity to survive and live in prosperity and wealth depends on our capacity to survive as a nation and on our readiness to promote collective interest.
>
> (Chia 2010: 67)

In another speech from the same year, he stressed that: 'it is a great task for Singapore to allow evolution of the multiracial and multicultural society, which, once independent, must transform itself into a united nation. (…) Education will be crucial for this evolution' (Chia 2010: 67).

State-building goals found reflection in education through the gradual adoption of English for communication. To avoid protests from various ethnic groups, the language was instituted as a compulsory secondary language. In practice, this turned English into the primary language in the public arena, even if no formal steps were taken to that effect. School programmes also included elements of cultural values and ethics reflecting a common, pan-Asiatic root shared by all inhabitants of the city-state. Much attention was devoted to the meaning of 'good citizenship', which involved poring over biographies of Singapore's pioneers and leaders, and learning about the role of the military and the police, and of the state's multicultural ideology (Chia 2010: 139).

Singapore numbers among the few states in the world to successfully predict the coming transformations and implement a plan of building up new competencies in the society. The state's dedicated organ for matters of education – the Council for Vocational and Technical Education comprised experts from various ministries – formulated a correct prognosis of the demand for abilities and planned centrally organised actions geared towards bringing them to the citizen. Though it is often easier said than done, the anticipated effects were actually accomplished, and, even more improbably, the specified abilities turned out to have been well suited to the demands of the day. Singapore consistently followed the policy of top-down planning of development of competencies, applying corrections on the go and adjusting to further stages of progress (Ashton, Green, James, and Sung 1999; Rodan 1989).

Though many states attempted to follow Singapore's policy course, few managed to achieve comparable results, both in terms of accuracy of predictions and efficiency in meeting the stated goals. During the 1960s and 1970s, South Korea repeatedly passed five-year plans for developing abilities (Adams and Gottlieb 1993; Brown, Green, and Lauder 2001), but consistent failures – which led, among others, to an oversupply of persons with higher education – convinced the country to abandon this strategy of progress. Singapore remains a global exception in that regard, its size and peculiar political organisation – sometimes referred to as enlightened authoritarianism – likely contributing to the successful planning of the demand for abilities.

Singapore's Economic Development Board, responsible for coordinating all matters related to direct foreign investment since 1961, engaged in negotiations with foreign partners, debating, among others, the need for adequately trained cadres. Foreign investors were required to provide their own managers and engineers to train the local cadres, whether at the workplace, or by sending them for training at the seat of the given corporation. This led to the formation of joint institutes of technology: German–Singaporean, Japanes–Singaporean, and French–Singaporean. During the 1980s, as well, the government of Singapore conducted an intervention aimed at improving the advanced competencies of the workers. Employers who offered low wages were burdened with a special tax providing operating resources for the Skills Development Fund, which, in turn, supplied the financing for in-house training in advanced competencies for employees. Major investments were also made in polytechnic education and the organisation of state-run research and development centres.

Singapore also took the lead in reforming education. In contrast to Japan and the Republic of Korea, the government did not face resistance from schools and parents opposed to the transition from learning by rote to focusing on problems. Today, the schools teach by setting out from a specific question and moving towards more theoretical issues through practical solutions. Singapore is also renowned for demanding a very high degree of competency from teachers, and the profession commands immense prestige as well as wages to match, comparable to those in the commercial sector – another facet that makes the state unique in global terms.

All analyses of the so-called economic miracle in East Asia highlight the role of education in this process. Access to qualified cadres encouraged major foreign direct investments in the region. The scientific-technical potential also informed achievements in increasing productivity and reorientation of the economies towards the production of ever-more advanced wares with higher added value. This occurred both at the turn of the 1970s, when efforts were put into developing the heavy and electronic industries, and a decade later, when the aforementioned countries stimulated the development of more advanced industries, both by transfer of technologies and some innovations developed domestically (Rodan 1989).

As in continental Europe, developments in education pre-dated industrialisation, meaning that human capital emerged before the demand for it did. Both

Japan and the other Asian tigers boasted universal access to primary education already at the onset of industrialisation. Subsequently, parallel to the industry, a dynamic development – both quantitative and qualitative – of middle schooling took place. In 1960, primary-level schooling in these states was universal, even as other developing states posted lower enrolment rates. In turn, secondary education remained relatively unpopular into the 1960s, with just 20 per cent enrolled in Hong Kong and 33 per cent in Taiwan. Expansion only began in mid-1970s, with over 60 per cent enrolment in Singapore and over 95 per cent in South Korea, the other states placing in between those two poles of the spectrum (Tilak 2002). Asian tigers enjoyed the advantage in education over other developing states both in terms of levels of participation and average years of schooling per citizen.

However, a simple review of indicators cannot provide an unambiguous answer whether the rising advantage caused the achievement of a higher stage of advancement or resulted from it. Most likely, it was the product of a feedback mechanism, in which higher education levels translated into economic progress, which, in turn, fostered higher education levels.

East Asian states not only improved their enrolment rates in record time, but also developed their universities, including those crucial for industrialisation – initially towards the traditional industrial technologies, but increasingly reorienting towards electronics by the 1990s. These states operated in conditions of constant brain drain and loss of talent, mostly to the benefit of the United States. After an initial increase in education levels following World War II, South Korea experienced a significant outflow of talent abroad in the 1960s. The ruling elite became increasingly aware of the problems posed by the loss of cadres. In response to this challenge, they devised a set of public policies geared towards extending the nation's technological capabilities, and thus reducing dependence on foreign enterprises for know-how. In 1966, Korea Institute of Science and Technology was established, modelled on analogous institutions in the USA. Its cadres were recruited from among Koreans employed in top-quality research institutions in the West. It played a major part in introducing Korean enterprises to the rules of R&D activity. On the other hand, USAID credits enabled the establishment of another institute for applied research, Korea Advanced Institute of Science, whose activities were tailored to the demands of industrial firms such as Samsung and Goldstar, as well as Hyundai and Daewoo, and which provided another opportunity for scholars educated abroad to return home. In 1982, the two institutions merged to create the Korea Advanced Institute of Science and Technology.

Though Korean universities are not among the best globally, the country boasts over 100 technical universities and just as many traditional universities with high-quality programmes. Korean universities can reform and improve the quality of their research output very quickly. The recruitment is competitive, and a significant proportion of the students spend at least a proportion of their studies abroad. Diplomas from leading American schools command high prestige. The stays are paid for both by the government and by private enterprises. Much as their Japanese counterparts, Korean companies regularly provide their employees with high-quality training. Major companies typically operate their own, expertly organised research centres and make significant investments in technology transfers from other states.

While the industrialisation of Korea occurred under significant support from the government, in recent decades, major companies achieved a stable international position with the public sector largely withdrawn from its role as coordinator of their development. Korean enterprises exemplify the successful transformation from a strategy of adaptation and imitation to one of risky innovation. Local companies achieved success in sectors that usually give preference to liberal market economies rather than coordinated ones, of which that of the Republic of Korea is an example. However, the reforms of the past twenty years have altered the shape of some of the local institutions, bringing the state closer to a liberal market model (Kang 2010: 520, 2015).

China: change in progress

In terms of education and science, at the outset of Deng Xiaoping's economic reforms, the People's Republic of China was hugely overburdened by the negative legacies of the Cultural Revolution. Over the span of more than a decade, the state's universities and research institutes were closed down or put to completely unproductive use. As a result, the state needed time to make up for the delay. China's economic success after the reforms of the turn of the 1970s relied on competitive advantages based primarily on access to massive amounts of cheap labour, which attracted industrial production and enabled its development at an unprecedented pace and scale. However, the state could not compete in areas where knowledge was required; this potential is only now being created. Education and science reforms began in 1976. Towards the end of the 1970s, China sent thousands of scientists specialising in areas considered crucial for the state to the United States and other Western countries for one- or two-year training programmes. Meanwhile, Chinese universities educated tens of thousands of people to produce cadres capable of engaging in productive activities requiring current scientific and technical knowledge (Kennedy 1987: 585).

In the 1990s, enrolment levels in higher education in China saw a swift uptake. At the beginning of the decade, the rate for the eighteen to twenty-two age bracket amounted to barely 3 per cent; by 2000, it rose by 10 percentage points, reaching almost 25 per cent in the early 2010s. The scale of this quantitative change is astounding, particularly when the extent of China's population is taken into account (Wu and Zheng 2008; Zha 2011). Yet, this increase continues to pose questions with regard to quality, since teaching standards are impossible to control in view of such a drastically changing scale. Though the expansion of higher education in China began in 1999 at the behest of the government, it gained broad social support shaped, among others, by the respect for education peculiar to the Confucian tradition. While at the outset the enrolment rate on the tertiary level amounted to 2.5 per cent in China and 5 per cent in India, by 2006 the proportions were reversed: the levels in China rose to 22 per cent, while India recorded 12 per cent. The two states also diverge in their aspirations in this area: the PRC's goal for the years 2017–2020 is 40 per cent, while India contents itself with just 20 per cent (World Bank 2007).

China has been attempting to form a group of elite universities, of which at least a few would rank in the global first league. For this purpose, the so-called 211 Higher Education Project was initiated in 1993, which selected 100 best Chinese universities (5 per cent of the total) responsible for 80 per cent of all doctorates and receiving 70 per cent of all government funds for basic research. The year 1998 saw the initiation of the so-called Project 985, geared towards providing support for an even narrower selection of nine institutions identified as China's future Ivy League. The Chinese are also responsible for the creation of the so-called Shanghai Ranking, the most famous classification of universities – and an instance of the country's cultural investment in hierarchies – designed to help China assess its standing in the world of science (Wojciuk, Michałek, and Stormowska 2015).

The dynamic of migration of Chinese students to Western states clearly indicates that the quality shortages at the local universities are increasingly made up for by learning abroad. Every year, roughly one million Chinese students attend universities around the world. Between 1999 and 2008, the number of Chinese students moving to Great Britain or Australia increased twofold, to Germany – tenfold, and to France – fourfold (Constant, Tien, Zimmermann, and Meng 2012). The largest group attended schools in the USA, which experienced a doubling of the Chinese student population in the period in question. In the academic year 2008–2009, there were 27,500 doctoral students and over 26,000 BA students from China in the USA. China attempts to secure the return of these foreign diploma holders, but the evident impact of this policy cannot hide the brain drain occurring on a major scale. In 2001, the percentage of Chinese graduates returning home was 14.5 per cent; by 2008, the rate increased to 38.5 per cent, meaning roughly 70,000 persons (China Statistical Yearbook 2009: 20–28). China also boasts the most foreign programmes and chapters operating in cooperation with local institutions – over 850. More than 150 institutions – mostly from Great Britain, Australia, and the United States – offer a double diploma to those studying in China, which makes it possible to reduce the costs of temporary relocation.

The state occupies the most significant position among those that seek to import knowledge. Only between 2000 and 2008, the number of Chinese doctors who have benefitted from foreign apprenticeship programmes has increased fourfold. An even higher increase – five times – was recorded in the number of scholars with a doctoral degree who organise such stays independently, for instance, by using post-doctoral training offered at Western universities (Educational Statistical Yearbook of China 2010). Today, elite Chinese universities employ only Chinese and foreign holders of diplomas from the finest American and European institutions. This practice is applied, for instance, by the Shanghai Jiao Tong University. Among the highest-ranked universities, English is increasingly becoming the language of communication (Zha 2011: 463).

The Chinese strategy of developing higher education and science is based primarily in quantitative expansion, second, in internationalisation, and third, in diversification of quality of institutions. The latter derives from the assumption that having a large number of decent universities is less productive than building up the potential of the few top institutions. As a result, the disparity between Chinese universities is increasing in all areas, the rule being, the winner takes all. Yet, the state has no institution in the top 100 of the Shanghai Ranking, and continues to trail Japan and Hong Kong in terms of quality. Brain drain still poses a problem, particularly with regard to the most gifted students – of those who pursue doctoral studies at American universities, 90 per cent continue to fail to return to China. Aside from infrastructure and expenses, the local academic culture suffers from lack of freedom and autonomy of research. It is also typified by strong government regulation, in political, economic, and administrative terms. In the humanities and social sciences, oversight continues to be exercised with regard to the content of the teachings.

In spite of dynamic change and improved participation and education levels in the society, China remains significantly behind the most developed states. Though illiteracy was almost completely eradicated (in 2008, only about 6 per cent of the Chinese were illiterate), enrolment rates in secondary and tertiary education remained stuck at a far lower level than in the most developed states. With the rapid economic development and expansion of industrial production, the state suffers from shortages of the necessary competencies and the inadequacy of those available to the requirements of the labour market. The demand for technical abilities exceeds the supply. In 2009, the ratio of supply to demand for specific qualifications was 1.43 for the lowest-ranked positions, 2.24 at the senior technical level, and 2.28 for experienced engineers. Of the almost five million university graduates in 2009, 1.4 million possessed competencies not favoured by the labour market (World Bank 2007). In 2005, only 160,000 of the over 1.5 million Chinese engineers had sufficient qualifications to warrant employment in multinational corporations – a number not dissimilar to that posted by Great Britain (Farrell and Grant 2005). Chinese education reforms after the Cultural Revolution promoted general competencies rather than vocational schooling. Between 1990 and 2008, the enrolment rate at the middle level increased over seven times, from 4.6 million to 80.5 million persons; in the same period, the number of pupils in the vocational school system rose from three million to 7.7 million, that is, roughly two and a half times. While the development of high schools was a success, the supply of vocational training does not meet the demand, and vocational schools tend to offer inferior quality schooling (Witt and Redding 2014).

Though companies could organise training to mitigate the deficit created by public education, the heavy rotation of workers discourages such investment. In many areas, it amounts to around 30 per cent a year, and in extreme cases can even reach 10 per cent a month (Smyth, Zhai, and Li 2009). Companies compete fiercely for that relatively minor group of workers equipped in sufficient qualifications, which does nothing to help the case of establishing a system of training provided for by the employers. A debate is raging whether China, supposedly still Communist, but in practice increasingly capitalist, follows the model of a coordinated market economy or the liberal variant. In its official discourse, the state subscribes to an active development policy, suggesting proximity to the coordinated model promoted by Japan and the Asian tigers, but in practice, most analyses indicate that the local institutions are more reminiscent of a liberal market economy (Witt and Redding 2014; Walter and Zhang 2012). The Chinese education system is nothing like those found in coordinated economies, and even in this regard the institutions betray a liberal market approach to organisation, with all its attendant faults that may prove an obstacle to the state's development if it follows the path of industrialisation through advanced technical abilities.

Conclusion

On the global map of science and knowledge, the United States occupies a central position, enjoying superiority in practically all aspects. Their dominance is also of a normative character and it often translates into the ability to set the tone of scientific debate, influence theoretical and methodological trends, and deploy powerful discourses of science from the position of a global power. The centre creates networks with other powerful players, mostly the major English-speaking countries: Great Britain, Canada, and Australia. The European Union continues to play a significant part, but its long-term position is uncertain. On the one hand, it attempts to compete with the USA according to rules largely defined by the superpower; on the other hand, it rejects some American ideas, proposing alternative rules of action. The third key region in this area is Asia, which is typified by the broad variety of its component parts. Singapore, Korea, and Japan number among important locations on the global map of science and knowledge, but their strength continues to lie in lightning-fast adoption of the latest knowledge and its adaptation to industrial implementations, rather than independent pursuit of breakthroughs in human cognition. In the last decade, the Republic of Korea has made significant advances in risky innovations, but its scientific potential remains lower than that of the leading states in this area. China, in turn, has experienced an unprecedentedly fast quantitative rise and harbours major ambitions of attaining the status of a superpower. In qualitative terms, however, in spite of efforts to build up elite institutions, it remains locked at a level far removed from the global leaders. In this respect, the future of China is still in the making.

Given that the policy recipes for science and innovation are applied *mutatis mutandis*, to the extent of their capacity and with regard for local peculiarities in every country, global competition is on the rise, changing the landscape of education systems, science, and innovation, as well as significantly affecting the conditions of operation of universities. Competition is increasing: universities adapt to the conditions of the market more frequently, accepting an increasingly business-oriented identity in an effort to retain their position as the producers, disseminators, and users of knowledge and competencies. The activities of academic institutions are particularly affected by changes in the rules of knowledge production, especially the globalisation of science, and the international competition for talent. The divergence of demographic processes, globalisation of labour markets, increasing mobility of students and scientists, and specific public policies aimed at stimulating and shaping the science sector to the demands of the state's global competitiveness, are also of special significance. In Europe, strategies and goals of the EU policy geared towards unifying some of the institutional arrangements between member states with a view to increasing its global competitiveness are added to this structure.

The process of internationalisation of science is also shaped by the inclusion of the quickly developing Asian powers, primarily China and India. A part of industrial production is being shifted outside of the OECD, where rising numbers of subcontractors are already operating. Major corporations increasingly move their research and development activities outside of their countries of origin in the global centre. The heart of global economy and politics shifts towards Asia, and states in that region – much as their counterparts in the OECD – invest in education, universities, research, and innovation, bringing on a decline of the West's relative impact on the progress of science and higher education. Without a doubt, the USA is still ahead of the pack due to the accumulated capital allocated in universities as well as innovative enterprises. It also benefits continuously from an influx of new talent from all over the world thanks to its immigration policy, and even more so because of its attraction for talented persons from across the world who dream of careers in the academia or the R&D sector. With China, in turn, the USA shares an ambition that other states do not harbour – the drive towards superpower status in science and knowledge, which sees the USA continuously escape forward and China mobilise its immense potential to make up for delays in development. It is uncertain whether China will advance beyond the role of the recipient of scientific and technical knowledge, in which it excels in the same way that Japan did before, to achieve advanced science and radical technological innovations.

Though human capital and the progress of knowledge are factors for economic growth, if it occurs at an excessive speed or in the wrong direction, negative consequences should be expected. James Heckman, Lance Lochner, and Christopher Taber (1998a, 1998b) indicate that a drastic increase in the supply of people with higher education can lead to a decrease in wages previously accorded for given qualifications. This, however, is a micro-level effect of significance to some workers, but not necessarily as important or deleterious for the economic policy of the state; in fact, in some cases it might prove beneficial in that regard. Yet, one clear negative consequence is the decline in the quality of instruction that usually accompanies quantitative expansion. When that occurs, the overburdened universities cannot provide the necessary infrastructure, let alone cadres, quickly enough.

Many specific studies concerning particular education systems indicate that the expansion and globalisation of education contributes to social inequality, even as better education can become the means of improving one's opportunities

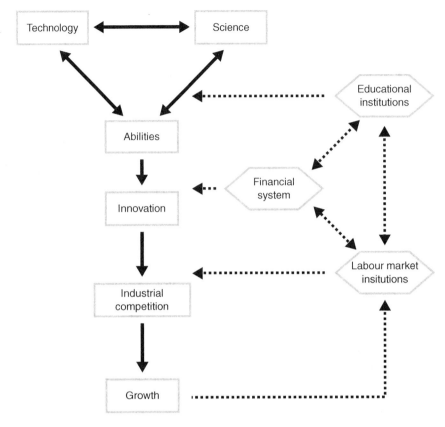

Figure 4.19 Ties between education, science, and innovation and other sectors.
Source: own elaboration based on Amable 2003: 86.

for social advancement. The globalisation of educational competition alters the rules of the game; the highest standard in a given country is increasingly commonly defined as the highest standard in the world (or rather, the standard thought to be the highest). As a result, local standards lose in relative prestige and come to be perceived as semi-peripheral or peripheral.

The economic aspect of education and science derives its significance not only from the potential present in the area, but also from interactions between human capital, the science sector which produces ideas, the technology sector which translates these ideas into artefacts, and the productive sector which introduces prototypes onto the market. The efficiency of this interaction depends primarily on the three sets of institutions and their mutual relations and synergy: the system of education and training that provides an adaptable, well-trained labour force; the financial system that defines the temporal horizon for innovation and production and plays a vital role in the selection and funding of investments; and the labour relations system that indirectly determines competitiveness of pricing and other aspects, such as the quality of cooperation within relations of production (Amable 2003: 86).

There is a clear global inequality in scientific potential, since advantages enjoyed by the best and most developed universities enable the concentration of talent. The most gifted scholars are drawn in by the leading institutions, which offer the most favourable working conditions both in terms of wages and intellectual inspiration. Harvard University, the richest in the world, has an endowment of US$35 billion; the second-richest Yale University – over US$20 billion. These amounts vastly exceed the complete yearly expenses on higher education and science in most states. Pure market forces favour the strongest, leading to the formation of clusters of scientific institutions operating in a synergetic relationship with enterprises and the government sector. The most famous clusters are located in the San Francisco area in California and on the East Coast of the USA – mostly in Boston and other cities in New England. In this regard, the concentration of scientific activity is even more pronounced than in industrial production. In spite of the rise in the average level of technological knowledge, those in the lead can still escape forward in almost all countries of the world.

The conviction voiced by Christopher Freeman (Freeman and Louçã 2001), that the ability to establish a well-drilled system of development and accumulation of knowledge is a critical condition of the overcoming of delays in development, remains valid. Roberto Mazzoleni and Richard R. Nelson (2009: 382), too, observe in the conclusion of their past analyses that education and science constitute a significant factor in the processes of making up for economic delays. In particular, they note the significant migration between countries, which sees citizen of a state in the process of developing travel abroad to gain education and then return to their home country. Of particular significance is the adaptation of lessons from other countries, mediated by academic institutions and student and staff exchanges. However, achieving a developmental leap requires more than just the absorption of knowledge and technologies by an avant-garde of scholars – one still needs the entire complex of organisational and institutional innovations that can provide the means to exploiting that insight (Mazzoleni and Nelson 2009: 385).

Today, states that are competitive in the area of science and innovative are described through a set of characteristics typically represented by means of indicators and benchmarks. Due to the complexities of quantifying the area in question, the measures of human capital and innovativeness proposed by various international organisations induce numerous controversies, necessitating cautious application (Dzierzgowski 2012: 28–30). Analyses reflect not merely the parameters of science and industry captured by the indicators, but in most cases also the operation of the national innovation systems. This enables a discussion of the intensity of R&D, both in terms of outlay (especially public and private expenses on education and R&D) and effects.

The contemporary moment is characterised by a relative decrease in significance of the military sector because, in contrast to the 1940s and 1950s, technologies derived from research conducted for military purposes have not yielded comparably revolutionary civilian applications in recent decades. Since the dawning of the Second Industrial Revolution, military technologies belonged among those most strictly tied to the transgressing of the boundaries of human knowledge. This relationship became even more apparent after World War I, which saw the first use of chemical weapons – the fruit of labours of German science in the second half of the nineteenth century. From that point on, scientific progress constituted the condition of possibility of such ground-breaking technologies of military use as electronics and computers, space technology, and atomic energy, and basic research became a factor of the military power of a state (Gilpin 1968: 24, 1981: 132, 160, 165). However, as the example of the USA indicates, large expenses on investments in military R&D no longer yield comparably ground-breaking discoveries for civilian use the way they did in the mid-twentieth century. The question of the scale of the burden shouldered by the state in this regard also evokes axiological doubts.

The financial crisis of 2007–2008 led many states to change the course of their policies in search of fiscal stability, which mostly entailed public expense limitations. The maintenance of the outlay on the creation of abilities among the citizen, science, and infrastructural investments for business use meant the limitation of the extent of the policy of innovation in many states, such as Great Britain. Though the role of innovation for future economic development was not put to question, more weight was attached to the approach that discouraged state intervention in the shape of funding for early development. Instead, the belief that public intervention is only needed to correct the imperfections of the market returned to vogue. In this view, aside from expenses on expanding abilities and infrastructure, the state's involvement can only be endorsed in relation to basic research whose results are visible in a longer temporal horizon and potential applications are unpredictable and incalculable, which leads the market to provide insufficient support; in certain Western states, other forms of public intervention are actively discouraged (Mazzucato 2011: 49).

Notes

1 Unless otherwise stated, all data presented in this chapter come from statistics provided by the National Science Foundation (www.nsf.gov) and were collected in 7–10 July 2015.
2 See Fulbright Notable Alumni 2014, Bureau of State and Cultural Affairs, Washington, DC, http://eca.state.gov/files/bureau/fulbright_notable_alumni-2014_0.pdf (accessed 14 June 2015).
3 States classified according to the Human Development Index (2014), in accordance with the division deployed by the UNDP. HDI>0.8: very highly developed states; HDI from 0.7 to 0.8: highly developed states; HDI from 0.7 to 0.55: middle development states; HDI<0.55: poorly developed states; source: http://hdr.undp.org/en/data (accessed 10 July 2015).
4 This way of organising public institutions is sometimes described as New Public Management. More about the impact new management paradigms on education institutions in Poland can be found in Kordasiewicz and Sadura (2017) and Herbst and Rok (2014).
5 China, India, Japan, Malaysia, Singapore, the Republic of Korea, and Taiwan.

6 OECD statistics from that period use the category to refer to Belgium, France, West Germany, the Netherlands, and Great Britain.
7 Data obtained during a conversation with Claes Hagn-Meincke, an officer of the Danish Ministry of Education (9 April 2013).

References

A Bill for the More General Diffusion of Knowledge, Virginia 1779, http://edweb.sdsu.edu/People/Dkitchen/TE655/jefferson_a.htm (accessed 8 August 2015).
Adams, D. and E.E. Gottlieb (1993). *Education and Social Change in Korea*. New York: Garland Publishing.
Amable, B. (2003). *The Diversity of Modern Capitalism*. Oxford: Oxford University Press.
Ashton, D., F. Green, D. James, and J. Sung (1999). *Education, Training and the Global Economy*. Cheltenham: Edward Elgar.
Attewell, P. and K.S. Newman (eds) (2010). *Growing Gaps: Educational Inequality Around the World*. Oxford: Oxford University Press.
Bashir, S. (2007). *Trends in International Trade in Higher Education: Implications and Options for Developing Countries*. Washington, DC: World Bank.
Block, F. (2008). Swimming against the Current: The rise of a Hidden Developmental State in the US. *Politics & Society* 36(2): 169–206.
Bowles, S. and H. Gintis (1975). The Problem with Human Capital Theory: A Marxian Critique. *The American Economic Review* 65(2): 74–82.
Brown, P., A. Green and H. Lauder (2001). *High Skills: Globalisation, Competitiveness and Skill Formation*. Oxford: Oxford University Press.
Bush, V. (1945). *Science The Endless Frontier*. Washington, DC: United States Government Printing Office, www.nsf.gov/od/lpa/nsf50/vbush1945.htm (accessed 3 June 2015).
Carrington, W. and E. Detragiache (1998). How Big is the Brain Drain? *IMF Working Paper* 98(102).
Chia, Y.T. (2010). The Loss of 'World Soul' in Education?: Culture and the Making of the Singapore Developmental State, 1995–2004 (PhD dissertation). University of Toronto.
China Statistical Yearbook (2009). Compiled by national bureau of statistics of China, www.stats.gov.cn/tjsj/ndsj/2009/indexeh.htm (accessed 8 October 2015).
Constant, A., B. Tien, K. Zimmermann, and J. Meng (2012). China's Latent Human Capital Investment: Achieving Milestones and Competing for The Top. *Journal of Contemporary China* 22(79): 109–130.
Cummings, W.K. (1980). *Education and Equality in Japan*. Princeton, NJ: Princeton University Press.
Cummings, W.K. (1995). The Asian Human Resource Approach in Global Perspective. *Oxford Review of Education* 21(1) 67–81.
Dosi, G., P. Llerena, and M. Sylos Labini (2006). The Relationships between Science, Technologies and their Industrial Exploitation: An Illustration Through the Myths and Realities of the So-Called 'European Paradox'. *Research Policy* 35(10): 1450–1464.
Dzierzgowski, J. (2012). Gospodarka oparta na wiedzy: niespełnione obietnice i problem umiejętności (PhD dissertation). Warsaw: Instytut Socjologii UW.
The Economist (2015). Whose Brains are Draining?, 1 July, www.economist.com/blogs/graphicdetail/2015/07/daily-chart (accessed 30 October 2017).

Educational Statistical Yearbook of China (2010). CNKI, Knowledge Network Service Platform, http://tongji.cnki.net/overseas/EngNavi/HomePage.aspx?id=N2012010030&name=YZKRM&floor=1 (accessed 8 June 2015).

Farrell, D. and A.J. Grant (2005). *Addressing China's Looming Talent Shortage*. New York: McKinsey Global Institute.

Freeman, Ch. and F. Louçã (2001). *As Time Goes By: From the Industrial Revolutions to the Information Revolution*. Oxford: Oxford University Press.

Freeman, Ch. and A. Young (1965). *The R and D Effort in Western Europe, North America, and the Soviet Union*. Paris: OECD.

Fuchs, E.R.H. (2010). Rethinking the Role of the State in Technology Development: DARPA and the Case for Embedded Network Governance. *Research Policy* 39(9): 1133–1147.

Gilpin, R. (1968). *France in the Age of the Scientific State*. Princeton, NJ: Princeton University Press.

Global Demand for English Higher Education (2014). London: Higher Education Council for England.

Goldin, C. and L. Katz (2010). *The Race between Education and Technology*. Cambridge, MA: Harvard University Press.

Green, A. (2013). *Education and State Formation: Europe, East Asia and the USA*. Basingstoke: Palgrave Macmillan.

Heckman, J., L. Lochner, and Ch. Taber (1998a). Explaining Rising Wage Inequality: Explorations with a Dynamic General Equilibrium Model of Labour Earnings with Heterogeneous Agents. *Review of Economic Dynamics* 1(1): 1–58.

Heckman, J., L. Lochner, and Ch. Taber (1998b). General-Equilibrium Treatment Effects: A Study of Tuition Policy. *American Economic Review* 88(2): 381–386.

Herbst, M. (2012). *Edukacja jako czynnik i wynik rozwoju regionalnego*. Warsaw: Wydawnictwo Naukowe Scholar.

Herbst, M. and J. Rok (2014). Equity in an Educational Boom: Lessons from the Expansion and Marketization of Tertiary Schooling in Poland. *European Journal of Education* 49(3): 435–450.

Innovation Union Scoreboard (2014). http://bookshop.europa.eu/en/innovation-union-scoreboard-2014-pbNBAY14001/?CatalogCategoryID=Gj0KABst-5F4AAAEjsZAY4e5L (accessed 14 May 2015).

Jemielniak, D. and D.J. Greenwood (2015). Wake Up or Perish: Neo-Liberalism, the Social Sciences, and Salvaging the Public University. *Cultural Studies: Critical Methodologies* 15(1): 72–82.

Johnson, Ch. (1995). *Japan: Who Governs?: The Rise of the Developmental State*. New York: W.W. Norton & Co.

Kang, N. (2010). Globalisation and Institutional Change in the State-Led Model: The Case of Corporate Governance in South Korea. *New Political Economy* 15(4): 519–542.

Kang, N. (2015). The Middle-Income Trap: A Sociological Interpretation. A paper presented at the Society for the Advancement of Socio-Economics (SASE) annual conference. The London School of Economics and Political Science, London, 2–3 July 2015.

Katz, M. (1976). The Origins of Public Education: A Reassessment. *History of Education Quarterly* 16(4): 381–407.

Katzenstein, P.J. (1985). *Small States in World Markets*. Ithaca, NY: Cornell University Press.

Kaysen, C. (1965). Federal Support for Basic Research. In *Basic Research and National Goals. A Report to the Committee on Science and Astronautics*, March 1965.

Kennedy, P. (1987). *The Rise and Fall of Great Powers*. New York: Vintage Books.
Kohli, A. (2004). *State-Directed Development: Political Power and Industrialization in the Global Periphery*. Cambridge: Cambridge University Press.
Kordasiewicz, A. and P. Sadura (2017). Clash of Public Administration Paradigms in Delegation of Education and Elderly Care Services in Post-Socialist State (Poland). *Public Management Review* 19(6): 785–801.
L'Émigration des scientifiques et des ingénieurs vers les États-Unis (1966). *Le Progrès Scientifique* 93: 38–53.
Lesher, R. and G. Howick (1966). *Assessing Technology Transfer*. Washington, DC: National Aeronautics and Space Administration.
McDonough, K. and W. Feinberg (eds) (2003). *Citizenship and Public Education in Liberal Democratic Societies: Teaching for Cultural Identity and Cosmopolitan Values*. Oxford: Oxford University Press.
Mazzoleni, R. and R.R. Nelson (2009). The Roles of Research at Universities and Public Labs in Economic Catch-Up. In M. Cimoli, G. Dosi, and J. Stiglitz (eds), *Industrial Policy and Development: The Political Economy of Capabilities Accumulation*. Oxford: Oxford University Press.
Mazzucato, M. (2011). *The Entrepreneurial State*. London: Demos.
Meyer, J.-B. and M. Brown (1999). *Scientific Diasporas: A New Approach to the Brain Drain*. Paris: UNESCO.
Motoyama, Y., R. Appelbaum, and R. Parker (2011). The National Nanotechnology Initiative: Federal Support for Science and Technology, or Hidden Industrial Policy? *Technology in Society* 33(1): 109–118.
OECD (2008). *Higher Education to 2030, vol. II: Globalisation*. Paris: OECD.
OECD (2013). *OECD Science, Technology and Industry Scoreboard 2013: Innovation for Growth*. Paris: OECD.
Painter, F.V.N. (1896). *A History of Education*. New York: D. Appleton & Co. (facsimile: Elibron Classic series 2006).
Price, D.K. (1954). *Government and Science*. New York: New York University Press.
Rodan, G. (1989). *The Political Economy of Singapore's Industrialisation*. London: Macmillan.
Scott, P. (1998). Massification, Internationalization and Globalization. In P. Scott (ed.), *The Globalization of Higher Education*. Buckingham: The Society for Research into Higher Education/Open University Press.
SKBF (2010). *Swiss Education Report* www.skbf-csre.ch/fileadmin/files/pdf/bildungsmonitoring/Education_Report_2010.pdf (accessed 30 October 2017).
Smyth, R., Q. Zhai, and X. Li (2009). Determinants of Turnover Intentions among Chinese Off Farm Migrants. *Economic Change & Restructuring* 42(3): 189–209.
Tauxe, Ch. (2004). La maturité ne vaut-elle plus rien?. *L'Hebdo* 19 August 2004.
Taylor, J.O. (1835). *The District School*. Philadelphia, PA: Carey, Lea & Blanchard.
Tilak, J.B.G. (2002). *Building Human Capital in East Asia: What Others Can Learn*. New Delhi: National Institute of Educational Planning and Administration.
Tyack, D. (1974). *The One of the Best Systems: A History of American Urban Education*. Cambridge, MA: Harvard University Press.
UNDP (2012). *Human Development Report*. Paris: UNESCO.
UNESCO (2005). *EFA Global Monitoring Report*. Paris: UNESCO.
UNESCO (2011). *School and Teaching Resources in Sub-Saharan Africa*, www.uis.unesco.org/Education/Documents/ib9-regional-education-africa-2012-en-v5.pdf (accessed 18 June 2015).

Walter, A. and X. Zhang (eds) (2012). *East Asian Capitalism: Diversity, Continuity, and Change*. Oxford: Oxford University Press.

Wende, M. C., van der (2004). Introduction. In Jeroen Huisman and Marijk C. van der Wende (eds), *On Co-Operation and Competition: National and European Policies for Internationalisation of Higher Education*. ACA Papers on International Co-Operation. Bonn: Lemmens.

Witt, M. and G. Redding (2014). China: Authoritarian Capitalism. In M.A. Witt and G. Redding (eds), *The Oxford Handbook of Asian Business Systems*. Oxford: Oxford University Press.

Wojciuk, A. (2014). International Power Dimensions of Higher Education in the Age of Knowledge. *Stosunki Międzynarodowe – International Relations* 1(49): 219–228.

Wojciuk, A. (2018). Higher Education as a Soft Power in International Relations. In Y. Watanabe (ed.), *Handbook of Cultural Security*. Cheltenham: Edgar Elgar.

Wojciuk, A., M. Michałek, and M. Stormowska (2015). Education as a Source and Tool of Soft Power in International Relations. *European Political Science* 14(3): 298–317.

World Bank (2007). *Enhancing China's Competitiveness through Lifelong Learning*. Washington, DC: World Bank.

Wu, B. and Y. Zheng (2008). Expansion of Higher Education in China: Challenges and Implications. *China Policy Institute Discussion Paper* 36.

Zha, Q. (2011). Understanding China's Move to Mass Education from a Policy Perspective. In Ruth Hayhoe, Jun Li, Jing Lin, and Qiang Zha (eds), *Portraits of Chinese Universities: In the Move to Mass Higher Education*. Heidelberg: Springer.

5 Structural factors
Governance, institutions, norms, transnational regimes

The final chapter of this work focuses far more consistently on the structural aspect of power, namely, international – or transnational, given the involvement of entities other than states and intra-governmental organisations – governance in education and science. The theory section presents a detailed conceptualisation of the structures of governance that underscores this analysis. It perceives governance as a multi-layer and multi-level phenomenon involving both macro-structures (such as the manner of organisation and functioning of the world economy), various intermediate layers (the *meso* level), and local discourses that can significantly affect the configuration of the areas in question in a given state or region. Structures of governance define the context in which state and non-state entities operate; they decide which values are appreciated, ascribed prestige, and where the power of a state in an international context is drawn from. Therefore, they represent an impersonal, structural perspective on power. Due to their complexity, an all-encompassing analysis of the structures of governance is impossible to achieve. For this reason, attempts to study governance necessitate a choice. In my approach to examples of structural power, I chose to focus on one of the transnational regimes that operates in these fields. Traditionally, education and science were not considered a matter of importance for international intergovernmental organisations, but rather one of internal policy. Cooperation and coordination on a limited scale was only found among developing states and involved developmental policy and aid, with UNESCO playing a major role (Finnemore 1996). Traditionally, the normative and cultural aspects of education and science also attracted interest from the Council of Europe, which organised meetings of ministers and representatives to foster debate and exchange of experiences. Since the 1960s, the OECD began to involve itself in these areas, encouraging its members to increase their interest in these fields as well as responding to the demands of the highly developed countries. Its main goal was to devise indicators, collect statistics and improve their quality, and provide governments with reviews of their policies. Similar services were provided by the World Bank. Today, the OECD is the biggest player in educational governance, while also exerting an influence on scientific policy and R&D. Studies conducted as part of Programme for International Student Assessment (PISA), under the auspices of the OECD, are provided with a highly detailed analysis in this chapter.

Today, science is more globalised than education, in part because of indicators and international comparisons. In contrast to education, still shaped by public authorities, governments, and regional governing bodies as regulators and controllers, science is endowed with a much higher degree of autonomy peculiar to the universities themselves, and functions in a much more international context. Governance in science is also affected more comprehensively by various private entities, responsible, for instance, for the influential rankings that define the key conditions of operation of the universities and of the implementation of public policies, which become, in fact, a part of the structure of governance in this area not regulated by the state. One instance of that is the famous, though controversial, so-called Shanghai Ranking (ARWU), mentioned on numerous occasions in this work. One should note here that the various indicators differ in status and reliability; while PISA depends on an advanced, if not uncontested, psychometric methodology, university rankings famously affect government policies and the activities of higher education institutions in spite of their high selectivity and reductionism (Rauhvargers 2013).

The PISA study warrants attention for the impact it has had on education due to the widespread media attention it attracts, the influence it has on policy directions, and being repeatedly referenced in justifications for government decisions as well as in the pronouncements of at least some of the interest groups operating within national systems. I claim that the PISA study and influential international university rankings constitute distinct forms of transnational regimes. The first part of this chapter is devoted to a description of select aspects of the theory of transnational regimes, which will serve to explicate this level of governance and to prove that the empirical case in question indeed represents that kind of a regime. The problem of the significance of statistical data for public policy – the so-called governance by numbers – will also be addressed.

Transnational regimes as a level of governance

International comparisons, which constitute an increasingly significant layer of structures of governance in education and science, can be seen to form a kind of transnational regime. The theory of international regimes developed in the 1980s and 1990s was initially dominated by a state-centric perspective which sought to explain the effects of bargaining by focusing on the shape of the institutions, the distribution of burdens and duties, hegemonic leadership, and the social processes of learning (Hasenclever, Mayer, and Rittberger 1997). During the last decade, the focus shifted from the state towards non-state actors (DeSombre 2006; Grande and Pauly 2005; Josselin and Wallace 2001). In particular, it is believed that private participants, including those representing business, are gaining an influence on the negotiations and the formation of institutions and international norms (Arts 2000; Josselin and Wallace 2001; Cutler, Haufler, and Porter 1999; Hall and Biersteker 2002; Falkner 2003, 2008; Fuchs 2007; Levy and Newell 2005). The evolution of this approach within international relations studies over the course of the past three decades produced an image of contemporary transnational regimes that fits the theoretical model of governance deployed in this work.

According to Stephen Krasner (1982b: 185) international regimes consist of formal and informal, explicit or implicit principles (factual convictions, cause-and-effect mechanisms), norms (e.g. concerning actions categorised within rights and duties), rules (in particular, guidelines for action), and decision-making procedures (dominant practices for making and implementing group choices) around which actor expectations converge in a given issue-area. They allow for power to be exerted in specific issue-areas from a structural perspective. As institutions, regimes do not possess the agency that typifies international organisations. Early on, Oran Young (1982: 284) approached international regimes from a firmly state-centric perspective, underlining the role dominant powers play in the emergence of spontaneous, negotiated, or imposed rules by way of a combination of coercion, co-optation, and manipulation of incentives. Krasner (1982a: 499), in turn, claimed that international regimes typically form when the continuity of the international system is disturbed by powerful states pursuing their own goals. Thus was the study of transnational regimes born, and the theory went on to give ever more room to non-state entities, eventually achieving the terminological shift from 'international' to 'transnational'.

Marc Levy, Oran Young, and Michael Zurn (1995: 272) were among the first to observe that transnational regimes can be tacit, that is, exhibit regularity while relying on implicit rules and informal norms. In such cases, no mechanisms for ensuring compliance are necessary. Regimes can emerge by way of spontaneous formation – dispersed, bottom-up, and uncontrolled – as well as through negotiations; they can also be imposed (Young 1983). Spontaneous emergence occurs when expectations converge without any conscious effort on the part of the participants, whose involvement results from the formation of social practice. Most importantly, this means that the ordering of an area can occur without any legal rules (Ellickson 1991).

Scholars of transnational regimes can be divided into behaviourists and cognitivists. Behavioural explanations of the emergence and conduct of those regimes look to the interests and power wielded by the actors, relying on a methodological individualism which treats subjective preferences as a given exogenous to the particular reality. From this perspective, socialisation in an international system is relatively weak. For a regime to exist in this perspective, agents must submit to the rules, though total compliance is not obligatory (Young 1989; Zacher 1987: 174). Cognitive approaches shift the focus from behaviour towards intersubjective meanings and shared understandings – the so-called convergence of expectations (Kratochwil and Ruggie 1986: 764). Those approaches treat the preferences and actions of agents as being rule-driven, not only endowing international regimes with a regulatory role, but also identifying them as constitutive for the interests of the actors. In light of this conviction, it is impossible to argue that the efficiency of a regime can only be measured by the degree of an actor's subordination to the rules (Hasenclever *et al.* 1997: 164). Non-compliance alone cannot justify the belief that an international regime is absent. In this context, scholars focus not only on the causal mechanisms, but also – and primarily – on analysing the emergence and dynamic of common, intersubjective understandings. This latter perspective is consistent with the theoretical model of governance deployed in this work.

As far as educational and scientific regimes are concerned, international comparisons have become a condition of possibility for obtaining the knowledge needed for governance. As Joseph Nye (1987: 380) notes, learning can alter the strategy of a state, and in extreme cases even lead to changes in the policy goals in an area. One of the most famous studies of the diffusion of innovation, including institutional innovations, was conducted by Everett Rogers (2003: 14), who concluded that it occurs when innovation is communicated by way of specific channels among the participants in a given social system. The significance of an innovation is determined by the cognitively available choices made by actors who seek to develop common understandings and discover the effects of specific innovations by sharing experiences. Common conventions and cooperation protocols are needed at the boundaries, where this exchange takes place. Practices are adapted when they appear to be more effective than the alternatives. In terms of significant normative evaluations, Rogers contends that diffusion typically occurs slowly and resembles a laborious and complicated reconstruction of identity rather than the mechanical dissemination of information (Haas 1990: 23). The process unavoidably involves the questioning of previous policy goals and the search for new ones, along with the accompanying instruments. These activities engage both international organisations and national experts and governments. Contemplation and the search for recipes also often occur within epistemic communities. Thus, international regimes form in a dispersed manner, and the process itself, along with its effects, remains beyond the control of any single agent.

Even without mechanisms of enforcing compliance, a regime can become effective as its participants learn and socialise, which becomes its peculiar form of coordination. Uncertainty is an indelible part of a complex, deeply interdependent world. In this environment, decision-makers, whether in public or private entities, require knowledge and expert advice. The reduction of uncertainty is one of the objectives of transnational regimes (Hasenclever *et al.* 1997: 141). These regimes enable the establishment of new perspectives on, and approaches to, the nature of the problem that the actors want to see resolved. They help generate ideas concerning the tools that might prove useful in facing the given challenges, and enable the sharing of experiences of the relative efficiency of specific manners of implementation. In its further consequences, the regime obviously can seek to reopen debates in the normative layer, questioning previous convictions, and redefining the nature of the problem and the interests of the actors. Norms, rules, discourses, and practices are not set in stone.

The increasing interdependence and interlinking of individuals, non-state actors, and states in various areas demands a supranational answer to questions concerning efficient policies and proper behaviours.

This leads to the questions: how much convergence has to exist between actors for a transnational regime to emerge? Are all agents required to accept the proposed interpretations and the manner of their implementation in a given area of international relations? Were that the case, no transnational regime would ever have emerged. It seems, however, that before states decide if and how to cooperate in solving a problem, they have to achieve a degree of consensus as to its nature and extent, as well as the relationship it has to other areas of activity and the challenges they face. Failing that, the convergence of expectations is unattainable (Haas 1992: 29). Regimes are therefore not merely static descriptions of norms and rules – they can constitute a vital means of learning and socialisation for international entities, leading to a convergence of interests, and then of state policies.

Regimes can emerge intentionally, but also spontaneously; the latter occurs when actors are socially integrated within an international system and consequently create norms (Dessler 1989; Kratochwil 1989; Puchala and Hopkins 1982; Young 1980, 1982). Participants cannot predict all of the consequences of their actions and may be surprised by the effects. Regimes provide an environment for agents, define goals, values, and the extent of that which is appropriate and practical. Thus, they can affect the activities of actors within the system without determining them (Arts 2000: 534). Negotiations and the implementation of a regime are mediated by the participants, rules, resources, and the distribution of capabilities, which render some actors more effective in establishing these institutions. Typically, however, the institutions are not easily controlled: even when they are present and marked by significant efficiency, such regimes can provide only soft coordination. Some agents actively resist entry inclusion in them or sharing in their assumptions. Transnational regimes are thus more akin to evolving, dynamic, and contestable processes than a set of well-grounded and stable rules maintained by way of coercion.

Finally, neo-Gramscian and Foucauldian approaches to international regimes expose the processes of defining, ordering, normalisation, and stabilisation of particular meanings, rules, beliefs, ideas, and norms concerning politics, which emerge during socialisation. From this perspective, all beliefs concerning 'good practices' are normative, benefitting some more than others – in other words, they always include a more or less covert aspect of power. Regimes and the effects of their functioning thus indelibly involve tension and contestation. The extent and intensity of resistance differ in time and between regimes – in some cases, conflicts and clashes can occur deep below the surface, lending an air of stability and order to the regime. In such instances, a specific group of actors achieves success in legitimising its own discourse and absorbing competing discourses, but this condition always inevitably proves to be precarious. Regimes belong to a broader structure of governance and larger processes, influencing events on the local, national, regional, and global level as well as being influenced in return (Young 2008: 757–760).

Regimes change when new problems emerge, old ones gain new significance, new actors enter the field of play, their interests change, new understandings appear, and the balance of power shifts (Hasenclever *et al.* 1997; Levy *et al.* 1995; Young 1991). Within specific regimes, actors experience the changes either as a limitation or as an expansion of options. The boundaries of regimes are subject to contestation, negotiation, and change (Haas 1980). The very organisation of specific areas is also subject to change – for instance, when actors emerge who can successfully alter the definition and understanding of a given problem within a regime. As interests shift, the discourses which legitimise specific meanings can weaken and open themselves up to change. The existence of deeply varied interests and the absence of a broadly accepted understanding or consensus as to the right approach to managing an area increase the likelihood of appearance of a complex and inconsistent regime spread across spaces controlled by other institutions. Due to the divergent understandings and interests of the actors, antinomies, inconsistencies, ambivalences, and mutually exclusive norms can coexist.

One of the central research problems in this field concerns the reasons for and means by which states have established effective institutions to address specific problems, while other issues – even very urgent and demanding attention – were not subjected to such institutionalisation (Hasenclever *et al.* 1997: 37). Neoliberal institutionalists perceive this as a product of agent interests – seeking to maximise efficiency, actors will only succeed in establishing those institutions that serve their interests (Keohane 1984: 80). From this perspective, a regime can only emerge when it benefits all sides – when each actor will gain from its existence. It is also necessary to know the distribution of pay-offs in a given game. In his polemic with Robert Keohane, Oran Young stresses that purely utilitarian explanations cannot be completely satisfying in this context given that negotiations, once they occur, are conducted in conditions of insecurity of results, and the distribution of positive and negative consequences is unclear. Thus, states will attempt to compromise to the extent that the results are unpredictable, establishing principles that are reasonably just for all players, ensuring commonly acceptable results so long as they reflect the accepted rules of the game (Young 1994: 102). Regimes are thus more likely to appear once states accept them as fair and aligned with their own interests. Their emergence becomes even more likely in case of external crises. The absence of effective leadership, on the other hand, can become an obstacle (Young 1994: 110–114). The arrival of transnational regimes is accompanied by a feedback effect in which the institutions are shaped by the convictions of the actors and then shape their preferences in turn, affecting the manner in which they view their interests. One should note, though, that the fact of sharing intersubjective knowledge does not by itself ensure international cooperation.

Transnational regimes often give birth to epistemic communities, that is, networks of experts and political decision-makers who accept the foundations of specialist knowledge in a given area (Haas 1989). These communities have access to knowledge on causal relations among social and physical phenomena which is considered reliable and useful. They agree on a basic level as to the kinds of actions that would result in gains and increased welfare for a given community, and in some cases, humanity itself. They also intersubjectively share the same convictions concerning the criteria of scientificity, truth, and the verification of scientific hypotheses.

In education and science, regimes that exert the greatest influence on the structures of governance on a supranational level are, first, informal – that is, free from any clear and unambiguous norms – and second, implicit rather than explicit. Yet, they influence national debates as well as the decisions taken by public and private entities.

Most international relations theories assume that structural factors can affect all agents – including states. While the so-called second image theories, including Kenneth Waltz's (1979) theory which popularised the term, describe the means by which the internal characteristics of a state affect its actions on the international arena – among others, its capacity to modify the structure of the international system (Waltz does not recognise such a capacity), the so-called reverse second image theories define how factors on the supranational level affect the internal shape of a state. Considerations on the impact of supranational governance on the actions of states fit within the paradigm of reverse second image theories. From a broader perspective, the pursuit of an explanation for the activities of an entity on the structural level typifies all structuralist approaches in social science. As Peter Gourevitch (1978) observes, the pursuit of the answer to the question why national systems look the way they do often leads to the identification of the international system as the explanatory variable. National systems can grow out of supranational ones.

Today, the belief that systemic conditions determine state policy (particularly in the peripheries) is peculiar almost exclusively to a narrow group of Marxists representing certain approaches within world-system theory (Wallerstein 1974). Most scholars in this field accept that national policies mediate and adapt these norms, adjusting them to a lesser or greater degree to the local context. While particular premises from the world-system level may thus elicit responses on the level of the state, these responses are embedded in the local conditions (Gourevitch 1978: 901).

Approaches that explain similarities between different education systems in the world in terms of mimetic isomorphism – as discussed in Chapters 2 and 3 – along with Alexander Gerschenkron's claims concerning the conscious character of the development policies enacted by states involved in catching up with the global leaders, can also be seen as a part of the same approach. Both the imitation of the form of modern statehood that succeeded in the West – the object of knowledge dissemination – and the search for strategies of economic development that could serve as a response to the new international economic configuration are, first, instances of the pursuit of knowledge about successful practices in a given area, and second, reflections of a structural consensus concerning the basic goals, functions, and organisational forms the state should take in specific fields. Due to their dispersion, lack of grounding in lasting institutions, and especially the fact of their macro nature, those phenomena cannot be called transnational regimes. However, they would surely fit in the category of governance as defined here, since they have contributed to structures of governance at different times and continue to act within them. These structures of governance, in turn, contain the understanding of the power of the state on the international arena at a given moment.

Though transnational regimes in education and science are an invention of the past few decades, it cannot be said that supranational governance only began to affect these areas with their arrival. In fact, the belief that a certain supranational regime operates there signifies that the convergence of norms between the national systems occurs at a higher pace than in regular diffusion. The emergence of transnational regimes around international comparisons of education systems discussed in this chapter differs from the previous stages primarily in intensity.

The role of international comparisons: governance by numbers

The analysis of the development of statistics (data, indicators, and benchmarks) in the service of governance and the so-called evidence-based policy constitutes a separate, extensive field of research. I refer to works within this problematic only to the extent that they provide me with observations relevant to the subject of this work, since one of the claims I am putting forward involves the international comparisons that give birth to informal and implicit transnational regimes. Soft coordination in education and science makes extensive use of various indicators, both on the side of expenditures and of effects, with the latter – owing to their persuasiveness – gaining in significance over the past few decades and providing a much stronger impulse for the formation of transnational regimes.

Theodore Porter (1996), author of the classic work on the role of numbers in public policy, proposes that statistical data, indicators, charts, and graphs be treated as specific communication strategies; more critical approaches would describe them as discursive practices. Due to their nature, these strategies are associated with specific communities, consisting primarily of scholars. The peculiarities of statistics and quantitative data lie in part in the fact that information on the results of studies and analyses is relayed in a standardised manner, which enables the unification of the multiplicity and variety of contexts, events, and transactions. After all, as a form of language, mathematics is highly structured and governed by much stricter rules than natural languages are. Its very use requires competency and discipline. The criteria of access for its users are identical all over the world, so long as they intend to use it competently. The development of this type of knowledge requires the imposition of an equal standard of collecting information that can then be processed. If this is achieved, the knowledge described in the language of mathematics becomes easily accessible to experts throughout the world, immediately universal and free from its native context. Numbers share qualities that render them more mobile, stable, and susceptible to various combinations as carriers of information than is the case with words (Robson 1992).

Counting enables the isolation of the defining feature of an object of this process, while leaving all other characteristics aside. The complexity of the phenomenon is reduced while the transfer of information about it is facilitated.

The frequently sophisticated methodologies deployed in measurements of complex phenomena yield results, which, on the one hand, can be easily digested and memorised, while on the other drawing closer to the sphere of the objective, away from the less reliable 'subjective opinion'. Numbers easily stabilise the content they carry because they usually depend on an at least minimal agreement between the experts concerning the manner in which certain phenomena and objects are to be measured. Statistics standardise and reinforce homogeneity, and sometimes merely the illusion thereof, thus enabling comparisons and connections between realities heretofore completely distinct. They serve to enhance debate on the sources of success and failure, contributing to the formation of new rules and prescriptions, which then reflexively affect the actors, modifying their behaviour.

Rationalisation is among the features that global norms are at least believed to possess. David Strang and John Meyer (1993) even refer to the 'theorisation of reality', as an indelible part of globalisation. It is based on the search for general, abstract rules that serve as sources of recommendations unattainable through local knowledge. These models contain causal and normative arguments concerning the right courses of action for various actors, from nation-states to individuals. Though this 'global' knowledge is considered rational, it is rarely unambiguous and does not provide a unified system assigning a clear direction to all activities. It is more reminiscent of a toolbox or a repertory actors mine for what they need to or can use (Swidler 1986: 277). Thus, it is only reasonable to expect competing solutions rather than a single recipe for all, and furthermore, active users rather than passive and unreflecting imitators.

In this context, arguments which have the status of scientific knowledge are treated with particular respect. The absence of a general model warranting even a basic theoretical description makes the dissemination of a given norm harder and therefore less likely. The theorisation of certain practices in education and science, driven by the analysis of successful systems, facilitates the diffusion of practices and patterns. Such theoretical formulas can assume drastically varied forms – from simple terms and typologies to highly abstract, complex, and rich models. Theorisation and quantification lend order to diffusion, facilitating the communication that accompanies it and contact between the usually loosely connected actors. Thanks to an extensive collection of indicators, the disseminated knowledge contains information on the response a similar system exhibited to a given situation and the resulting effects, justifying the expectation that comparable action (if adapted to a different state) will yield comparable results. All 'similar' states are encouraged to follow this practice and assume similar priorities. Theoreticians can become the key links in the diffusion process provided their arguments are persuasive and clear (Strang and Meyer 1993). Like quantitative data, practices which become the object of theory can be detached from their original context with greater facility and travel freely.

The adaptation of 'a solution that works', a pattern based in scientific knowledge or 'evidence', confers prestige on both the entity that provides the pattern and that which appropriates it, declaring on the side of modernisation. Some international organisations and groups of experts offer institutional or third-party support to states which seek to efficiently implement modernisation. As a result, a growing number of issues are subjected to an international debate and rationalisation, leading to the emergence of a degree of organisation in this structure, with subsequent issue-areas manifesting more or less informal and often implicit transnational regimes.

Porter (1996: 8, 27), too, observes that quantitative data are particularly valuable to the bureaucracy, engaged in a constant search for justifications of its own decisions motivated by the absence of a public mandate conferred through elections, let alone any divine right. To justify one's decision with specific data is the most objective manner of disclosing one's motives, and it steals much of the wind from potential opponents, nullifying the weight of charges of arbitrariness and favouritism, which public administrators tend to face. Scientific evidence confirms the just and impartial demeanour of the decision-makers and provides an easy tool for rationalisation. Statistical data are endowed with great powers of persuasion in this context.

Adherence to norms connotes legitimation (Barnett and Finnemore 2004). However, as the theoretical perspective assumed in this work indicates, interactions with norms and structures are not free from relations of power. This should not be taken to mean that the acceptance of norms is necessarily elicited by force or strategic calculation. In this view, strategic thinking itself, like other forms of social action, is much more rationalised than rational. External criteria of assessment of this rationality often command more respect than their national counterparts (Meyer and Rowan 1977). For numbers to affect the society, they need to be respected by the people they refer to and whose behaviour they are supposed to affect. International comparisons of the abilities of schoolchildren, of the quality of universities, and of other parameters in education and science operate according to the same mechanism as grading at school or in national exams. Their efficiency as a structure of governance is dependent on the extent to which their indications are perceived as correct and relevant for the context in which the grading takes place. With that ensured, they can impart a direction on the very activities they are assessing. Thus, numbers create norms – both the most gentle and the most persuasive form of power (Porter 1996: 45). This phenomenon, which Foucault described as governmentality, is captured in the famous saying of management experts: 'Be careful what you measure, because that is what we are going to produce.'

The use of quantification and measurement in social sciences and political analyses evokes much scepticism, particularly on the left and among the conservatives. This work represents a moderate view on the use of data in public policy, recognising many examples of productive deployment among the obvious abuses. In themselves, these practices are not deleterious or beneficial – their effects depend on the shape of the given indicator, the interpretation of the study, and the specific application. However, effects cannot always be predicted in entirety: actors have limited control over the use made of the data, and the regimes are not easily controlled.

Focusing on the benefits, one might point out that because of its unifying and impersonal character, the use of data as basis for political decisions reinforces egalitarianism by naturally abstracting from the privileges enjoyed by the elites and treating all actors within specific groups equally. Already in 1932, Harold Lasswell observed that the use of formal language is as distant as possible from monarchism. In his view, the American political system's love affair with quantitative, objectified data derived precisely from its democratic character. Meanwhile, the British system was less susceptible to formal models of understanding and communication because the local political and administrative leaders formed a tight milieu. Faith in numbers grows out of the belief in progress; most statistical analyses of societies can be associated with the desire to improve the living conditions of workers, children, the poor, women, and 'racial' or ethnic minorities (Porter 1996: 77, 80). Due to the ties between evidence-based policies, and other rationalisations of political decisions, and modernisation, participation in particular international regimes based on 'objective and certain knowledge' is currently perceived as a source of prestige in itself, a symbol of reverence for values that typify civilised, progressive states (Löwenheim 2008).

On the other hand, though, excessive reliance on numbers can be harmful due to the ease with which they transgress disciplinary and state boundaries, which entails the lessening of the depth of contextualisation and evasion of key questions. The medium that allows the different needs, aspirations, and goals to be voiced in a common language can thus provide faulty guidance for decision-making. In many cases, it is tacit knowledge – the very opposite of statistical data – that contains the most valuable lessons. Another risk involved in governance by numbers is the excessive concentration on indicators, whose specificity cannot communicate the precise worth of a given value or good. In other words, the influence this measurement system exerts on the attitudes of actors can lead the bad (and easily quantified) money to drive out the good – whether through inadequacy of measurement, or omission due to faulty calibration of the system. Governance by numbers carries the same opportunities and threats as meritocracy and technocracy – though it does away with various forms of clientelage with efficiency, a valuable and unique part of a culture may be lost in the process.

Today, measures, indices, rankings, and other international comparisons are a part of governance.[1] They can politicise or depoliticise issues, shift particular fields into different layers of the structures of governance, or strengthen some social identities at the expense of others. They also foster relationships of knowledge and truth, which transgress borders, shaping a space for new questions and enabling various modes of surveillance, communication, and activity (Krause Hansen and Mühlen-Schulte 2012: 455). Due to the aforementioned peculiarities of statistical data, regimes based on international comparisons can represent a significant degree of autonomy with regard to agents, and the norms and rules that coalesce around these statistical comparisons can be more susceptible to evolution than other institutions established through social processes. Numbers entrench norms and, due to strong legitimation as 'hard science', can become an obstacle to the introduction and legitimation of alternative frameworks for structures of governance, leading the contesting elements to face greater difficulties when institutionalising competing values.

The PISA study as an example of a transnational regime

The PISA (Program for International Student Assessment) study constitutes another stage of the process of devising indicators and seeking out effective educational policy solutions for members of the OECD. The organisation, whose efforts exerted an increasing influence on the public policies of its members and international governance over the past two decades, has been the subject of relatively few scholarly works. Only recently did three monographic studies of the OECD see print (Woodward 2010; Martens and Jakobi 2010; Carroll and Kellow 2011). Here, the transnational regime formed around the PISA study is analysed as an instance of an informal, networked structure of governance, erected in the twenty-first century by way of consent and cooperation, and formed in part by characteristic epistemic communities that combine expert knowledge in social sciences – mostly of quantitative nature – with involvement (in expert capacity) in advising governments.

The peculiarity of the OECD and its role in educational policy

The Organisation for Economic Cooperation and Development (OECD) was established in 1961, a reformation of the Organisation for European Economic Cooperation (OEEC), an entity devised by the United States in 1948 to administer the Marshall Plan. Since its inception, the OEEC supported liberal democracy and market economy as a sort of economic counterpart of NATO. The organisation played a key part in promoting the so-called evidence-based policies and benefitted in return from the development of that approach by becoming a leading international think-tank. Statistics, reports, and studies published by the OECD are an irreplaceable tool for devising public policies in developed states, and increasingly also in those that aspire to this elite designation. Today, the organisation is widely recognised for providing highly reliable knowledge and recommendations based on it. Education figures among the areas where the role of the OECD increased the most thanks to the development of a set of various indicators and international comparisons.

Peter Carroll and Aynsley Kellow (2011) observe that the OECD is characterised by soft coordination, which consists in forming communities of experts around major themes – communities which can become so tight that one could characterise them as epistemic communities, and which include public policy analysts, representatives of administrations, and politicians, from both the organisation itself and its member states. The process of formation of these communities took many years and occurred spontaneously – it coincided with standard activities of the OECD, previously limited to peer-reviews of the policies of member states (the so-called peer-review process). This instrument was in place already in the OEEC, as a control mechanism for spending of the resources provided by the Marshall Plan, which provided public reports on government activities in that regard. Already at that time, the peer-review mechanism was free from any means of enforcement, relying primarily on enticement and persuasion (Carroll and Kellow 2011: 34). Since its inception, the OECD has been using a very limited set of direct instruments of reward and punishment for convincing member states to implement the political solutions promoted by the organisation, which did not include financial incentives.

During the second half of the 1970s, like other international organisations, the OECD shifted the focus from Keynesian economic recipes to a more neoclassical model, a practice that continued in the following decade (Carroll and Kellow 2011: 69). The 1990s, in turn, brought an expansion of the membership of the organisation with the inclusion of post-Communist countries, Mexico, the Republic of Korea, and subsequently also Chile and Israel. In addition, cooperation with non-members – Brazil, China, India, Indonesia, Russia, and South Africa – increased. The organisation, which includes some thirty-seven member-states, cooperates with over 100 other countries. Today, it is in the lead in the use of information technologies, expanding and reinforcing connections between experts while improving access to different data on the states. The feedback loop caused by the 'promotion' of this approach, furthered by the broader trend of developing statistics for the purposes of public policy, led to an increased demand for data and analyses enabling 'evidence-based' activity. The major EU report – *Eurydice* (2009) ascribes to the PISA study, as well as to PIRLS (Progress in International Reading Literacy Study) and TIMSS (Trends in International Mathematics and Science Study), a significant role as a starting point for the discussion on the quality of education. *Eurydice* indicates that roughly a third of European states experienced a marked increase of demand for higher quality information on teaching effects following the studies; more importantly, external exam systems became much more popular. The OECD also benefitted from an ever-clearer connection between human capital and knowledge and economic welfare. During the 1990s, these factors put the organisation in a favourable position, allowing it to significantly expand its involvement in educational governance.

Richard Woodward (2010) contends that the OECD has had spectacular achievements in cognitive and normative aspects of governance. Its member states agree as to the fundamental values promoted by the organisation, which facilitates the creation of norms and institutions around the OECD and its undertakings. Even today, it plays the role of a laboratory of sorts for public policies in many areas (Lingard, Taylor, and Rawolle 2005). These approaches to governance are flexible and easily adapted to new conditions. In many areas, the OECD can be perceived as a network of networks.

Kerstin Martens and Anja Jakobi (2010: 2) claim that the structures of governance that surround the OECD emerge, first, with the appearance of new ideas and their spread, second, through public policy evaluation, and third, from the production of data. The authors relate the various descriptions applied to the

OECD in studies, which are said to reflect the unusual character of the organisation: 'a curious creature, an amalgam of a rich man's club, a management consulting firm for governments, and a legislative body, idea inventor, idea arena, idea agent, idea merchant, and idea authority'. Robert Cox (1987: 259, 359) describes it as a body that contributes to the achievement of consent, operating in the name of a 'transnational managerial class'; for Anne-Marie Slaughter, in turn, it is the 'the quintessential host of transgovernmental regulatory networks, as well as a catalyst for their creation' (2004: 46).

The OECD does not merely provide states with recipes for action, but also with a space for framing common responses to the problems diagnosed with the help of the organisation; the eventual convergence of interests between these entities is a result of negotiation. Because of that, they cannot be reduced to simple conveyor belts, but rather actively partake in the production of consent. This semi-independent think-tank has no legal or financial instruments for intervention. Its efficacy is due solely to the establishment of consent and peer pressure (Rinne, Kallo, and Hokka 2004: 455–456; Lingard and Grek 2007: 3–5). Therefore, the governance that the OECD is inscribed in is mostly structural in nature.

Since its emergence in 1961, the OECD had an immediate interest in education. In the early stages, the organisation's activities in this regard were defined by a theory of modernisation that prioritised the promotion of technology, mathematics, and science. In time, the 'human factor' in educational policy became more apparent as a condition of progress. Planning in education seemed indispensable for the necessary number of scientists and engineers to be produced (Papadopoulos 1994: 21). During subsequent conferences organised under the auspices of the OECD, increased outlay on education was advocated as an investment in the economy (Papadopoulos 1994: 37, 40). The 1961 meeting titled 'Economic Growth and Investment in Education' played a seminal role in this respect.

Further institutionalisation of activities in this area included the establishment of Centre for Educational Research and Innovation (CERI); two years later, the Committee for Educational Workers and Engineers was renamed the Committee for Education, finally legitimising the OECD's involvement in the field (Papadopoulos 1994: 63). The 1970s saw many more organisational changes, with education increasingly associated with the labour market. Social issues rose to prominence at the time, particularly the question of equal opportunity, providing an impulse for the OECD to invest more broadly in education (Papadopoulos 1994: 74–91). The 1980s, in turn, were dominated by the problem of increasing unemployment among the young and demographic transformations; attention also turned to the shifting socio-economical context and ties between education and socio-economic growth (Henry, Lingard, Rizvi, and Taylor 2001: 64). Meanwhile, the form of the OECD's engagement in education evolved. While during the 1970s, it was limited to debates over public policy, the 1990s saw an expanded approach, involving more policy reviews conducted at the behest of governments, and the production of ever more data (Martens and Jakobi 2010:

164). In 2002, the organisation established the Directorate for Education, further enlarging the significance of the area within its structures, even as no meaningful financial or legal instruments have been attached to the body.

Already in the 1960s and 1970s, the OECD began to collect quantitative data from member states and construct indicators. From the outset, these activities were accompanied by a demand for an efficiency assessment of the systems and for a comparison of educational expenses in particular states. In the 1960s, the first handbook for educational statistics was devised to unify standards, but the quality of the data left much to be desired. The only thing the OECD could do was to plead with the states to be more thorough and follow the guidelines. Obtaining precise, reliable data about so many systems was too much for one organisation, and scientific comparisons were not yet possible at the time. Thus, activity in the area of education remained marginal, with few publications appearing (Papadopoulos 1994: 190). Up until the 1960s, its main achievement was to note the shortage of data. At the time, the OECD lacked a structure of governance for education. Though information on the importance of data could modify state policies in some cases, there was yet no transnational coordination or convergence of expectation which the organisation now specialises in (Martens and Niemann 2009).

It was only in the 1990s that a qualitative change occurred in this respect – the organisation built up its capabilities of generating educational data, shifting accents from expense analysis to the search for effects and efficiency indicators. With data collection under control, comparisons and analyses became much more reliable. By developing the benchmarks, the OECD achieved recognition for its input into developing educational statistics, with results published yearly in *Education at a Glance*. The organisation continues to optimise thirty-six basic indicators, striving to maintain the capacity for comparisons between particular periods. New benchmarks are also established to improve the capabilities for comparisons and the usefulness of existing data.

The PISA study and state policy

The OECD gained worldwide fame in the field of education thanks to the PISA study. The most advanced of all international indicators in the field, PISA studies measure the effects rather than the outlay and are conducted under complete control of the OECD, which eliminates the possibility of incomplete information that occurs when states report on their own achievements. After the OECD resigned from developing indicators in the 1970s, the American government took a decade to pick up on the notion, postulating the creation of tools that enabled the assessment of the quality of national education systems by way of international comparisons. The immediate impulse for the initiative came from a report published in 1983, titled *Nation at Risk: Imperatives for Educational Reform*, which uncovered serious deficits in the American school system. Ronald Reagan's administration turned to the OECD, asking for help in identifying the causes of poor performance of American schools, and international comparisons provided the means (Martens and Jakobi 2010: 172). In contrast to other international studies assessing the abilities of students and adults previously conducted by the IEA (International Association for the Evaluation of Educational Achievement) as a research project, the measurements applied by the OECD were meant to serve public policy first and foremost. Thus, from the beginning, they were considered a useful tool for decision-makers. However, work on the project only gathered pace ten years later, in part thanks to interest from France, whose new, left-leaning government headed by Lionel Jospin sought arguments for a reform promoting equal opportunity among students. At the time, it was thought that a comparison between the French system and its foreign counterparts would provide the means of exerting pressure, since the solutions applied in France seemed far from egalitarian. Additionally, the idea of such comparisons continued to receive support from the United States. The establishment of PISA was immediately preceded by a series of actions initiated by another OECD programme, the so-called DeSeCo (Definition and Selection of Competencies: Theoretical and Conceptual Foundations). Implemented in 1997–2005, which was geared towards identifying key competencies of universal value from an international standpoint. Lack of knowledge about those competencies would render international comparisons impossible. In addition, they would help define the general goals of the education systems and lifelong learning (LLL).

The project involved specialists in different fields: sociologists, economists, anthropologists, psychologists, historians, education experts, statisticians, evaluators, political decision-makers and analysts, members of labour unions, employers, and other interest groups (Murray, Owen, and McGaw 2005: 34). Their work consisted in months of debates and consultations, lasting until an acceptably consistent, common knowledge was achieved within this highly varied group of professionals from different states. The DeSeCo programme fostered an approach to abilities based on the criterion of market demand, which includes both cognitive and non-cognitive elements of competency, useful in the formation of an 'flexible, adaptive, innovative, creative, self-directed, self-motivated and responsible ... learner, worker, citizen, family member, or consumer' (Murray *et al.* 2005: 36).

In 1994–1998, in turn, the OECD conducted an international comparison of abilities as part of the International Adult Literacy Survey (IALS), which looked at adult competencies in literacy. The first such undertaking in history, it combined the assessment of reading skills with an international perspective, providing a completely new context for the organisation's activities and increasing its influence. Though previous studies compared mathematical skills in different countries (e.g. TIMSS), in this case, the identical set of skills that was the subject of the comparison was represented in various different languages. In mid-1990s, this was a new and astounding instrument with a potential that encouraged the development of similar tools.

The three cycles of measurement provided the first internationally comparable, longitudinal database on literacy defined as a specific skill consisting in the ability to digest information, as well as a manner of behaviour. The object of the study was to provide knowledge for political decision-makers responsible for the LLL, as well as social policy and the labour market. It became another step towards the formation of a common, consistent, international discourse on competency and ability development (Murray et al. 2005: 39).

The competencies assessed by the IALS were then presented as the essential ingredient of a flourishing society, without which, according to the study, 'globalisation, technological change and organisational development' could not be met. The measurement tool itself was described as innovative, capable of transgressing contextual boundaries between systems and applicable in states of different languages and cultures, as well as guaranteeing an unprecedented accuracy of results in open questions-based testing. The development of universal standards of measurement of literacy provided another opportunity for the strengthening of ties between government experts, their counterparts in the OECD, officials representing individual states and the organisation, and commercial enterprises involved in educational assessment (Murray et al. 2005: 43).

The DeSeCo and IALS programmes fostered a transnational network of experts that continues to cooperate on subsequent editions of PISA, constituting – in the eyes of at least some scholars – a form of an epistemic community. Over numerous meetings conducted for the purpose of implementing the two projects, the aforementioned body of experts formed a largely common, compromise version of knowledge about key competencies and the significance of measuring them. The belief in the significance of this venture was also affirmed (Freeman 2008). In the years that followed, this epistemic community grew in strength, thanks in part to the significant methodological complexity of PISA. The degree of advancement of its psychometric tools seriously limits access for those outside of the cohort of experts, and even within this group, only a relatively small section of persons specialising in quantitative methods can understand the detailed solutions applied to these measurements (Goldstein 1998). The ability to raise potential methodological doubts is reserved for the few specialists by default (Steward 2014).

PISA as a set of norms and rules

The peculiar development of international comparisons conducted by the OECD, which helped foster a sort of transnational regime, is partially responsible for the efficiency of this structure of governance. Over countless sessions, workshops, and conferences, a broad understanding of the goals and the means to their achievement was worked out while the axiological positions of the members converged. The norms developed during this process gained broad legitimacy thanks to this inclusive and wide-ranging formula of cooperation (Grek 2013). Its research into efficient policies for knowledge-based economies, human capital, key competencies, and lifelong learning turned OECD into a major player shaping the meaning, understanding, and normative aspect of education.

The PISA study, which is the subject of this section, is thus not separate from the broader context of OECD activities. However, PISA is the element that achieved the most notoriety and influence on educational policies of states. This standardised tool for assessment of the abilities of fifteen-year-olds – in many states, individuals at the end of compulsory or common education – is designed to measure knowledge and skills acquired as part of compulsory schooling which are considered vital for 'full participation in social life'. In three-year cycles, the study assesses literacy and mathematical and scientific reasoning without reference to the content of the programmes of instruction in different countries – instead, it focuses more comprehensively on the practical applications of knowledge and abilities that one may come across in everyday life. These abilities number among those considered the most useful on the labour market, and high levels of facility in them is thought to attract foreign investment. PISA also collects data concerning the socio-economic status of the family of the pupils and the schools they attend. The data are compared between different editions of the study (aside from the first one), which enables longitudinal analyses.

The reconstruction of the aims that led the states to partake in the PISA study and the context of the undertaking was conducted on the basis of source material from the OECD. For this purpose, I analysed the contents of 271 documents for the years 1990–2014, found in the OECD archives at the organisation's seat in Paris and available for researchers, in November 2014. At its inception, this analysis of PISA as a transnational regime was supposed to rely exclusively on sources in the organisation's archive, but the query indicated that the OECD documents I could obtain access to were highly schematic and formulaic, and very underwhelming as sources of insight into the formation of the regime. As a result, I was forced to use existing detailed analyses in this area, which rely on a much broader empirical material. In spite of the shortcomings of the resources available at the OECD archives, they provided me with the insight that by the end of the 1990s, when the study took its final shape, the broad consensus with regard to its basic goals and assumptions had already been achieved. Experts representing the organisation and the states participating in the study had experienced a far-reaching convergence of expectations and understanding concerning the most significant challenges to education in the period of transformation to the so-called knowledge-based economy. Below, the reader will find the conclusions drawn from the analysis of the source material.

The narrative of the creation and continuation of the study, as well as the official motivations of the states, remain constant between documents – a fact that finds expression in the frequent use of near-identical statements, and even whole paragraphs, in various contexts. Three major motives for organising the study are indicated. First, it is stressed that PISA considers effects rather than expenditures, as had been the case thus far, which allows for the states and their systems to be compared in terms of efficiency. Second, it is highlighted that the study has international ramifications, which enhances its usefulness and viability as a source of inspiration for reforms in other countries. The third repeatedly invoked justification concerns the labour market and the adequacy of the competencies in question from the perspective of its demands in conditions of globalisation.

Table 5.1 Participation in subsequent cycles of PISA

PISA 2000		PISA 2003		PISA 2006		PISA 2009		PISA 2012	
32*		41		57		67		65	
OECD	OECD non-members	OECD	OECD non-members	OECD	OECD non-members	OECD	OECD non-members	OECD	OECD non-members
28	4	30	11	30	27	30	37	34	31

Source: own elaboration of data from the OECD.

Note

* The number of participants mostly comprises states, but in some cases, city, district, and other school systems can partake. No state resigned from participation – instead, new ones join the study; cities and minor systems do sometimes opt out.

The theme of modernisation is also visibly present, particularly in such categories as the 'skills of tomorrow', human capital, and knowledge-based society, as well as notions related to effective management and efficient public policy under limited resources. Many documents voice a deep conviction that the results of the PISA study should be presented in a manner that would motivate reform.

According to its authors, the regularity with which the study is conducted – every three years, with the nine-year cycle providing an in-depth view of the progression of results in mathematics, literacy, and scientific reasoning – enables the monitoring of the effects of reform, which are only apparent after a while and require a familiarity with the trends to be properly assessed. The cyclical aspect of the study allows states to gradually construct a detailed profile of the abilities of their students and correlate these results with other indicators and the analysis of institutional changes (Schleicher 2006: 31). The exceptional character of the study also derives from the fact that the programme involves over sixty states, including thirty from the OECD. Such an extensive scale increases the analytic capabilities of the data generated by the OECD.

The OECD itself presents the programme as an exceptional venture due to its political implications and the fact that, from the perspective of political decision-makers, it provides a stable reference point that enables the monitoring of the evolution of education systems.

> Governments and the general public need solid and internationally comparable evidence of educational outcomes. In response to this demand OECD has launched the PISA. OECD/PISA will produce policy-oriented and internationally comparable indicators of student achievement on a regular and timely basis. The assessments will focus on 15-year-olds, and the indicators are designed to contribute to an understanding of the extent to which education systems in participating countries are preparing their students to become lifelong learners and to play constructive roles as citizens in society.
> (OECD 1999a)

> PISA, has become the world's premier yardstick for evaluating the quality, equity and efficiency of school systems. But the evidence base that PISA has produced goes well beyond statistical benchmarking. By identifying the characteristics of high-performing education systems PISA allows governments and educators to identify effective policies that they can then adapt to their local contexts.
> (OECD 2014)

The conviction is apparent that today's world needs more than the national programmes of quality control – effective policies are impossible without reliable data, which become all the more useful when set against other systems. According to the OECD, they enable the identification of political and institutional solutions, and the information provided by PISA can allow politicians to find the factors that decide educational success (Schleicher 2006: 23).

In light of the documents I analysed, the foremost challenge for the politicians is to equip the citizen with the abilities that will allow them to achieve success in a globalised economy (OECD 2012). One oft-repeated claim stipulates that welfare depends largely on the quality of education, which expands human capital and provides citizen with opportunities (OECD 1999b, 2003). PISA is designed to focus on key competencies from the perspective of the labour market and adjust to the conditions of globalised international competition (OECD 2000). The goals of the programme include encouraging the states to invest in social development and social justice. From the outset, many of its documents highlighted its rootedness in the notion of equal opportunity in education, as expressed through the promotion of those education systems, which are typified by egalitarianism understood as low incidence of students with the lowest scores and limited between-school variation in results.

> Most importantly, the report sheds light on countries that succeed in achieving high performance standards while at the same time providing an equitable distribution of learning opportunities. Results in these countries pose challenges for other countries by showing what it is possible to achieve.
> (OECD 2004)

A large proportion of documents devoted to education in the OECD archive concern indicators, the practicalities of their creation, evaluation, and modification, and the problematic of data collection. The documents confirm that the creators of PISA derived its originality from the construction of the measurement on the basis of 'an innovative definition of the term literacy', that is, the ability on the part of the students to apply knowledge and abilities in several key areas, as well as to analyse, reason, effectively communicate, and solve problems, and interpret them in various real-life situations (Schleicher 2006: 31). The object of this assessment, therefore, is to discover to what extent the students can use the knowledge they possess for practical purposes (Schleicher 2006: 35). The focus is on what the students can 'make' with their knowledge, rather than on their ability to repeat everything they learned. In this manner, the PISA study posits itself as an alternative to other analyses, strictly bound to education programmes and devoted to measuring the knowledge students are expected to obtain according to the assumptions shaping the content of teaching that define the systems they function in.

The impact of the PISA study on state policy

The next step involves a review of some of the motives for states to initiate and continue participation in the PISA study. The analysis presented below does not constitute a complete reflection of the declared goals and motives; instead, it provides examples of the kinds of justifications that repeatedly figure in government papers and analytical reports compiled by think-tanks. The first description of the motives and justifications provided by the governments depends to a large degree on a detailed analysis of that problematic, and discusses such states as France, Belgium (specifically, the Francophone Walloon region), Germany, Hungary, Portugal, Scotland, and Romania (Carvalho 2009).

The most common justifications point to natural continuation, since the states in question have been involved at previous stages of the OECD's work. They also managed to amass experience thanks to participation in competing studies conducted by the IEA, though the latter have a more academic character and are less policy-oriented. As the documents prove, national experts cooperating with the OECD and advising governments in many countries played a crucial part in convincing the governments to the benefits the state could draw from participating in the study. The OECD's initiative in this regard coincided with plans for internal reforms, which put greater stress on collecting data on student achievements and using this data to design evidence-based policies. PISA resonated with contemporary intellectual trends in educational policy, in many cases going further than current national practice and providing tools of higher quality than those available to the governments. The prestige of the OECD as a symbol of modernisation in the 'developed world' mould attracted positive sentiments.

This last feature played a particularly crucial part in states which sought to pursue the global leaders, particularly the newly admitted members of the OECD, for whom participation in this organisation was a source of prestige. Such was the case, for example, with Hungary, for whom this allegiance served to underline its membership in the Euro-Atlantic world and adherence to its values, as well as to distinguish itself from those states of the former Eastern Bloc that did not take part in the study (Carvalho 2009: 88). Some states justified their participation by the example of others; media pressure was also cited – for instance, in Portugal – as were the arguments of experts themselves, who claimed that the tool would prove useful in politics. In the case of France, it was said that denial of participation would entail a loss of prestige, suggesting that the state had something to hide and solidifying the negative image of the state as an un-dynamic partner loath to face challenges (Carvalho 2009: 89). Furthermore, Hungary's participation was achieved not by the structures of governance, but rather by the circles of experts who had previously taken part in IEA studies, and who convinced the government to assign them the tasks involved in engaging in cooperation with the OECD team concerned with the establishment of methodologies for international comparisons in education (Carvalho 2009: 86–88).

The declared goals and motives of states indicate that the PISA study is an instrument of political legitimation of directions of reform, as well as promotion and control of certain priorities in educational policy. In Great Britain and Belgium (Francophone), it was viewed as an instrument for the so-called soft coordination, a relatively discreet means of disseminating and promotion of certain pedagogical, educational, and programmatic directions (Carvalho 2009: 89). Furthermore, in the case of France and the Francophone part of Belgium, the new approach to education as a measurable area attracted interest.

In some states, participation in the study correlated with the party in power. For instance, France's decision to join the study at the end of the 1990s was not met with fanfare and the government approached the results with scepticism to avoid antagonising the educational milieus. Yet, after 2003, in the context of planned reforms, it became a useful tool for the government headed by the UMP (l'Union pour un Mouvement Populaire) (Mons and Pons 2009: 38–39, 65–67). The cases of Scotland and Romania followed a similar pattern, with entry into the study coinciding with modernisation plans and reforms geared towards improved adjustment of the goals and the operation of the education systems themselves to the demands of international economic competition.

Many states questioned the methodology, claiming that the study promotes the Anglo-Saxon view of education and charging the OECD with taking a determinate, neoliberal approach to the society (Mons and Pons 2009: 20–22, 86–93, 34–35). Criticism concentrated first, on doubts concerning the very idea of comparisons and comparability and the normative aspect of such an approach, and second, on the entire paradigm which, critics claimed, subjected education to economic goals (Labaree 2014).

Numerous analyses were conducted to assess how the PISA study affects government policies in education. Stephen Heynemann and Bommi Lee (2012: 11) noted that twenty-one states implemented educational reforms in reaction to the results of their students in the TIMSS and PISA studies – nearly half of all states that took part in the studies. Reforms took various guises, from the introduction of standardised external exams, to the centralised development of programme frameworks in traditionally federal states, where the various regions have thus far enjoyed greater autonomy in shaping the content of teaching.

Sotiria Grek, whether independent (2009) or in cooperation with Jenny Ozga (Grek and Ozga 2010), analysed the cases of Scotland, England, Denmark, Sweden, and Finland, showing how the PISA study is incorporated into national policy. In their view, as the perception of education as a key factor of an economy's international competitiveness increased, the process of internationalisation – and, in some cases, of convergence between the systems – in this area intensified. The PISA study became one of the more conspicuous symptoms of this phenomenon, leading those states to perceive it as a political technology and a useful resource for governance. The so-called knowledge-based regulation that the OECD offers assumes that the indicators not only inform about the levels of absorption of competencies among students, but also indicate to the states where they are and where they should be given their other conditions. This knowledge is also a source of suggestions as to what direction the governments should take and how they should reform their institutions.

In states involved in the study conducted by the aforementioned authors, the degree of interest in transnational knowledge as well as the intensity of debate caused by the results of the PISA study has been uneven. The knowledge is processed, to an extent, by way of dialogue and mediation through the local conditions, as well as a reinterpretation of data, negotiation of their significance and solutions, and recontextualisation. Even where similarities appear between institutions and discourses in states with divergent historical and cultural traditions, the manner in which norms are adapted is always distinct due to differences in context, processes, and structures peculiar to the states (Ozga and Jones 2006). Thomas S. Popkewitz (2003) calls this the indigenous-foreigner phenomenon, addressing the peculiar form of mediation between the global standards and local applications. Such context-specific categories as the professionalisation of teaching or school autonomy gain a new status through research, transforming into an internationally legitimised knowledge, and are subsequently processed and digested in this modified sense in local systems, which results in peculiar effects. Alexander Wiseman (2010), in turn, claims that reforms conducted under the influence of PISA and the recommendations it contributes, produce similar, but not convergent systems. These processes are more akin to a diffusion of models encapsulated in the theory of mimetic isomorphism.

It should be noted though that the reports of the OECD are marked by exceeding care with regard to the differences between states and local conditions. Official documents provide no unambiguous recommendations from the organisation as to what the states should change in their education systems. Reports and analyses contain only highly circumscribed assertions referring to key facts and identifying successful cases. Still, the PISA study has spawned a set of interpretations and standard operational models. Knowledge and technologies lend support to modifications in national regulations, helping the governments implement reforms and legitimise the changes. Access to data concerning the results of different education systems facilitates the search for the so-called good practices and provides a starting point for answering the question of the most effective solutions. This knowledge is generated in unpredictable ways, and the results of the study had always yielded positive surprises as well as major disappointments. The results of the first study in 1999 were met with dismay in Germany, which scored far below expectations. In the United States as well, every new edition of the study sparks a debate on the unsatisfactory state of education, especially the wastage of talent of pupils from lower socio-economic backgrounds. Meanwhile, the 'discovery' of high education levels in Finland and Singapore, which had not been associated with quality education before, evoked quite different emotions. These surprises show that particular effects of the functioning of the regime in question are unpredictable and uncontrollable.

The announcement of results inevitably provokes debates on the sources of success and causes of failure of states. The winners receive appealing labels, such as 'strong performer' or 'successful reformer', providing an immediate boost to certain axiological models and thus turning into a source of international soft power for the given state (Wojciuk *et al.* 2015). The pace with which this is achieved exceeds that of the traditional diffusion of effective practices in the area of education, as described by John W. Meyer and Michael T. Hannan (1979), (see Chapters 2 and 4). Concurrently, states which post disappointing scores find themselves under increasing compulsion to change, which facilitates the mobilisation of resources for reform. Recognition as a 'successful state' results in countless study tours by experts from countries that sit lower in the table, looking for 'good practices' (Välijärvi, Linnakylä, Kupari, Reinikainen, and Arffman 2003; Sahlberg 2012; Darling-Hammond 2010; Tucker 2011).

Poland, too, used to be a destination for such visitors due to high marks among states at that stage of economic development as well as one of the greatest leaps in abilities measured by the PISA study (Herbst and Wojciuk 2016; Ripley 2013).

The functioning of a transnational regime can also be analysed from the perspective of agents. On the one hand, the effect of socialisation of states and governments to a certain common understanding concerning education, particularly its role in the process of economic development, cannot be underplayed. On the other, however, observation of examples of states that introduce reforms proves that the participants in the study were not only equipped in a certain kind of knowledge, but also actively engaged in attempts to use the existence of these institutions for their own purposes. Though the structure itself is uncontrollable, governments have a significant impact on OECD reports and official publications. If a government does not agree to the publication of specific data, they are suppressed. Furthermore, the OECD's recommendations are typically packaged in very general formulations, even as they manoeuvre between the varied interests of different states to help the governments in pursuit of reforms.

The results of PISA and various other indicators provided by the OECD and other organisations combine in a diffused and uncoordinated manner to produce an entire body of knowledge that develops continuously, generating new understandings, hypotheses, and norms. One particularly desirable part of that knowledge is the aforementioned 'good practices', that is, causal relations between specific institutional solutions and positive outcomes. The pursuit of 'proven scientific' knowledge about the mechanisms and rules governing social life that could prove useful in governance is highly pronounced. International ramifications and reliance on knowledge endow PISA with high legitimacy, thereby making the indicators it produces an influential means of coordination. These structures of knowledge are particularly convincing for the media, which tend to accept the results as given and ascribe to them a higher authority than, for example, to the results of national exams. The latter, after all, can only test the efficiency of the education system in terms of internal expectations, without reflecting on the actual ability of the students to succeed on the labour market. An international comparison also allows for the assumptions laying at the foundation of the educational structures of a state to be put to question.

Aside from influencing governments and reforms, PISA data constitute fertile ground for scientific research. A systematic review of publications devoted to the study published as reports and articles in different areas between 1999 and 2007 shows an increase of interest in the topic, particularly in economic sciences (Carvalho 2009: 12). The first group of publications uses PISA data for their own analyses; the second, put forward reflections on these results and the OECD analyses that accompany them. A third group disputes the theoretical and methodological grounds of the study. Most numerous, the texts from the first group indicate that the data fuel a debate, reinterpretation, and a shifting of accents (Carvalho 2009: 98).

The OECD operates in tension between the firmly liberal Anglo-Saxon model and the more social-democratic trend represented by some of its European members. This finds reflection in the set of values that always figure in the organisation's documents concerning education, one next to the other: efficiency and equality. The very economisation of considerations on education and its association with the labour market, stress on the achievement of global competitiveness by the state and elasticity of employment with the use of specific education while other aspects are left for the state to address, cause numerous criticisms. It is claimed that the organisation attaches too little importance to the significance of social cohesion and inclusivity or the strength of public education. The social-democratic critique of the notion of lifelong learning indicates that the concept encourages citizen to engage in a constant cycle of training and learning, acquiring new abilities and qualifications in preparation for increasing their chances in a never-ending process of seeking employment. By OECD recipes, the crisis of the welfare state will be resolved by its people once they take responsibility for raising their own qualifications to make themselves more 'employable'. 'Learning' is understood here as a peculiar perspective which identifies such an attitude as a vital part of the equipment of a citizen in an era of economic change, of the transition from the industrial to the post-industrial era. This attitude is accompanied by changes in the sphere of work, including the shift from physical to mental activity, from transforming material objects to amassing and processing information, from programmed tasks and routine activities to non-routine ones, and from roles resistant to change to ones that are often redefined.

The transformation of the process of education in view of those challenges involves, first, the transition from the passive approach of the learner to the engaged attitude of the active experimenter, and second, the move from teaching that informs and corrects mistakes in a hierarchical relationship to one that operates in an organic model, developing independence and responsibility in students. The PISA study suits this transformation because it does not involve itself in testing the ability of the students to memorise the blocks of knowledge described in the programmes, but rather focuses on the ability to apply the knowledge and abilities in key thematic areas in the practice of analysing, considering, and effectively communicating. Though some of the leftist critiques of PISA may be accurate, references to the aforementioned conceptualisation of governance by numbers seem more reminiscent of the hypothesis that statistics and international comparisons – for all their negative effects – can also become drivers of progress and emancipation.

Neoliberal bias is not the only error ascribed to the organisation (Meyer and Benavot 2013). Another common negative response to international comparisons predating the arrival of PISA purports that specific school systems are incomparable (Heyneman 1993). The study is criticised for a reductionist approach, assessing only those abilities that are cognitive, and among those, excessively highlighting those that are considered useful from an economic standpoint. Some sceptics dispute the belief that the competencies identified, which are considered universal, are actually decisive for economic success (Labaree 2014). Even those who agree that economic welfare is key to the success of states and societies also often stress the vital role of grit, lateral thinking – or, the ability to consider recognised problems from alternative standpoints – and creativity, motivation, determination, and cooperation, as well as social trust, which seriously affect human capital but are absent from the set of indicators deployed by the OECD. Some postulate the appreciation of who the students are instead of concentrating on what they can do.

Besides, other aspects of education are being invoked, which may lose significance as the normative visions involved in the international comparisons gains popularity. Here, there is no room for individual development broadly conceived, for aesthetic enjoyment, critical thinking, the expansion of an open mind, erudition, tolerance, cultural transmission, understanding of the society and of nature, social engagement, achieving personal goals or dreams, spiritual elevation, etc. Education can open the door to the world for the young, pointing out opportunities for the future and preparing them for various social roles. Only some of the tools needed to achieve these goals involve cognitive development; the experience of social and cultural exchange with other pupils and with teachers is at least as significant, in the same way that reading and discussing works of fiction is no less important for humans than literacy. Critics also claim that PISA mostly reflects the Anglo-Saxon approach to education, imposing a worldview on states which subscribe to a different tradition. Such arguments were deployed, for instance, by opponents of reform defending Germany's system and its peculiarities in response to the shock caused by the state's poor showing in the study (Münch 2014). Aside from promoting a specific type of student and teacher, the PISA study can contribute to the spread of a certain model of the political decision-maker. In this case, too, OECD papers leave no room for such considerations, which cannot be said about the media pronouncements of some of the specialists involved in the study, especially its internationally renowned creator, Andreas Schleicher. As an expert, he plays a decisive part in the popularisation of the knowledge derived from the PISA studies. His statements and recommendations are less restrained than the official reports of the organisation. In many press interviews and presentations at international summits and conferences devoted to education, Schleicher authoritatively promotes far-reaching conclusions and recommendations for governments, which, in his view, simply follow from the amassed data. For instance, at the International Summit on the Teaching Profession (ISTP) in New York in March 2011, he stressed that:

> states now have the opportunity to improve because they can diagnose problems objectively, rather than relying on the political intuitions of the decision-makers. This is fundamental. Nothing will improve if you do not measure it, which is why international comparisons matter. Looking at rankings, parents, teachers, and the authorities can apply comparisons and assess where their systems are in relation to those of other states in the OECD.... Having learned of the poor results their education system posted in one of

the previous studies, some politicians and experts of a less progressive mind phoned me to express their outrage. They said I expect their students to reflect on situations too far removed from their everyday life, which in their view was unfair. The short-sightedness of these people, which prevents them from noticing that both Chinese and American pupils know the answers to those questions, not only betrays the lack of readiness of the political decision-makers, but also highlights their unfavourable position in conditions of international competition.[2]

Transnational regimes tie the goals of education systems to the conditions of the global economy, proposing a path of evolution that could allow national education systems to optimise the position of the state within that economy. This is reflected, for instance, in narratives concerning the development of human capital for the so-called knowledge-based economy, in the promotion of a powerful culture of management of the system and a broadly conceived improvement of quality. The international aspect is expressed in the characteristic wording of statements concerning the mechanisms of change, including such terms as borrowing, learning, harmonising, diffusion of standards, and institutionalisation of interdependence. In this context, transnational regimes do not challenge the independence of states, but merely provide specific alternatives to institutional solutions and foster a discourse that underlines economic conditions and particular axiologies. The internalisation of education itself, on the other hand, is the most pronounced at the point where it meets the economy, in debates over human capital and lifelong learning (Dale 2005). The Organisation of Economic Cooperation and Development plays a crucial role within the aforementioned structures of governance and their interactions with actors, particularly states.

Conclusion

In spite of the doubts and potential weaknesses discussed above, the PISA study is a successful attempt on the part of the OECD to create indicators and build up structures of governance around them. The programme has largely resisted criticism owing to its widespread acceptance both among political decision-makers and scholars. In this case, international comparisons shape the debates and internal political initiatives by providing governments with benchmarks and regular updates in reference to the knowledge about how their states operate. As a result, the indicators and the accompanying reports and tools can succeed not only in moulding the debate on education and influencing public opinion, but also in coordinating state policy in that regard with the use of soft power (Carvalho 2009: 14–15). This transnational regime, which lends support to various, not always mutually consistent values, enhanced debates about education with different understandings of such issues as equality, efficiency, quality, employability, attaching them to questions of global competitiveness (Lindblad and Popkewitz 2004: xx–xxi). Education is generally a field with little tradition of supranational regulation, which is why potential transnational regimes appearing in this field are more likely to assume an informal shape and function implicitly.

As an international organisation, the OECD occupies much room in this analysis, suggesting a major agent. However, we are dealing here with a plurality of actors sharing diffused power and responsibility, and having very limited control over the process. According to the contemporary theory of transnational regimes and the model of governance assumed in this work, structures of governance are typified by the appearance of effects that are beyond the control of any single subject. Thus, it is a more fruitful venture to look at the effects of the regime than to search for strong agency in this context.

The norms spawned by the PISA study, on the one hand, promote efficiency, and their mode of operation partly consists in the production of an impulse/stimulus for greater competition. As a result, another area of social life is 'pressed' into greater rivalry. The rules and practices established in this context represent a more liberal approach. On the other hand, however, the level of public policy sees one of the most important leftist values – equality – being promoted. The results of the study indicate the negative impact of systems which assign elite character to quality education, where the socio-economic status of a child's family decisively affects its opportunities and results. Such is the case, for instance, with France, which experiences a significant divergence in quality levels between schools, with the best working exclusively with youth of a high socio-economic status. The case of Israel is similar, with PISA data being used in debates over divergence in quality of education offered to different social groups, among which the Arab youth fall prey to negative bias (Baudelot and Establet 2009).

This knowledge is a structure that generates important conditions of operation for states. Due to its area-specific nature and the placement at the intermediate layer of multi-level governance, it operates as a transnational regime, informally and implicitly. The impact of these structures on public policy takes place without any means of direct coercion, whether through incentives or punishments. In accordance with the expectations of the theory of governance by numbers, the efficiency of a regime is highly dependent on the perceived rationality of the decisions. International comparisons conducted with lesser or higher diligence provide justifications for political choices viewed as rigorous and scientific. Governments use the data to legitimise their policies. However, as analyses of reforms introduced in different states and justified with PISA results indicate, political decision-makers can draw even diametrically opposed conclusions from the same studies and react divergently to good and bad results alike. Though studies suggest what 'works in a given policy', they never provide straightforward answers. As these regimes coalesce, states are socialised and acquire knowledge and common understanding of goals and challenges of the future, with these interpretations serving as the grounds for the identification of interests and the best strategies for realising them. The interpretations are accompanied by a set of the so-called good practices and tools for the evaluation of public policy that suit the same 'paradigm' without necessarily exhibiting internal cohesion or a categorical tone. In the past two decades, changes in basic and higher education systems in different states followed similar paths in spite of the application of divergent solutions. Centrally designed coordination mechanisms were strengthened both in terms of administrative structures, teaching programmes, and the measurement of results. The importance of evaluation, monitoring, and various other tools ensuring accountability increased.

Chapter 2 discusses the role education played in the state-building process defined by the variously achieved centralisation of power. Globalisation alters the context, preventing states from exercising as much control as before over economic processes and flows, especially of capital. The demands of competition ramp up the pressure to transform the citizen not only into efficient entrepreneurs and consumers, but also for them to become competitive in a global context. As the instruments at its disposal change, the state often can no longer depend on regulation to the same extent it did before, and is thus motivated to look for new coordination mechanisms, including those perceived as soft. Globalisation also increases the dissonance between the democratic, constitutional, and social aspirations of the people, still moulded by the nation-states, and the ever-more difficult engagement in collective action through political processes inside a state. Multilateral and transnational regimes can sometimes increase a state's influence in some areas of social life, but they escape democratic – and often even political – accountability. States continue to play a decisive role in economic and social policy, but the changing international conditions force the political decision-makers to adjust their institutional frameworks to the new rules of the game.

At the same time, some states become increasingly conscious of the fact that the pursuit of optimal routes of progress for different societies cannot take place in separation from complex normative issues and internal peculiarities of a state. The belief in a single universal path to success is on the wane, as arguments abound for the interrelation between institutions and local cultures necessitating the adjustment of the former to the latter. Consciousness of these limitations informs the scepticism with which the likelihood identifying universal 'good practices' in public policy is approached. It also suggests the need for accepting the existence of many roads to the final goal.

Though the intensity of globalisation alters the conditions of their operation, the phenomena discussed here were present even before. One can surely observe a quantitative, if not qualitative, change. As Chapter 2 indicates, diffusion of patterns occurred in the nineteenth century, as well, but with much less clarity as to which practices were superior. Ultimately, however, the winning paradigms belonged to the West – even in Asia, dominated by the influence of the Japanese model established on the basis of German and, to an extent, American patterns. The study of the impact of governance on government behaviour allows for broader conclusions to be drawn with respect to the nation-states themselves. They prove that states are rooted in a broader, supranational environment and submit to the mechanisms of socialisation and stimuli that cannot be accounted for by reference to the traditional power wielded by some actors against others.

Such phenomena are best captured in approaches that include a structuralist component attuned to the diffusion of power, variety of agents, impersonality and indirectness of certain influences, and frequent absence or limitation of control over the effects of decisions.

The level of structures of governance in question, the transnational regimes, is only a part of governance, which includes both conditions of a much more macro nature, such as the stage of industrialisation or formally extant institutions and global discourses, and those from the micro perspective, affecting reality at the regional, national, or completely local level. The layers of the structure are built by a varied group of actors, neither of which exerts control over processes, and the evolution of order is not controllable. In contrast to the previous parts of this work, this chapter was devoted to the analysis of the more structural aspects of power in international relations rather than considering the agential side of the equation.

Notes

1 The roots of comparisons of education systems in a research mode reach back to the pioneering nineteenth-century works of Marc-Antoine Jullien, who published *Esquisse et Vues Préliminaires d'un Ouvrage sur l'Éducation Comparée* in 1817. In Asia, Nanijiro Nakajima's *Comparative Study of National Education in Germany, France, Britain and the USA* (originally published in Japanese), which appeared in 1916, achieved particular renown, with subsequent translations into other Asian languages – including Chinese – exerting an influence on the philosophy of learning, particularly in China. Reflections of this kind would subsequently expand throughout Europe and the United States, and then the rest of the world. Jullien and Nakajima's works discussed solely European examples, providing the impulse for the application of these paradigms elsewhere.
2 Source: own notes from the International Summit on the Teaching Profession in New York, March 2011.

References

Arts, B. (2000). Regimes, Non-State Actors and the State System. *European Journal of International Relations* 6(4): 5013–5542.
Barnett, M. and M. Finnemore (2004). *Rules for the World*. Ithaca, NY: Cornell University Press.
Baudelot, Ch. and R. Establet (2009). *L'élitisme Républicain – L'école française à L'épreuve des Comparaisons Internationals*. Paris: Seuil.
Carroll, P. and A. Kellow (2011). *The OECD: A Study of Organisational Adaptation*. Cheltenham: Edgar Elgar.
Carvalho, L.M. (2009). *Production of OECD's Programme for International Student Assessment (PISA)*, http://knowandpol.eu/IMG/pdf/o31.pisa.fabrication.pdf (accessed 10 August 2015).
Cox, R.W. (1987). *Production Power and World Order: Social Forces in the Making of History*. New York: Columbia University Press.
Cutler, C., V. Haufler, and T. Porter (1999). *Private Authority and International Affairs*. Albany, NY: State University of New York Press.

230 Institutions, norms, regimes

Dale, R. (2005). Globalisation, Knowledge Economy and Comparative Education. *Comparative Education* 41(2): 117–149.

Darling-Hammond, L. (2010). *The Flat World and Education, How America's Commitment to Equity Will Determine Our Future*. New York: Teachers College Press.

DeSombre, E. (2006). *Flagging Standards: Globalization and Environment, Safety, and Labor Regulations at Sea*. Cambridge, MA: MIT Press.

Dessler, D. (1989). What is at Stake in the Agent-Structure Debate? *International Organization* 43(3): 441–473.

Ellickson, R. (1991). *Order Without Law: How Neighbors Settle Disputes*. Cambridge, MA: Harvard University Press.

Falkner, R. (2003). Private Environmental Governance and International Relations: Exploring the Links. *Global Environmental Politics* 3(2): 72–87.

Falkner, R. (2008). *Business power and Conflict in International Environmental Politics*. Basingstoke: Palgrave Macmillan.

Finnemore, M. (1996). Norms, Culture, and World Politics: Insights from Sociology's Institutionalism. *International Organization* 50(2): 325–347.

Freeman, R. (2008). Learning by Meeting. *Critical Policy Analysis* 2(1): 1–24.

Fuchs, D. (2007). *Business Power in Global Governance*. Boulder, CO: Lynne Rienner Publishers.

Goldstein, H. (1998). Models for Reality: New Approaches to the Understanding of the Educational Process. Professorial lecture given at the Institute of Education, www.bristol.ac.uk/cmm/team/hg/models-for-reality.pdf (accessed 12 April 2014).

Gourevitch, P. (1978). The Second Image Reversed: The International Sources of Domestic Politics. *International Organization* 32(4): 881–912.

Grande, E. and L. Pauly (2005). *Complex Sovereignty: Reconstituting Political Authority in the Twenty-First Century*. Toronto: University of Toronto Press.

Grek, S. (2009). Governing by Numbers: The PISA 'Effect' in Europe. *Journal of Education Policy* 24(1): 23–37.

Grek, S. (2013). Expert Moves: International Comparative Testing and the Rise of Expertocracy. *Journal of Education Policy* 28(5): 695–709.

Grek, S. and J. Ozga (2010). Re-Inventing Public Education: The New Role of Knowledge in Education Policy-Making. *Public Policy and Administration* 25(3): 271–289.

Haas, P.M. (1980). Why Collaborate?: Issue-Linkage and International Regimes. *World Politics* 32(3): 357–405.

Haas, P.M. (1989). Do Regimes Matter?: Epistemic Communities and Mediterranean Pollution Control. *International Organization* 43(3): 377–403.

Haas, P.M. (1990). *Saving the Mediterranean: The Politics of International Environmental Cooperation*. New York: Columbia University Press.

Haas, P.M. (1992). Introduction: Epistemic Communities and International Policy Coordination. *International Organization* 46(1): 1–35.

Hall, R.B. and T.J. Biersteker (eds) (2002). *The Emergence of Private Authority in Global Governance*. Cambridge: Cambridge University Press.

Hasenclever, A., P. Mayer, and V. Rittberger (1997). *Theories of International Regimes*. Cambridge: Cambridge University Press.

Henry, M., Lingard, B., Rizvi, F., and Taylor, S. (2001). *The OECD, Globalisation and Education Policy*. Paris: Pergamon.

Herbst, M. and A. Wojciuk (2016). Common Legacy Origin, Different Paths: Transformation of Education Systems in the Czech Republic, Slovakia, Hungary and Poland.

Compare: A Journal of Comparative and International Education, doi: 10.1080/03057925.2016.1153410.
Heyneman, S. (1993). Quantity, Quality, and Source. *Comparative Education Review* 37(4): 372–388.
Heyneman, S. and B. Lee (2012). Impact of International Studies of Academic Achievement on Policy and Research. In L.A. Rutkowski, M. von Davier, and D. Rutkowski (eds), *Handbook of International Large-Scale Assessment: Background, Technical Issues, and Methods of Data Analysis*. London: Chapman and Hall Publishers.
Josselin, D. and W. Wallace (2001). *Non-State Actors in World Politics*. New York: Palgrave.
Keohane, R. (1984). *After Hegemony: Cooperation and Discord in the World Political Economy*. Princeton, NJ: Princeton University Press.
Krasner, S. (1982a). Regimes and the Limits of Realism: Regimes as Autonomous Variables. *International Organization* 36(2): 497–510.
Krasner, S. (1982b). Structural Causes and Regime Consequences – Regimes as Intervening Variables. *International Organization* 36(2): 185–205.
Kratochwil, F. (1989). *Rules, Norms and Decisions: On the Conditions of Practical and Legal Reasoning in International Relations and Domestic Affairs*. Cambridge: Cambridge University Press.
Kratochwil, F. and J.G. Ruggie (1986). International Relations: An Assessment of the Field. *International Organization* 40(4): 753–775.
Krause Hansen, H. and S. Mühlen-Schulte (2012). The Power of Numbers in Global Governance. *Journal of International Relations and Development* 15(4): 455–465.
Labaree, D. (2014). Let's Measure What No One Teaches: PISA, NCLB, and the Shrinking Aims of Education. *Teachers College Record* 116(9): 1–14.
Levy, D. and P. Newell (eds) (2005). *The Business of Global Environmental Governance*. Cambridge, MA: MIT Press.
Levy, M., O. Young, and M. Zurn (1995). The Study of International Regimes. *European Journal of International Relations* 1(3): 270–273.
Lindblad, S. and T.S. Popkewitz (2004). Educational Restructuring: (Re)Thinking the Problematic of Reform. In S. Lindblad and T.S. Popkewitz (eds), *Educational Restructuring: Perspectives on Traveling Policies*. Greenwich: IAP.
Lingard, B. and S. Grek (2007). The OECD, Indicators and PISA: An Exploration of Events and Theoretical Perspectives. ESRC/ESF research project on fabricating quality in education. *Working Paper*, 2.
Lingard, B., S. Taylor, and S. Rawolle (2005). Bourdieu and the Study of Educational Policy: Introduction. *Journal of Education Policy* 20(6): 663–669.
Löwenheim, O. (2008). Examining the State: A Foucauldian Perspective on International 'Governance Indicators'. *Third World Quarterly* 29(2): 255–274.
Martens, K. and A.P. Jakobi (eds) (2010). *Mechanisms of OECD Governance – International Incentives for National Policy-Making*? Oxford: Oxford University Press.
Martens, K. and D. Niemann (2009). *Governance by Comparison: How Ratings and Rankings can Impact National Policy Making In Education*. Paper presented at the International Studies Association (ISA). New York City, February.
Meyer, H.-D. and A. Benavot (2013). *PISA, Power, and Policy: The Emergence of Global Educational Governance*. Oxford: Symposium Books.
Meyer, J.W. and M.T. Hannan (eds) (1979). *National Development and the World System*. Chicago, IL: University of Chicago.

Meyer, J.W. and B. Rowan (1977). Institutional Organizations: Formal Structure as Myth and Ceremony. *American Journal of Sociology* 83(2): 340–363.

Mons, N. and X. Pons (2009). *The Reception of PISA in France*, http://knowandpol.eu/ IMG/pdf/o31.pisa.france.pdf (accessed 20 May 2015).

Münch, R. (2014). Education Under the Regime of PISA & Co.: Global Standards and Local Traditions in Conflict – The Case of Germany. *Teachers College Record* 116(9): 1–16.

Murray, T.S., E. Owen, and B. McGaw (2005). *Learning a Living: First Results of the Adult Literacy and Life Skills Survey*. Ottawa: Statistics Canada and the Organization for Cooperation and Development.

Nye, J.S. (1987). Nuclear Learning and U.S.-Soviet Security Regimes. *International Organization* 41(3): 371–402.

OECD (1999a). *Measuring Student Knowledge and Skills: New Framework for Assessment*. Paris: OECD.

OECD (1999b). *The PISA Assessment Frameworks: Monitoring Students Knowledge and Skills in the New Millennium*. Paris: OECD.

OECD (2000). *Measuring Student Knowledge and Skills: The PISA 2000 Assessment of Reading, Mathematical and Scientific Literacy*. Paris: OECD.

OECD (2003). *Literacy Skills for the World of Tomorrow: Further Results from the PISA 2000*. Paris: OECD.

OECD (2004). *Problem Solving for Tomorrow's World: First Measures of Cross-Curricular Competences from PISA 2003*. Paris: OECD.

OECD (2007). *PISA 2006. Science Competences for Tomorrow's World*, vol. I: *Analysis*. Paris: OECD.

OECD (2012). *PISA 2012 Results: Creative Problem Solving: Student Skills in Tackling Real-Life Problems*. Paris: OECD.

OECD (2014). *PISA 2012 Results: Creative Problem Solving: Students' Skills in Tackling Real-Life Problems*. Paris: OECD, http://dx.doi.org/10.1787/9789264208070-en.

Ozga, J. and R. Jones (2006). Travelling and Embedded Policy: The Case of Knowledge Transfer. *Journal of Education Policy* 21(1): 1–17.

Papadopoulos, G. (1994). *Education 1960–1990: The OECD Perspective*. Paris: OECD Publishing.

Popkewitz, T.S. (2003). National Imaginaries, the Indigenous-Foreigner, and Power: Comparative Educational Research. In J. Schriewer (ed.), *Discourse Formation in Comparative Education*. Frankfurt am Main: Peter Lang.

Porter, T. (1996). *Trust in Numbers: The Pursuit of Objectivity in Science and Public Life*. Princeton, NJ: Princeton University Press.

Puchala, D. and R. Hopkins (1982). International Regimes: Lessons From Inductive Analysis. *International Organization* 36(2): 245–275.

Rauhvargers, A. (2013). *Global University Rankings and Their Impact*. Brussels: European University Association.

Rinne, R., J. Kallo, and S. Hokka (2004). Too Eager to Comply?: OECD Education Policies and the Finnish Response. *European Educational Research Journal* 3(2): 454–486.

Ripley, A. (2013). *The Smartest Kids in the World: And How They Got That Way*. New York: Simon & Schuster.

Robson, K. (1992). Accounting Numbers as 'Inscription': Action at a Distance and the Development of Accounting. *Accounting, Organizations and Society* 17(7): 685–708.

Rogers, E.M. (2003). *Diffusion of Innovations*. New York: Free Press.

Sahlberg, P. (2012). *Finnish Lessons: What Can the World Learn from Educational Change in Finland?* Ashland, OR: Blackstone.
Schleicher, A. (2006). Fundamentos y cuestiones políticas subyacentes al desarrollo de PISA. *Revista de Éducación*, No. extraordinário, 21–43.
Slaughter, A.-M. (2004). *A New World Order*. Princeton, NJ: Princeton University Press.
Steward, W. (2014). Is PISA Fundamentally Flawed? *TES*, 24 September 2014, www.tes.com/article.aspx?storycode=6344672 (accessed 15 May 2015).
Strang, D. and J. Meyer (1993). Institutional Conditions for Diffusion. *Theory and Society* 22(4): 487–511.
Swidler, A. (1986). Culture in Action: Symbols and Strategies. *American Sociological Review* 51(2): 273–286.
Tucker, M. (ed.) (2011). *Surpassing Shanghai*. Cambridge, MA: Harvard Education Press.
Välijärvi, J., P. Linnakylä, P. Kupari, P. Reinikainen, I. Arffman, and J. Yliopisto (2003). *The Finnish Success in PISA – And Some Reasons Behind It*. Jyväskylä: Institute for Educational Research, University of Jyväskylä, https://ktl.jyu.fi/img/portal/8302/PISA_2003_screen.pdf (accessed 18 April 2015).
Waltz, K. (1979). *Theory of International Politics*. Reading, MA: Addison Wesley.
Wallerstein, I. (1974). *The Modern World-System: Capitalist Agriculture and the Origins of the European World-Economy in the Sixteenth Century*. New York: Academic Press.
Wiseman, A. (2010). *International Perspectives on Education and Society: The Impact of International Achievement Studies on National Education*. Emerald Insight, www.emeraldinsight.com/books.htm?issn=1479-3679&volume=13& (accessed 23 September 2015).
Wojciuk, A., M. Michałek, and M. Stormowska (2015). Education as a Source and Tool of Soft Power in International Relations. *European Political Science* 14(3): 298–317.
Woodward, R. (2010). The OECD and Economic Governance: Invisibility and Impotence? In Kerstin Martens and Anja P. Jakobi (eds), *Mechanisms of OECD Governance: International Incentives for National Policy-Making?* Oxford: Oxford University Press.
Young, O.R. (1980). International Regimes: Problems of Concept Formation. *International Organization* 32(3): 331–356.
Young, O.R. (1982). Regime Dynamics: The Rise and Fall of International Regimes. *International Organization* 36(2): 277–297.
Young, O.R. (1983). *International Cooperation: Building Regimes for Natural Resources and the Environment*. Ithaca, NY: Cornell University Press.
Young, O.R. (1989). The Politics of International Regime Formation: Managing Natural Resources and the Environment. *International Organization* 43(3): 349–375.
Young, O.R. (1991). Political Leadership and Regime Formation: On the Development of Institutions in International Society. *International Organization* 45(3): 281–308.
Young, O.R. (1994). *International Governance: Protecting the Environment in a Stateless Society*. Ithaca, NY: Cornell University Press.
Young, O.R. (2008). The Architecture of Global Environmental Governance: Bringing Science to Bear on Policy. *Global Environmental Politics* 8(1): 14–32.
Zacher, M.W. (1987). Trade Gaps, Analytical Gaps: Regime Analysis and International Commodity Trade Regulation. *International Organization* 41(2): 173–202.

Conclusion

This work set out to prove that education and science affect state power in the international arena. I based my analysis on the model, which includes agential and structural aspects in the conceptualisation of international power. Chapters 2 and 3, devoted to state-building processes and economic questions, were dominated by an agential perspective, concentrating on the mechanisms which had historically contributed to the international standing of states by securing improvements in education and science. The part that followed presented an international balance sheet in education and science and analysed examples of state strategies in this context. The final part, in turn, considered the structural aspect of power using a particular transnational regime as a reference point. I discussed both the theoretical underpinnings of the analysis – the theory of transnational regimes – and the characteristics of soft coordination peculiar to governance by numbers. The specific empirical example I used was the PISA study administered by the OECD, approached as an informal and implicit transnational regime. Structures of governance are highly complex – they include the macro level, such as the contemporary structure of the global economy, as well as the local, institutional and discursive microstructures. The cited example of a contemporary structure of governance in the shape of a transnational regime is thus merely a narrow section of a complicated reality; however, it uncovers some of the characteristic mechanisms of structural power in education and science. In the sequence of chapters, I presented detailed arguments in support of the claims put forward in Chapter 1.

This work highlights an important part of the contemporary social reality that has not been subjected to analysis from such a perspective as yet. Today, states attach more significance to the quality of education and science than was the case in the past and it is very likely that this tendency will continue. However, the direction of progress in education and science was not of interest to me, for all the heated debate it now provokes. Various aspects of globalisation and the development of communication and information technologies doubtless pose a challenge to the established organisational patterns of universities and science, but their impact is most obvious in schools. No one can provide a satisfactory answer as to how those fields should be reformed. While I concede that certain changes need to occur, prophecies of the impending demise of the institutions or a complete overhaul of teaching and learning have put me in a sceptical frame of mind.

Another major challenge to education comes from globalisation in politics and culture, with its increasing tendency to challenge the state-building powers of education, particularly its role in establishing civic identity and loyalty to the state. Fundamental problems concerning the future of humanity can no longer be resolved through a clash between national egoisms – anthropogenic global warming is symbolic of the contemporary situation. A patriotism reduced to minding one's own business is exposed as a faulty, short-sighted paradigm that could lead to unpredictable – and very likely catastrophic – results in the long run. In many states, the project of using education to inculcate loyalty to the fatherland, ever rooted in a particular view of the past and clear distinctions between us and them, is being redefined. One of the reasons for that are the migrations, which have put increasing numbers of people from various cultural backgrounds in the same schools and universities. Today, schools in developed states serve the crucial function of integrating the children of the immigrants; this does not involve only the complex question of identity, but also a socio-economic understanding of social cohesion.

One major unknown for the future of education are changes in the labour market and the depth to which they will occur – which professions will disappear, what will replace them, and, more broadly, what shape the process will take and whether it will truly diverge so drastically from what we know from history. This process will define the competencies and knowledge of use in the future. The belief that the division inherited from the Enlightenment, into a prestigious and qualitative, strictly academic education on the one hand and vocational training – often carrying negative connotations – on the other, resonates as deeply dysfunctional with me. Obviously, the point is not to 'deintellectualise' societies, but rather to devise a formula that would open new paths to diverse talents, allowing more people to fulfil their potential and achieve recognition.

The ability to cooperate and work in a group, which traditional schools and universities tend not to prioritise, will become key, for social as well as economic reasons. The degree to which this aspect is underplayed is astounding. Learning through group work is a natural and effective practice, which – if applied correctly – helps maintain concentration and interest among pupils and students, which not only improves the transmission of content and the formation of various abilities, but also reinforces cooperative attitudes so crucial for personal success and common welfare. Finally, the sense of purpose in learning, accompanied by motivation and consistent attention levels, plays a primary role in education. Discipline in the traditional sense is no longer attainable, and electronic devices provide access to knowledge at a moment's notice while emitting enormous amounts of stimuli that hinder concentration and persistence in search of solutions. For all the scepticism that prophecies of radical paradigm shifts in education evoke in me, I believe that it does face the question of the purpose of learning and of the means by which the sense of that purpose could be fostered among pupils and students. Today, the answer is no longer the same as in the era of modernisation during the Second Industrial Revolution.

Taking all these dimensions into account, one could say that changes in education and science will coincide with the evolution of structures of governance, particularly those that define the direction of changes within the state and economy, and the normative implications of these processes. Every state which aspires to the role of a world power needs a world-class scientific-technological base. The question of how states are going to use education in the future to build up power in the international arena remains unanswered. The same applies to the question of the future progress of economisation in various areas of social life and the evolutionary path of capitalism itself. In this context, I consider it apt to question whether the pursuit of political power and economic greed drive the progress of humanity or whether they constitute a burden – perhaps even a threat. Education and science are clearly among the fields where clashes between divergent values and axiological orders are especially palpable today, and their outcome will have a decisive impact on the future of states, societies, and international relations.

Index

Abramovitz, Moses 87
Acemoglu, Daron 10, 63, 79, 88, 112, 134
Adams, Donn 183, 185
Aghion, Philippe 77, 79
Aldcroft, Derek H. 16, 27
Almond, Gabriel 57, 79
Altenstein, Karl von 45, 120–121
Amable, Bruno 192–193, 195
Anderson, Benedict 54, 57–58, 79
Anderson, Perry 119, 134
Anderson, Richard Dean 67, 79
Appelbaum, Richard 79, 176, 197
Archer, Margaret S. 39–40, 41, 66, 79
Arffman, Inga 222, 233
Arrow, Kenneth 90, 134
Arts, Bas 200, 203, 229
Artz, Frederick D. 54, 65, 79
Ashton, David 94, 134, 184, 195
Attewell, Paul 143, 195
Autor, David 112, 134

Bacon, Francis 12, 60–61, 67, 79, 122, 137
Bairoch, Paul 16, 27
Bajaj, Monisha 54, 82
Ball, Stephen 129, 134
Barnett, Correlli 105, 134
Barnett, Michael 208, 229
Barro, Robert J. 89, 134
Bashir, Sujitha 143, 195
Baudelot, Christian 227, 229
Becker, Gary S. 86, 88, 94, 134
Becket, Thomas 46
Benavot, Aaron 224, 231
Bendix, Reinhard 56, 66, 75, 79
Bernstein, Gail Lee 137
Biersteker, Thomas J. 200, 230
Blanchard, Ian 27, 197
Block, Fred 127, 134, 171, 174, 176, 195
Boli, John 43, 44, 79, 82

Bourdieu, Pierre 38, 79, 231
Bowles, Samuel 38, 79, 129, 134, 169, 195
Brady, Henry E. 20, 27
Braudel, Fernand 109, 113, 134, 136
Brewer, Dominic J. 136
Brown, Mercy 163, 197
Brown, Philip 94, 134, 185, 195
Bruno, Giordano 13
Brynjolfsson, Erik 98, 112, 134
Buelens, Frans 135
Bukowski, Maciej 91, 93, 134
Burks, Ardath W. 124, 134
Bush, George W. 177
Bush, Vannevar 172–173, 175, 195
Butts, Freeman R. 42–44, 79

Caboto, Sebastiano 13, 51
Calhoun, Craig 58, 79
Calvin, John 43
Carrington, William 163, 195
Carroll, Peter 210–211, 229
Carvalho, Luis Miguel 220, 223, 226, 229
Castells, Manuel 77, 79
Cave, Peter 125, 135
Cerny, Philip G. 16, 27, 29, 79, 97–98, 129, 135
Chalotais, Louis-René de la 44
Chattopadhyay, Saumen 87, 90, 135
Cha, Yeow Tong 36, 79, 184, 195
Cimoli, Mario 90, 95, 135, 137, 197
Cipolla, Carlo M. 12, 15, 27, 30, 43, 52, 79
Clinton, Bill 177
Colbert, Jean-Baptiste 52–53
Collier, David 27
Collins, Randall 45, 79
Condorcet, Jean-Antoine de 44
Constant, Amelie 188, 195
Cooper, Richard 97, 135
Corrigan, Philip 30, 79

238 *Index*

Cox, Robert W. 212, 229
Cubberley, Ellwood Patterson 38, 80
Culpepper, Pepper 117, 135
Cummings, William K. 124, 135, 183, 195
Curie (Skłodowska-Curie), Maria 68
Curie, Pierre 68
Cutler, Claire 200, 229
Czaputowicz, Jacek 56, 78, 80

Dale, Roger 226, 230
d'Andrea Tyson, Laura 98, 139
Darling-Hammond, Linda 222, 230
Davier, Matthias von 231
Davis, Kingsley 35, 80
Dedrick, Jason 116, 137
Dee, Thomas 88, 135
Deng, Xiaoping 116, 187
Denison, Edward F. 89, 135
Descartes 13–14, 122
DeSombre, Elizabeth 200, 230
Dessler, David 203, 230
Detragiache, Enrica 163, 195
Diderot, Denis 44
Diebold, Claude 136
DiMaggio, Paul J. 78, 80
Dmowski, Roman 71, 78, 80
Dobrucki, Gustaw 72
Dosi, Giovanni 90, 135, 137–138, 183, 195, 197
Drake, Francis 51
Durkheim, Emile 34–35, 42–43, 80–81
Dzierzgowski, Jan 112, 135, 193, 195

Elias, Norbert 24, 27
Ellickson, Robert 201, 230
Engels, Friedrich 39
Esping-Andersen, Gosta 98, 117, 135
Establet, Roger 227, 229
Etzkowitz, Henry 99, 135

Falkner, Robert 200, 230
Falski, Marian 71, 80
Farkas, George 92, 135
Farrell, Diana 189, 196
Federowicz, Michał 117, 135
Feinberg, Walter 55, 81, 168, 197
Finegold, David 117, 135
Finer, Herman 48, 80
Finnemore, Martha 54, 80, 199, 208, 229–230
Fischer, Wolfram 46–53, 80, 120, 135
Fisher, Irving 86
Foucault, Michel 22, 27, 36–37, 80, 208
Frank, Andre Gunder 10, 27

Freeman, Christopher 99, 106–110, 112–113, 127, 135–136, 175, 178, 193, 196
Freeman, Richard 215, 230
Frobisher, Martin 51
Frederick V 31
Frederick the Great 31
Friedrich II 119
Friedrich Wilhelm I 49
Friedrich Wilhelm III 120
Fuchs, Doris 174, 196, 200, 230

Galileo Galilei 13, 18, 59
Galor, Oded 91, 115, 136
Gamble, Andrew 63, 80
Gellner, Ernest 17, 27, 58, 80
Gereffi, Gary 113, 115, 136
Gerschenkron, Alexander 95, 136, 205
Gibbons, Michael 99, 136
Gilpin, Robert 4, 7, 53, 68–69, 75, 80, 96, 111, 122, 136, 194, 196
Gintis, Herbert 38, 79, 129, 134, 169, 195
Goldin, Claudia 86, 134, 136, 171, 196
Goldstein, Harvey 215, 230
Goldstone, Jack A. 10–12, 14, 27, 62, 80
Goodman, Anthony 27
Gottlieb, Esther E. 183, 185, 195
Gourevitch, Peter 205, 230
Gramsci, Antonio 21, 38–39, 80
Green, Andy 32, 44, 63, 66–67, 76, 80, 94, 121, 124, 128, 168–169, 178, 185, 195–196
Green, Francis 94, 184, 195
Greenwood, Davydd J. 136, 161, 196
Grek, Sotiria 212, 215, 221, 230–231
Grieco, Joseph 84, 116, 136
Grosvenor, Ian 56, 81
Guizot, François 67
Guzzini, Stefano 1, 19, 21–23, 27, 140

Haas, Peter M. 202–204, 230
Hagn-Meincke, Claes 195
Hahn, Roger 52–53, 81
Ha, Joonkyung 93, 136
Hall, Peter 136
Hall, Rodney Bruce 200, 230
Hallinan, Maureen T. 24, 27, 30, 81
Hamilton, Alexander 104, 136
Hannan, Michael T. 75, 81, 117, 137, 222, 231
Hanushek, Erick A. 92–93, 136
Harris, John R. 27
Hasenclever, Andreas 200–204, 230
Hastings, Sally Ann 124, 137

Haupert, Michael 136
Hawkins, John 51
Hayhoe, Ruth 198
Heckman, James 92, 136, 191, 196
Henderson, Jeffrey 79
Henry, Miriam 212, 230
Herbst, Jeffrey 74, 81
Herbst, Mikołaj 74, 81, 87–88, 136, 141, 194, 196, 223, 230
Heyneman, Stephen 221, 224, 231
Hlond, August 73
Hobbes, Thomas 14
Hobsbawm, Eric J. 30–31, 57, 63, 77, 81, 105, 136
Hokka, Sanna 212, 232
Hollist, W. Ladd 28
Hopkins, Raymond 203, 232
Hopkins, Terence 113, 115, 136
Howick, George 173, 197
Howitt, Peter 93, 136
Huisman, Jeroen 198
Humboldt, Alexander von 45, 68
Humboldt, Wilhelm von 122

Ikenberry, John 136
Inkeles, Alex 57, 81
Iwakura, Tomomi 123

Jakobi, Anja P. 210–212, 214, 231, 233
James, Donna 94, 134, 185, 195
Jefferson, Thomas 167–168
Jemielniak, Dariusz 161, 196
Jędrzejewicz, Janusz 72–73, 81–82
João II 13
Johnson, Chalmers 107, 126, 136, 183, 196
Jones, Arthur J. 55, 81
Jones, Eric 10
Jones, Robert 222, 232
Jospin, Lionel 214
Josselin, Daphne 200, 231
Jullien, Marc-Antoine 229
Jun, Li 198

Kakowski, Aleksander 73
Kallo, Johanna 212, 232
Kang, Nahee 187, 196
Katz, Lawrence 134, 136, 171, 196
Katz, Michael 81, 168, 196
Katzenstein, Peter J. 6–7, 179–181, 196
Kaysen, Carl 174–175, 196
Kellow, Aynsley 210–211, 229
Kennedy, Paul 15, 17, 27
Keohane, Robert 204, 231

Kimball, Erin 20, 28
Kimko, Denis D. 92, 136
Kohli, Atul 81, 95, 137, 183, 197
Kohn, Hans 58, 77, 81
Koivu, Kendra L. 20, 28
Konarski, Stanisław 69
Kondratiew, Nikołaj 106, 109
Kordasiewicz, Anna 194, 197
Korzeniewicz, Miguel 113, 115, 136
Kot, Stanisław 69–70, 81
Kraemer, Kenneth 116, 137
Krasner, Stephen 201, 231
Kratochwil, Friedrich 231
Krause Hansen, Hans 209, 231
Kupari, Pekka 222, 233

Labaree, David 221, 225, 231
Lall, Marie 135
LaMond Tullis, Floyd 28
Landes, David S. 10–12, 14–15, 27–28, 44, 81, 105, 122, 137
Lasswell, Harold 209
Lauder, Hugh 94, 134, 185, 195
Lee, Bommi 89, 134, 221, 231
Lee Kuan Yew 183
Leibnitz, Gottfried Wilhelm 18, 53
Lesher, Richard 197
Levy, David 200, 231
Levy, Marc 201, 203, 231
Lévy-Leboyer, Maurice 16, 27
Leydesdorff, Loet 99, 135
Limoges, Camile 136
Lindblad, Sverker 226, 231
Linden, Greg 116, 137
Lingard, Bob 211–212, 230–231
Linnakylä, Pirjo 233
Lipset, Martin 36, 42, 45, 81
List, Friedrich 93, 137
Llerena, Patrick 183, 195
Lochner, Lance 196
Louçã, Francisco 109–110, 112, 135, 178, 193, 196
Löwenheim, Oded 209, 231
Lucas, Robert 89, 137
Louis XIV 52
Lukes, Steven 35, 81
Lundgreen, Peter 46–53, 80, 120, 135
Lundvall, Bengt-Åke 99, 106, 108, 114, 137
Luther, Martin 43

Mackie, John Leslie 27–28
Mahoney, James 20, 28
Mankiw, Gregory N. 95, 137

Marie Therese 31, 43, 119
Marx, Karl 10, 39, 106, 109
Martens, Kerstin 210–214, 231, 233
Mayer, Peter 200, 230
Mazzoleni, Roberto 126, 137, 193, 197
Mazzucato, Mariana 87, 96, 137, 174, 176, 194, 197
McAfee, Andrew 98, 112, 134
McCauley, Martin 17, 28
McCowan, Tristan 82
McCulloch, Gary 81
McDonough, Kevin 81
McEwan, Patrick J. 136
McGaw, Barry 214, 232
McLaren, Peter 129, 137
Meng, Jingzhou 188, 195
Meyer, Heinz-Dieter 231
Meyer, Jean-Baptiste 163, 197
Meyer, John W. 75, 81, 117, 137, 207–208, 222, 231–233
Michałek, Maciej 7–8, 144, 188, 198, 233
Miller, Pavla 31, 81
Milligan, Kevin 88, 137
Mincer, Jacob 86, 137
Mitter, Wolfgang 29, 81
Mokyr, Joel 12, 17–19, 28, 59–62, 81
Mons, Nathalie 221, 232
Moore, Barrington Jr. 121, 137
Moore, Phoebe 118, 129, 137
Moore, Wilbert E. 35, 80
Moretti, Enrico 88, 137
Mori, Arinori 124
More, Thomas 46
Morris, Ian 10, 27–28
Motoyama, Yasuyuki 176–177, 197
Mühlen-Schulte, Arthur 209, 231
Münch, Richard 225, 232
Murray, T. Scott 232

Nairn, Tom 63, 82
Nelson, Richard 90, 137
Nelson, Richard R. 126, 137, 193, 197
Newell, Peter 200, 231
Newman, Jennifer 27
Newman, Katherine S. 143, 195
Newton, Isaak 18
Niemann, Dennis 213, 231
Nolte, Sharon N. 124, 137
North, Douglass 84, 91, 138
Nove, Alec 17, 28
Nowotny, Helga 136
Nussbaum, Martha 77, 82
Nye, Joseph 202, 232

Obama, Barack 177
Okubo, Toshimichi 124
Orbán, Viktor 154
Oreopoulos, Philip Enrico 88, 137
Owen, Eugene 232
Ozga, Jenny 221–222, 230, 232

Painter, Franklin V.N. 120, 138, 167, 169, 197
Papadopoulos, George 212–213, 232
Park, Chung-Hee 183
Parker, Rachel 176, 197
Passeron, Jean Claude 38, 79
Passim, Herbert 124, 138
Pasteur, Ludwig 68
Pauly, Louis 200, 230
Perez, Carlota 113, 135, 138
Persson, Torsten 77, 79
Petty, William 133
Phelps, Edmund 95, 137
Piłsudski, Józef 72, 78
Plant, Raymond 134, 138
Polanyi, Karl 37, 82
Pons, Xavier 221, 232
Pomeranz, Kenneth 10, 28
Popkewitz, Thomas S. 222, 226, 231–232
Porter, Michael 99–104, 113–114, 138
Porter, Theodore 200, 206, 208–209, 232
Porter, Tony 229
Powell, Walter W. 78, 80
Prettner, Klaus 91, 138
Price, Don K. 171, 197
Pritchett, Lant 91, 138
Puchala, Donald 203, 232

Raciborski, Jacek xii, 54, 82
Ramirez, Francisco 44, 82
Rauhvargers, Andrejs 200, 232
Rawolle, Shaun 211, 231
Reagan, Ronald 176, 213
Redding, Gordon 189–190, 198
Reich, Robert B. 98, 138
Reinert, Erik 114, 138
Reinganum, Jennifer 106, 138
Reinikainen, Pasi 222, 233
Ricardo, David 93, 104, 138
Richelieu, Armand Jean 65
Rifkin, Jeremy 98, 138
Rinne, Risto 212, 232
Ripley, Amanda 223, 232
Rittberger, Volker 200, 230
Rizvi, Fazal 212, 230
Robson, Keith 206, 233
Rodan, Garry 184–185, 197

Rodrik, Dani 91, 138
Rogers, Everett M. 113, 138, 202, 232
Rok, Jakub 194, 196
Rokkan, Stein 36, 42, 45, 81–82
Romer, Paul M. 89–90, 95, 137–138
Roosevelt, Franklin Delano 172
Rosenberg, Hans 49, 82
Rousseau, Jean-Jacques 62, 65, 70, 74, 82
Rouzet, Dorothee 77, 79
Rowan, Brian 208, 232
Ruggie, John G. 231
Rush, Benjamin 167–168
Russell, Susan Garnett 54, 82
Rutkowski, David 231
Rutkowski, Leslie Ann 231

Sadura, Przemysław 194, 197
Sahlberg, Pasi 222, 233
Samuelson, Paul A. 113, 138
Saussure, César-François de 62, 82
Say, Jean-Baptiste 61, 82
Sayer, Derek 30, 79
Schilling, Heinz 42, 82
Schleicher, Andreas 218, 219, 225, 233
Schlereth, Thomas J. 57, 82
Schmidt, Vivien 133, 139
Schriewer, Jürgen 232
Schultz, Theodore W. 139
Schumpeter, Joseph A. 106, 109, 113, 136, 139, 181
Schwab, Klaus 103, 139
Schwartzmann, Simon 136
Scott, Peter 136, 159, 197
Sedláček, Tomáš 85, 139
Seton-Watson, Hugh 65, 82
Sharif, Naubahar 108, 139
Slaughter, Anne-Marie 212, 233
Smil, Vaclav 17, 28, 93, 111–112, 139
Smith, Adam 55, 58, 82, 85–86, 93, 104, 139
Smith, David 57, 81
Smyth, Russell 189, 197
Soete, Luc 113, 138
Solow, Robert 87, 89–90, 139
Soros, George 154
Soskice, David 117–118, 136
Spinoza, Baruch de 14
Spruyt, Hendrik 74, 82
Steward, William 215, 233
Stiglitz, Joseph 135, 137
Stixrud, Jora 92, 136
Stormowska, Marta 7–8, 144, 188, 198, 233
Strang, David 74, 82, 207, 233

Strange, Susan 4, 7, 21, 28
Swaan, Abram de 36, 82
Swidler, Ann 207, 233
Sylos, Labini Mauro 183, 195

Taylor, J. Orville 168, 197
Taylor, Sandra 211–212, 230–231
Teece, David 138
Thatcher, Margaret 178
Thatcher, Mark 133, 139
Thelen, Kathleen 105, 117, 119, 139
Thomas, Aquinas 11
Thomas, Robert 84, 138, 222
Tien, Bienvenue 188, 195
Tilak, Jandhyala B.G. 94, 139, 186, 197
Tilly, Charles 36, 46, 80, 82, 135
Tomasello, Michael 133, 139
Trow, Martin 136
Tucker, Marc 222, 233
Turgot, Anne Robert 44
Tyack, David 56, 82, 168, 197

Unterhalter, Elaine 82
Urzula, Sergio 92, 136

Välijärvi, Jouni 222, 233
Vauban, Sébastien de 52
Vaughan, Michalina 66, 79
Verba, Sidney 57, 79
Vespucci, Amerigo 13
Vickers, Edward 135
Vogel, Ezra F. 15, 28

Wallace, William 200, 231
Wallerstein, Immanuel 113–115, 136, 205, 233
Walter, Andrew 190, 198
Waltz, Kenneth N. 205, 233
Washington, George 167
Weber Eugen 65, 83
Weber, Max 10, 13, 45, 83
Webster, Noah 167–168
Weil, David 91, 136
Wende, Marijk C. van der 182, 198
Whitehead, Alfred N. 111
Wiseman, Alexander 222, 233
Witkowski, Wojciech 74, 83
Witt, Michael 189–190, 198
Wojciuk, Anna 7, 20, 28, 78, 80, 144, 151, 153–154, 162, 188, 198, 222–223, 230, 233
Woodward, Richard 210–211, 233
Wössmann, Ludger 92–93, 136
Wu, Bin 187, 198

Yliopisto, Jyväskylän 233
Young, Alison 107, 136, 175, 196
Young, Oran 201, 203–204, 231, 233

Zacher, Mark W. 201, 233
Zarycki, Tomasz 83, 113, 139
Zeldin, Theodore 67, 83

Zha, Qiang 187–188, 198
Zhai, Qingguo 189, 197
Zhang, Xiakoe 190, 198
Zheng, Yongnian 187, 198
Zimmermann, Klaus F.N. 188, 195
Zurn, Michael 201, 231
Zysman, John 98, 139